A Spectrum Approach
to
Mood Disorders

Norton Professional Books

A Spectrum Approach
to
Mood Disorders

Not Fully Bipolar
But Not Unipolar—
Practical Management

James Phelps, MD

W. W. Norton & Company

Independent Publishers Since 1923

New York • London

For information about permission to reproduce selections from this book,
write to Permissions, W. W. Norton & Company, Inc.,
500 Fifth Avenue, New York, NY 10110

For information about special discounts for bulk purchases, please contact W. W.
Norton Special Sales at specialsales@wwnorton.com or 800-233-4830

Manufacturing by RR Donnelley Harrisonburg
Production manager: Christine Critelli

Library of Congress Cataloging-in-Publication Data

Names: Phelps, James R., 1953– , author.
Title: A spectrum approach to mood disorders : not fully bipolar but not
    unipolar : practical management / James Phelps.
Description: First edition. | New York, N.Y. : W. W. Norton & Company, Inc.,
    [2016] | "A Norton Professional Book." | Includes bibliographical
    references and index.
Identifiers: LCCN 2015046821 | ISBN 9780393711462 (hardcover)
Subjects: | MESH: Mood Disorders—therapy | Bipolar and Related
    Disorders—therapy | Antipsychotic Agents—therapeutic use
Classification: LCC RC537 | NLM WM 171 | DDC 616.85/2706—dc23
LC record available at http://lccn.loc.gov/2015046821

W. W. Norton & Company, Inc.
500 Fifth Avenue, New York, N.Y. 10110
www.wwnorton.com

W. W. Norton & Company Ltd.
Castle House, 75/76 Wells Street, London W1T 3QT

1 2 3 4 5 6 7 8 9 0

Dedication

Just as we're reaching the point of truly understanding depression as a disorder of mind *and* brain; just as we're reaching the point of recognizing nature and nurture as inseparable; and just as we're realizing that people who are not like us are humans too, with the same rights—comes a potential for sliding backwards, in the face of overpopulation and climate change. This book is dedicated to my children: their generation inherits our increasing wisdom, and an increasing challenge to hang on to it.

Contents

Acknowledgments

Deepest thanks to my patients over the last 25 years, and their families, who have taught me so much about mood disorders and resilience and recovery. Likewise I am indebted to the contemporary pioneers whose research and clinical insights form the foundation of this book, particularly Drs. Fred Goodwin, Gary Sachs, and S. Nassir Ghaemi. Dr. Ghaemi's gracious mentorship-at-a-distance supported my closet academic tendencies. Without his recognition and direction, none of my writing opportunities, including this book, would have arisen. He and colleague Ron Pies are our generation's finest psychiatrist-philosophers.

Almost as important for a closet academic is a generous, accomplished librarian. Ken Willer has steadily searched for and provided the full text of hundreds of articles requested, many of which are cited herein. My thanks to The Murray Memorial Library and Samaritan Regional Medical Center for making his professional services available to me and others.

Meanwhile, I am grateful for the warm support I've received from colleagues who have always understood why the ideas in this book are so important to me, particularly Mike and Tania May, and Rick Bingham. Tam Kelly, Bob Caldwell and Dana Hilliard, John Gottlieb and other insurrectionists at the International Society for Bipolar Disorders are responsible for any excesses of enthusiasm, having egged me on for years now. Likewise my wife Anna-Maria Phelps has endured hours of talk about bipolarity, helped me avoid alienating people with it, and provided unending encouragement for my continued efforts to help people understand it.

The office staff at Samaritan Mental Health have taken exceptionally good care of me, as well as my patients, for over 15 years. They have created the opportunity for me to keep my head down and focus on the work and the learning. Foremost among them is Ms. Heidi May-Stoulil, who always leads by example: dedication, hard work, and always asking, "What's best for the patient?" Thanks for all the laughs, the bureaucratic lead blocking and early warning systems, and the patience with my ideas.

For having worked within the rules while enabling me to provide the education I wished to convey, bringing together providers efficiently and professionally, I am deeply indebted to Kristine Shirley and Brad Pankalla. Their support enabled many hours of free care in my practice and in our local free clinic. We had a great Robin Hood gig going there for a few years.

The PESI organization, led by Claire Zelasko, has enabled me to reach another large group of providers over the years. Their team has given me a national reach I'd not have had otherwise. Thank you for the support and the encouragement and all the work it takes to put those programs together.

Finally, at Norton Professional Books, I am fortunate to have had guidance from their entire editorial team, especially Deborah Malmud, who knows what to keep, what to cut, and how to get an author to do it.

A Spectrum Approach
to
Mood Disorders

Dichotomies are useful for education,
communication, and simplification.
Unfortunately, simplicity is useful, but untrue;
whereas complexity is true, but useless.
　　　　　　　　　　　　　　—Vieta and Suppes (2008)

A Spectrum View Better Fits Reality, But What Happens to Diagnosis?

Violet. Blue. Yellow. Though these words denote specific colors, most everyone understands that they are simply points on the continuum of the electromagnetic spectrum. "Orange" helps identify a general location on that spectrum but is not a different phenomenon than "red": it is still light, but at a different wavelength.

Likewise, in a spectrum approach to mood disorders, the various bipolar diagnoses are recognized as points on a continuum, with myriad variations between the named entities. A *spectrum* model of mood disorders, as shown in Figure 1.1, better describes what we see in patients than a yes/no system. This is not a radical idea. The director of the Harvard-associated mood disorders clinic suggested a decade ago that rather than asking "Does this patient have Bipolar Disorder or not?" we should ask "How bipolar is he?" to place the patient on the mood spectrum (Sachs, 2005).

Similarly, David Kupfer, who recently served as the chair of the *Diagnostic and Statistical Manual of Disorders* (5th ed.) (DSM-5) effort, coauthored a study titled "The Mood Spectrum in Unipolar and Bipolar Disorder: Arguments for a Unitary Approach" (Cassano et al., 2004). Pause for a moment and look at that title and year. They found that patients with recurrent Major Depression often had manic symptoms.

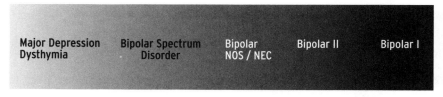

Figure 1.1. **The mood spectrum**

Some had none or few, some had many; and in between was a smooth continuum. Based on their data, the authors concluded that a "spectrum approach is useful in making a more accurate diagnostic evaluation in patients with mood disorders."

Genetic data also support a spectrum view. Two hundred twenty-six separate genes have been associated with bipolar disorder (Nurnberger et al., 2014). Although these likely sort into a few major pathways, as has recently been shown in schizophrenia (Arnedo et al., 2015), even 5 major bipolar pathways, each with just 10 variations, would have 250 different combinations. That certainly mirrors clinical experience, where it seems there are nearly as many bipolar variations as there are patients: each person has a different mix of depression and manic experiences. Some patients only have manic symptoms (though interestingly we still call their illness "bipolar" without much hesitation). Most patients experience hypomania as a rare island in a sea of depression, though each archipelago is different. Some patients' symptoms are always mixed, never purely polar. To date no one has produced clear evidence to suggest that these many variations can be divided cleanly into unipolar and bipolar categories. There is no natural cutoff, no place to "carve between the joints" (Phelps et al., 2008).

Indeed, Dr. Kupfer attempted to steer the DSM-5 toward changing from a categorical system (dichotomous, yes/no, cutoff-based) toward a "dimensional" (jargon term for spectrum-based) system (Adam, 2013; First, 2006). This proved to be too big a leap. Instead he published separately his conclusion about the relationship between Major Depression and bipolar disorders:

[T]he difficulty in identification of a clear boundary between the two disorders suggests that they might be better represented as an affective disorders continuum, with variable expressions of bipolarity representing dimensions of underlying pathophysiologic processes. (Phillips and Kupfer, 2013)

Fortunately, as noted by many (e.g., Parker, 2008), there is no need to abandon one model in favor of another. At the ends of the spectrum, where criteria are clearly met, a categorical system has the advantages noted in this book's epigraph: "dichotomies are useful for education, communication, and simplification." But many people with mood problems are not found at these poles. Authors of a large U.S. epidemiologic study, the National Catchment Area replication, concluded years ago: "there is growing clinical and epidemiologic evidence that major mood disorders form a spectrum from major depressive disorder to pure mania." They pointed out that "nearly 40% of study participants with a history of major depressive disorder had a history of subthreshold hypomania" (Merikangas et al., 2007).

We need a system to detect those patients and address the symptoms of mid-spectrum patients, everyone whose diagnoses lie between unipolar depression and Bipolar I. That is the focus of this book.

A Case Example

Imagine that your next new patient is Ms. Arguello, a 35-year-old woman. She has been depressed for several months. Later you establish that her thyroid values are normal (TSH 1.2 mIU/L) and she has no major ongoing medical problems or new symptoms suggestive thereof, so her depression appears to be a primary mood disorder. As per your routine, you work out the timeline of her current and previous episodes, looking for external events that might have been triggers for her symptoms. She reports that this episode, like many prior, "came out of the blue."

As you know, if Ms. Arguello has a history of hypomania or mania at any point in her life, this episode of depression is a bipolar depression. And thus the search begins once again: has she had any prior symptoms that suggest hypomania or mania? Many factors limit this search. Time is almost always inadequate. There are many symptoms to query; and as reviewed in the next chapter, her family history and multiple other similarly relevant elements of her history are also important. (Many practitioners have difficulty remembering all these symptoms and elements—I did—and resort to mnemonics like DIGFAST, which unfortunately capture less than half of the necessary information. Chapter 2 presents a simple alternative.)

Moreover, Ms. Arguello may not be able to assist in this search if she does not understand what is being sought. She may know about mania, but most patients do not know that subtler forms exist, nor what they feel like. One recent study found that only 22 percent of patients who'd previously had a hypomanic episode recognized it as such (Regeer et al., 2015). Indeed, one could ask: when does an experience become a symptom, and not just a normal variation in mood, energy, or activity? Let's try using a spectrum lens to address that question.

The "Wedge" of Hypomania

The Spectrum Collaborative Project (14 researchers in three centers around the world) found that hypomanic/manic symptoms in patients with mood disorders form a remarkably smooth continuum from absent to fully manifest (Cassano et al., 2004), as in the schematic Figure 1.2.

At Point A, no hypomania is present at all. The diagnosis here is major depressive disorder, or one of the other unipolar variations: for example,

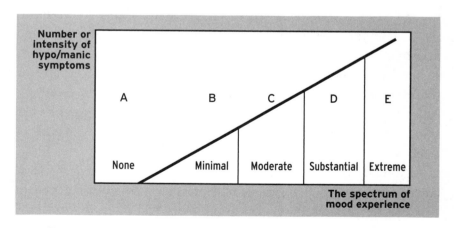

Figure 1.2. **The continuum of hypomanic/manic symptoms among patients with mood disorders**

dysthymia or adjustment disorder with depressed mood. At the other end of the spectrum, Point E, full manic symptoms are present. The diagnosis is Bipolar I. But in between lie many variations.

One way to recognize some of the intermediate variations is to lay out bipolar symptoms by intensity, as in Table 1.1. (These features are episodic in cyclic mood disorders. But they can be steadily present as temperamental traits—e.g., "hyperthymic," between B and C).

Should Ms. Arguello have had the manic symptoms of Point E, her diagnosis is not likely to be missed. Even Point D ought to be relatively easily identified. But consider Point B. These symptoms hardly differ from the rest of her experience and do not clearly differ from experiences many people have who do not have a mood disorder at all. Indeed, at this level, these are not "symptoms." They definitely do not warrant hauling out the "bipolar" label. People with depression who have had Point B experiences will be understandably mystified to hear that they warrant the same diagnostic label as patients with Point E experiences. Yet they are, likely unbeknownst to them, on that continuum.

For patients at Point B, their diagnosis may hinge primarily—ironically—on whom they see. A practitioner with a strong spectrum bent may find all these subthreshold symptoms very telling, and invoke bipolarity, though not Bipolar Disorder. Another practitioner who sticks to the DSM criteria would diagnose Major Depression. Fortunately, other data can help determine such a patient's degree of bipolarity, so that these very subtle symptoms, highly subject to interpretation by the patient and practitioner, are not the only information on which to make a very important judgment. For example, family history is accepted as relevant here, but there are at least 10 other factors which, like family history, change the probability of bipolar disorder. These are reviewed in Chapter 2. For now, recognize that patients at Point B will present with depression, and only the most detailed dredging of their history will reveal potentially hypomanic experience.

Moving along this continuum, Point C presents a similar but less daunting challenge. If these symptoms persist for four days or more, some clinicians will diagnosis bipolar disorder, but others will not find such symptoms compelling because by the patient's report, they are not noticed by other people.

Table 1.1. **Symptoms of bipolarity across the mood spectrum**

Symptom	Point A	Point B	Point C	Point D	Point E
Distractability	No manic symptoms	Slightly unfocused	Notable difficulty staying on task	ADD could be invoked	Nonfunctional
Insomnia	No disturbance	6 hours or less, sometimes broken	4 hours or less, frequent awakenings	2 hours or less, waking too early	Nights of no sleep at all
Grandiosity	No extremes of self-esteem	Pleased with accomplishments, abilities, prospects	"Life of the party," charismatic	Intrusively self-confident, irritating	Grandiose; "narcissistic," unshakeable beliefs in self
Flight of ideas	Nothing unusual	Many ideas about many things	Highly creative, making rapid connections	Experiencing many unrelated ideas at high speed	Psychotic disconnection of thought (highly tangential to loose)
Activity level	Unremarkable	Highly energetic, engaged	Multiple projects at quick pace	So many projects, not completing them, bouncing one to another	Constant motion, ineffectual
Speech	Normal prosody	Quick but not otherwise remarkable	Rapid speech, occasionally difficult to follow	Very rapid speech, losing most listeners	The proverbial "fire hose"
Impulsive risk	Safe or minimally risky behavior	Some choices regrettable and not thought through in advance	Increased risk taking, impulsive	Spending hundreds of dollars, increased "sex, drugs and rock-and-roll"	Spending sprees far beyond means; illegalities, dangerous choices

Of course there are no real Points B or C. These merely indicate positions on a spectrum. But if there is no line to be drawn between normal experience and overt hypomania, then where does unipolar depression become "bipolar?" Here the categorical DSM system cannot cope: a *dimensional* system is necessary to help guide patients and clinicians toward an understanding of prognosis and appropriate management.

Alarums and Excursions

Before we move on to explore the spectrum approach, the alarm many practitioners experience at a broadening of the concept of bipolar disorders warrants attention. First, my apologies for sounding as though I disdain contrary opinion. It is valuable and often well founded. Somehow the very word "bipolar" triggers deep disagreements and discord between well-meaning providers. Invoking the B-word can take us into a realm that seems more like politics and religion than medical science. (Perhaps that has not been your experience, in which case I am glad for you; it has certainly been mine.) Appendix A presents data from social psychology research that suggest differences in clinicians' mood diagnoses may reflect moral values like "do no harm," "respect authority," and "do not violate taboos," more than different findings from patient histories. If you've struggled with colleagues over bipolar diagnoses, I commend Appendix A to you.

One of the main concerns about a spectrum approach to mood disorders is that it expands the breadth of bipolarity and could lead to overdiagnosis of bipolar disorders. For example, a widely cited study examined the accuracy of community providers' diagnoses and found that over 50 percent of patients who had been told they have bipolar disorder did not meet criteria for this diagnosis in a structured interview. Appendix B presents details of that important study, including the underdiagnosis rate of 30 percent, and examines—in simple terms—important statistical determinants of the predictive value of clinical diagnoses.

But from a spectrum view, overdiagnosis and underdiagnosis are not possible. If there is no real dividing line between unipolar depression and bipolar disorder, then there is no line to be over or under. There can be disagreement over where to *draw* a line, and disagreement about adherence to the line once drawn. But these arguments will all be based on attempts to divide what is manifestly a smooth continuum. Let's see what happens if we try to manage patients with that continuum clearly in view: first, how to determine, with rigor, where on the spectrum patients might be; how to understand their mixed states from a spectrum view; how to handle the highly overlapping symptoms of borderlinity, post-traumatic stress disorder, and attention deficit/hyperactivity disorder; and then turn in the remainder of this book to treatment approaches for mid-spectrum presentations.

Chapter 2

Increasing Rigor and Improving Communication:
Non-manic Markers and the Bipolarity Index

Early in training, you were taught to include a family history of mental health problems in your initial evaluation and have likely been doing so ever since. Why? When I ask this question in large groups, nearly everyone reports they routinely ask for a family history because they know that a close relative with a reliable history of bipolar disorder changes the odds that the patient's depression is bipolar, not unipolar.

But there are 10 other markers of bipolar disorder that also increase the probability of bipolar disorder. Why aren't these features incorporated in the DSM, if they're so important? Because the DSM's diagnostic criteria are, by convention, symptoms only. The non-manic markers of bipolar disorder are common clinical findings, but not symptoms per se.

The Non-manic Bipolar Markers

Just like a reliably positive family history, when these other markers are present, the probability that depression is *bipolar* depression goes up. Some of these associations are stronger than others (see Table 2.1).

Table 2.1. **Non-manic markers of bipolar disorder and their relative strengths**

Relative strength	Variable
Strong	First-degree relative with reliable diagnosis of bipolar disorder
	First episode of depression between ages 18–24
	Postpartum depression
	Highly recurrent episodes of depression
	Ever psychotic (without drugs, etc.)
	Transient hypomania/mania on antidepressant
Less strong	Very short episodes of depression, with rapid onset and offset
	Antidepressant loss of response (a.k.a. "Prozac poop-out")
	Having tried more than three antidepressants
	Seasonality of mood
	"Atypical depression" features when depressed: hypersomnic, hyperphagic, leaden anergy, mood reactivity

Where did this list come from? The data have been accumulating over many years, but the entire list was described and formally characterized in an invited review by Ghaemi, Ko, and Goodwin (2002). It has since been explored further and reiterated in most reviews of bipolar diagnosis, including several from the International Society for Bipolar Disorders (ISBD) (Mitchell et al., 2008; Phelps et al., 2008).

In their 2002 review, Dr. Ghaemi and colleagues characterized Bipolar Spectrum Disorder as the presence of bipolar markers *in the absence of a history of hypomania*. Although clearly emphasizing that mood disorders exist on spectrum, in a concession to the reigning categorical approach to diagnosis, they offered criteria and cutoffs for Bipolar Spectrum Disorder:

A. At least one major depressive episode

B. No spontaneous hypomanic or manic episodes

C. Either of the following, plus at least two items from criterion D, or both of the following plus one item from criterion D:

   1. A family history of bipolar disorder in a first-degree relative

   2. Antidepressant-induced mania or hypomania

D. If no items from criterion C are present, six of the following nine criteria are needed:

1. Hyperthymic personality (at baseline, nondepressed state)
2. Recurrent major depressive episodes (more than three)
3. Brief major depressive episodes (on average, <3 months)
4. Atypical depressive symptoms
5. Psychotic major depressive episodes
6. Early age of onset of major depressive episode (<age 25)
7. Postpartum depression
8. Antidepressant "wear-off" (acute but not prophylactic response)
9. Lack of response to three antidepressant treatment trials

Even mood specialists who express concern about bipolar overdiagnosis have encouraged systematic assessment of these factors in bipolar diagnosis; for example, Phil Mitchell in a follow-up invited review (2012).

How does one remember all these items? You may have found it difficult to remember all seven DSM B criteria and relied on the DIGFAST mnemonic (distractibility, impulsivity and irresponsibility, grandiosity, flight of ideas, activity increased, sleep decreased, talkativeness). But worse yet, you actually need to remember 11 DSM items, if you count the A criteria: elated, expansive, or irritable mood and increased energy. With the non-manic markers, you have another 11 items to recall, right when you need them, while sitting with a patient.

Recognizing this problem, clinical wizard Ron Pies devised a mnemonic for the non-manic markers (Pies, 2007). I joked with him that this would be beyond most practitioners, who like me have difficulty memorizing DIGFAST. Nevertheless, his list demonstrates that DIGFAST alone does not capture all the relevant elements in bipolar diagnosis. We'll get to a simpler way of handling all this soon, but for your amusement at least, Dr. Pies' mnemonic is shown in Table 2.2.

Non-manic Markers Are Broadly Applicable

If it makes sense to take a family history when trying to understand the nature of a patient's depression, it makes sense to get information about all these other non-manic markers as well. And if it makes sense to get this information when the patient presents with *depression*, it makes

Table 2.2. **The WHIPLASHED mnemonic**

W	Worse or "wired" when taking an antidepressant
H	Hypomania, hyperthymic temperament, or mood swings by history
I	Irritable, hostile, or showing mixed features in depression
P	Psychomotor (retardation or agitation)
L	Loaded family history of affective illness (not necessarily just bipolar disorder)
A	Abrupt onset or termination of episodes
S	Seasonal or postpartum pattern of depression
H	Hyperphagia or hypersomnia
E	Early age of onset of depression
D	Delusions, hallucinations, or other psychotic features

sense to get it when the patient presents with any other symptom for which bipolar disorder is in the differential diagnosis:

- Depression, obviously, as we're considering here
- Psychosis, because Bipolar I can present with psychosis, including auditory hallucinations and delusions (paranoid, as well as grandiose; even disorganized)
- Substance use disorders, which can present with all manner of mood symptoms and overlap extensively with mood disorders
- Anxiety disorders, as the symptom of anxiety has been described in an ISBD review as a "core symptom" of bipolar mixed states (see Chapter 3)
- Post-traumatic stress disorder (see Chapter 4)
- Personality disorders, particularly borderline and narcissistic (see Chapter 4)
- Attention-deficit disorder, which especially in children is highly comorbid with bipolar disorder, but also shares many of the same criteria, making for very complex differential diagnosis (also in Chapter 4)

This list includes the majority of common psychiatric disorders, does it not? Thus a hard look for bipolarity is warranted in nearly every patient we see. Instead of later having arguments about whether the patient has bipolar disorder, a spectrum approach simply suggests that practitioners lay out all 22 items relevant to bipolar disorder. That's a tall order for busy practitioners. Fortunately, a team based out of Harvard and Boston came up with a relatively simple way to do this: the Bipolarity Index. Combined with a questionnaire to elicit most of these data, the Index is not difficult to prepare.

The Bipolarity Index

In 2004, Gary Sachs, then head of the Harvard-associated mood disorders clinic, was just getting under way with the massive research program called STEP-BD (Systematic Treatment Enhancement Program for Bipolar Disorders). In part for that program he and Nassir Ghaemi and others developed what they called the Bipolarity Index (Sachs, 2004). With just five components, it is easier to recall and report than WHIPLASHED. Because it also includes the DSM criteria, it provides a summary of all data relevant to bipolar diagnosis.

The Bipolarity Index begins with traditional DSM criteria, then includes the non-manic markers:

1. Hypomania/mania   20 points
2. Family history   20 points
3. Age of (mood) onset   20 points
4. Course of illness   20 points
5. Response to Rx   20 points

(Course of illness contains several features: ever psychotic, postpartum depression, highly recurrent, rapid onset/offset, seasonality, and brief episodes or constant hyperthymia.)

Note that the authors gave *80 percent of the weight* to the non-manic markers. Without using it quantitatively, the Index is simply handy for organizing the relevant findings regarding bipolarity. If all practitioners were to present a Bipolarity Index of their findings on this key rule-out diagnosis, the rest of us could come along later and benefit fully from the earlier assessment.

By contrast, when I read a chart and find "no manic symptoms reported," I have no idea how systematic, diligent, or thorough the search for these features was. Ironically, unless I have reason to trust that whoever preceded me did a thorough evaluation, I would have more data to go on if instead of a clinical interview, the patient had simply filled out one of the common bipolar screening tools such as a Mood Disorders Questionnaire or Bipolar Spectrum Diagnostic Scale. Does this imply that I do not trust my colleagues on this? Well, ask yourself: are you really assessing 22 features when you screen for a history of hypomania or mania? I don't know of anyone who routinely does that without a tool (such as the one described below).

More important, with all the data reported, a subsequent practitioner can arrive at her own conclusions regarding the key question from the spectrum view: "How bipolar is this patient?"

Quantitative Use of the Bipolarity Index

The original Bipolarity Index also specified how to weight findings within each of the five sections. These weights have been validated in an independent sample by Chris Aiken, who demonstrated that with a cutoff of 50 points, the Index had extremely high sensitivity (0.91) and specificity (0.90), using the MINI 6.0 as a gold standard (Aiken et al., 2015).

The five dimensions each contain up to 20 points, as shown in Table 2.3. Don't attempt to memorize how many points are awarded for which presentations. Suffice it to recognize that even within the dimensions, considerable thought has been given to these presentations. They are not all equal: some are "more bipolar" than others, and many features are spectrums themselves.

The Bipolarity Index provides a systematic way to organize all of the relevant findings and present them to others. It showcases the importance of non-manic markers. It demonstrates that spectrum thinking is not radical or novel: one of the premier U.S. research teams, the STEP-BD, designed a spectrum instrument in 2004. The 2015 validation study by Aiken and colleagues shows that the original authors were remarkably accurate with their initial distribution of points and overall weighting. But how would a clinician actually use it in practice?

Table 2.3. **The Bipolarity Index**

Episode characteristics (DSM symptoms)	
20	Prominent euphoria or grandiosity
15	Mixed state with full manic and full depressed symptoms
10	Hypomania, cyclothymia, or manic after antidepressant (within 12 weeks)
5	Hypomanic after antidepressant, or subthreshold hypomania, psychotic or postpartum depression
2	Recurrent unipolar depression or ever psychotic
Family history	
20	At least one first-degree relative with clear bipolar disorder (BD)
15	• Second-degree relative with clear BD or • First-degree relative with depressions and behavioral evidence suggesting BD
10	• First-degree relative recurrent depressions or schizoaffective disorder or • Any relative with clear BD or recurrent depressions with behaviors suggesting BD
5	• First-degree relative with a substance use disorder or • Any relative with possible bipolar disorder
2	• First-degree relative with possible recurrent depressions or • First-degree relative with anxiety (including PTSD or OCD), eating disorder, or ADD/ADHD
Age of onset (first depression)	
20	15–19 years old
15	Less than 15 or between 20 and 30
10	30–45
5	After age 45
Course of illness and associated features	
20	Recurrent, distinct manic episodes separated by at least two months of full recovery
15	Same as above but hypomanic; or same but or incomplete recovery between episodes
10	• Any substance use disorder (except nicotine/caffeine) or • Psychotic only during mania or • Legal issues when manic
5	• More than three prior episodes of depression or • Recurrent hypomania but with incomplete recovery between episodes or • Borderline PD; anxiety (including PTSD and OCD); eating disorder; hx of ADHD or • Gambling or other risky behaviors or • Behavioral evidence of perimenstrual exacerbation of mood symptoms

continued

2	• Baseline hyperthymic temperament when not manic or depressed or • Marriage three or more times (including to the same individual) or • Starting a new job and changing it within a year, twice or more or • More than two advanced degrees
Response to treatment	
20	• Full recovery within four weeks of treatment with a mood stabilizer
15	• Full recovery but within 12 weeks, or relapse within 12 weeks of stopping treatment or • Switch to manic or mixed within 12 weeks of starting an antidepressant or increasing the dose
10	• Worsening dysphoria or mixed during antidepressant Rx (not akathisia, anxiety, sedation) or • Partial response to one or two mood stabilizers or • ntidepressant-induced new or worsening rapid cycling
5	• Three antidepressants with no response or • Switch to hypomania or mania with antidepressant withdrawal
2	• Near-complete response to antidepressant withdrawal within a week

Reprinted from *Journal of Affective Disorders, 177,* pp. 59-64, copyright (2015), with permission from Elsevier

The Bipolarity Index in Practice: Use a Questionnaire

I can't remember 22 items, especially while also managing the complex interpersonal process of an initial interview. Many practitioners can't reel off even the DSM criteria, as I've discovered in workshops. Yet here I am advocating that you gather all 22 elements for nearly every patient whom you see. Since your adherence to the Bipolarity Index approach depends on your perception of its feasibility, I suggest using a questionnaire to gather these data.

Several questionnaires are available to screen for bipolar symptoms, but only one incorporates the non-manic markers. When questionnaires are used as screening tools in primary care, their predictive value is so low that Britain's National Health Service has explicitly recommended they not be used (NICE, 2014a). Fortunately, adding the non-manic markers to these questionnaires improves predictive value dramatically. Adding the non-manic markers to the routine psychiatric database may be the only way to get the predictive value of psychiatrists' diagnoses over 50 percent, according to one analysis (Phelps and Ghaemi, 2012). A summary of that analysis is presented in Appendix B.

For all these reasons, with permission of the author, I have added questions eliciting the non-manic markers to Dr. Pies's Bipolar Spectrum Diagnostic Scale (BSDS)—a multiply validated bipolar screening questionnaire that performs as well or better than the more well-known Mood Disorders Questionnaire (MDQ) (Ghaemi et al., 2005; Jeong Jeong et al., 2015; Vázquez et al., 2010). Either would do, but the MDQ has been copyrighted and thus cannot be modified. The resulting two-page questionnaire, MoodCheck, is a public sector instrument available for download at PsychEducation.org.

Parts A and B are the original BSDS questions. The BSDS now has at least eight validation studies supporting its use. Part C has been added to the BSDS; obviously, it's a family history screener. Part C has one validation study: adding it to the MDQ improved the MDQ's performance in children and adolescents (Algorta et al., 2013). The rest of Part C asks two questions important in the primary care setting. Part D provides information for the rest of the Bipolarity Index. Shaded areas help remember which answers carry more weight: the darker the shading, the more statistically meaningful the finding.

Though it was originally designed for use in primary care, the psychiatric outpatient program I am affiliated with uses the MoodCheck in our pre-evaluation questionnaires to standardize information gathered about bipolarity for every new patient. This has worked very well. The version shown here has several features designed for primary care providers: self-scoring, patient education, and the U.S. Food and Drug Administration (FDA) antidepressant warning in plain English (in case the questionnaire suggests low probability for bipolarity and antidepressants are considered). It can be modified as warranted for any clinic.

MoodCheck

Part A. Please place a check after the statements below that *accurately describe you*

During times when I am not using drugs or alcohol:	
I notice that my mood and/or energy levels shift drastically from time to time.	
At times, I am moody and/or energy level is very low, and at other times, very high.	
During my "low" phases, I often feel a lack of energy, a need to stay in bed or get extra sleep, and little or no motivation to do things I need to do.	
I often put on weight during these periods.	
During my low phases, I often feel "blue," sad all the time, or depressed.	
Sometimes, during the low phases, I fell helpless or even suicidal.	
During my low phases, my ability to function at work or socially is impaired.	
Typically, the low phases last for a few weeks, but sometimes they last only a few days.	
I also experience a period of "normal" mood in between mood swings, during which my mood and energy level feels "right" and my ability to function is not disturbed.	
I then notice a marked shift or "switch" in the way I feel.	
My energy increases above what is normal for me, and I often get many things done I would not ordinarily be able to do.	
Sometimes during those "high" periods, I feel as if I have too much energy or feel "hyper".	
During these high periods, I may feel irritable, "on edge," or aggressive.	
During the high periods, I may take on too many activities at once.	
During the high periods, I may spend money in ways that cause me trouble.	
I may be more talkative, outgoing or sexual during these periods.	
Sometimes, my behavior during the high periods seems strange or annoying to others.	
Sometimes, I get into difficulty with co-workers or police during these high periods.	
Sometimes, I increase my alcohol or nonprescription drug use during the high periods.	
Total	

Part B. The statements in Part A (not just those checked) describe me
(circle one of the answers below)

Not at all (0)	A little (2)	Fairly well (4)	Very well (6)

Add the numbers in parenthesis in Part B to your checkmark total from Part A _____

Part C.

Please indicate whether any of your (blood) relatives have had any of these concerns:					
	Grandparents	Parents	Aunts/ Uncles	Brothers/ Sisters	Children
Suicide	☐	☐	☐	☐	☐
Alcohol/Drug Problems	☐	☐	☐	☐	☐
Mental Hospital	☐	☐	☐	☐	☐
Depression Problems	☐	☐	☐	☐	☐
Manic or Bipolar	☐	☐	☐	☐	☐
Has a health professional ever told you that you have manic-depressive illness or bipolar disorder?				Yes	No
Have you ever attempted suicide?				Yes	No

Part D.

How old were you when you first were depressed? *(circle one)*	As long as I can remember	Grade School	Middle School	High School	18-24	>24
How many episodes of depression have you had?	One		2-4	5-6		>10
Have antidepressants ever caused: *(circle all that apply)*	Excessive energy	Severe Insomnia	Agitation	Irritability	Racing thoughts	Talking a lot
How many antidepressants have you tried, if any?	None	1	2	3		>3
Has an antidepressant you took worked at first, then stopped working?	No			Yes		
Do your esipsodes *start* gradually, or suddenly?	Gradually		Can't say	Suddenly		
Do your episodes *stop* gradually, or suddenly?	Gradually		Can't say	Suddenly		
Did you have an episode after giving birth?	No		Within 6 months	Within 2 months		Within 2 weeks
Are your moods much different at different times of year?	No effect of time of year			Yes, seasonal shifts		
When you are depressed, do you sleep differently?	No		Sleep less		Sleep more	
When you are depressed, do you eat differently?	No		Eat less		Eat more	
When you are depressed, what happens to your energy?	Nothing	It varies a lot		Very low	Extremely low, can hardly move	
In episodes, have you lost contact with reality? (delusions, people thought you were odd)	No			Yes		

If your total score from parts A and B is **greater than 16**, or if you have **lots of circles** in shaded boxes on this page, you may need to learn more about "mood swings without mania". See www.PsychEducation.org. This is something to learn about, not necessarily about *you*.

If your total score from Parts A and B is **less than 10**, and you have **few circles** in shaded boxes on this page, antidepressants are probably okay, if you and your doctor choose to use them. They can occasionally cause: unusual thoughts, including violent and suicidal ones; irritability; too much energy; and severe sleep problems. Contact your doctor if you think any of these might be happening to you.

Your Name _____   Date _____

Figure 2.1. MoodCheck questionnaire

Practical Implications of a Spectrum Approach to Depression

When a provider sees a new patient with depression, she and the patient quickly arrive at a distinct fork in the road: to the left lie the treatments for unipolar depressions and to the right, the treatments for bipolar disorders. Which is the right path? The DSM has always approached this as though there is one correct answer: match the patient with the path. This can be finessed or postponed to some degree if psychotherapy is the treatment, but when a medication is chosen, providers and patients must choose: turn left and choose an antidepressant, or turn right and choose a mood stabilizer. Where along the spectrum from unipolar to bipolar should patients eschew the left fork in favor of the right?

From a spectrum view, the answer is not a black-and-white decision but a judgment call to be made with the patient. Consider: quetiapine and lithium have evidence for efficacy all the way across the spectrum. Were it not for quetiapine's greater risks, it could easily be justified as an antidepressant for Major Depression. Even lamotrigine may have benefit in unipolar depression, although this is not certain (Reid et al., 2013). But lithium and quetiapine are rarely chosen for unipolar depressions because they are perceived by practitioners and patients to have more risks than antidepressants. In the case of quetiapine, this is correct, but not so clear for lamotrigine and low-dose lithium, properly managed (more on this in Chapters 7 and 8).

The big judgment call is about antidepressants. A categorical diagnostic approach asks "Does the patient have bipolar disorder?", and clinicians judge whether to use an antidepressant from the diagnosis. A spectrum approach ends up framing the question differently: "How many antidepressants should be tried before switching strategies to a mood stabilizer with antidepressant effects?" Figure 2.2 presents a possible set of answers as an example of this shades-of-gray approach.

Using a Bipolarity Index should help the practitioner educate the patient as to roughly where along this continuum she lies, and thus how to approach this decision about antidepressants. Fortunately at least nine alternative treatments have as much evidence for efficacy as antidepres-

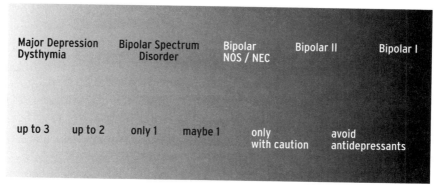

Major Depression Dysthymia	Bipolar Spectrum Disorder	Bipolar NOS / NEC	Bipolar II	Bipolar I
up to 3 up to 2	only 1 maybe 1	only with caution		avoid antidepressants

Figure 2.2. **A mood spectrum approach to antidepressant decision making**

sants at the Bipolar I end of this spectrum, and far less risk of making bipolar disorders worse (detailed in Chapter 12).

As a brief example of how this all might work, consider Ms. Brecker, who has just been seen in her primary care clinic and evaluated for depression. Her PHQ-9 (a standard measure of depression) is 18, moderate to severe. Her MoodCheck BSDS score of 12 suggests significant bipolarity but not DSM-level bipolar disorder. It shows that she's had an episode of postpartum depression; she has had >10 episodes since then. Her positive family history is confirmed by asking about her mother's treatment and learning that lithium helped avoid hospitalizations, which ensued when it was not taken. Thus she is clearly bipolar enough to warrant caution with an antidepressant. She is instructed to read about "more than depression but not manic" using the Diagnosis and Treatment pages at PsychEducation.org and come back in a week.

On her return, she notes that she can now recognize episodes of mild hypomania in her history, with symptoms she had not thought were part of the mood pattern, just strings of "really good days I try to take advantage of, when they show up." This new history tips the balance more firmly away from antidepressants. Her primary care provider explains lamotrigine's risks and titration schedule and refers her to an in-house psychologist for further bipolar psychoeducation and depression management training.

Ms. Brecker's case was relatively simple. More often, patients have trauma histories and anxiety complicating diagnostic assessment. Positive bipolar screens often detect borderlinity, not bipolarity, or the two may both be present. In the next two chapters, we explore anxiety as manifest in mixed states, then borderline symptoms and their differential diagnosis relative to bipolarity, and a similar analysis for post-traumatic stress disorder; all from the spectrum perspective.

Chapter 3

Anxiety Is a Bipolar Symptom?
Mixed States and Differential Diagnosis

Anxiety is not just a common comorbid symptom, it is a *bipolar* symptom—at least in mixed states. Mixed states are associated with dramatically increased suicide attempt rates compared with depression alone. For these reasons, a thorough understanding of mixed states is essential. A spectrum perspective helps one understand and explain mixed states and their confusing differences in models and terminology.

Mixed Conceptions of Mixed States

Diagnosing bipolar disorders is difficult. Helping patients understand and accept the diagnosis is difficult. Often, finding an effective treatment is difficult. How unfortunate, then, that our nomenclature makes the job harder. Using the term "bipolar disorder" for the middle of the mood spectrum as well as for fully expressed manic-depressive illness surely does not help with the patients' understanding and acceptance. The very term "bipolar disorder" invokes a picture of north and south poles—polar opposites.

This leaves us working backward to invoke a different image of depression and manic-side symptoms somehow combining. Thinking in terms of a graph rather than poles helps, as in Figure 3.1.

The DSM-III did not include mixed states at all. The DSM-IV named only the upper right corner of Figure 3.1 as a mixed state, a single point. As soon as the DSM-IV was published, Susan McElroy and colleagues (1995) from the University of Cincinnati presented a different way to envision mixed states. She and her team regarded the entire territory of the graph as potential mixed states and were clearly saying that the DSM-IV view was too limited. Instead, their graph acknowledges a continuum of admixtures of depressive and hypomanic/manic symptoms: a spectrum approach. There are no cutoffs. One can be "a little mixed." One could ask "How mixed is this depression?"

Clinching the appropriateness of a spectrum view of "mixity," a STEP-BD team looked at the frequency of manic-side symptoms during an episode of bipolar depression (Goldberg et al., 2009). They found a remarkably smooth continuum from zero manic symptoms to as many as seven. Twenty-five percent of patients had just one manic symptom. Beyond that, there was no cutoff point to separate a clearly mixed from a somewhat mixed group. The authors of the multicenter BRIDGE study found the same result (Angst et al., 2011). As they summarized, "the distribution is not bimodal."

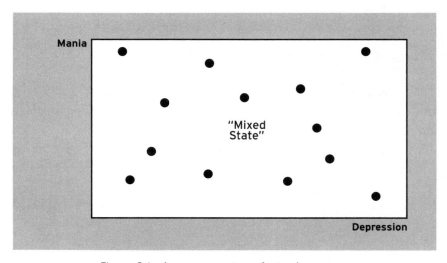

Figure 3.1. **A spectrum view of mixed states**

Mixed States as Waves

Another model of mixed states that allows smooth distributions of manic and depressed symptoms was put forth by Dean MacKinnon and Ron Pies (2006). In their "waves" model, individual mood symptoms are allowed to vary independently of one another: mood, energy, and speed of thought/creativity can all shift at different rates. When all three go up at the same time, we call that a manic episode. When all three go down together, we call that a depressed phase. What if mood is down but energy and speed of thought are up? That would be an agitated depression, right? This has no formal name in the current nomenclature, though it is common. The Mackinnon/Pies model deftly encompasses this variation.

Just as deftly, their model also explains intra-episode variations in mood and energy. Many patients, on seeing the graph of symptoms in Figure 3.2, have exclaimed something like "Oh, now I see, that's me."

In this figure, black represents depression, white represents manic-side symptoms, and shades of gray are various degrees of mixed states, from mostly depression (lighter gray) to mostly manic (darker gray). These shades result from combining the three "waves" of mood, energy, and speed of thought when they are all varying at different rates, creating varying combinations. For example, high energy but low mood would create a medium gray. High energy, low mood, and low speed of thought as well would create a lighter gray. All three going up at once yields black; and so on. Note the absence of symptom-free phases, the "well interval" that is prominent in classic Bipolar I. Patients in the middle of the mood spectrum, riding a roller coaster of mixity as many do, have difficulty recognizing themselves in typical descriptions of bipolar disorder, which emphasize discrete phases of depression, hypo/mania, and well intervals. For them the waves model makes

Figure 3.2. **The continuously varying experience of mixed states as waves**

more sense: they can see their experience in the constantly varying shades of gray.

The Experience of Mixed States

What do mixed states actually *feel* like? This is hard to capture in a few paragraphs: they can be so intense, and so varied. A common ingredient, however, is too much energy, very negative energy. Physically this feels like agitation, "antsy", can't sit still. Alone, this sensation is indistinguishable from "akathisia", a well-known side effect of some antipsychotics. But in a mixed state, this physical excess energy is almost always accompanied by a mental excess energy as well, where akathisia (from the Greek *kathisis*, to sit down; akathisia is literally an inability to sit still) is almost exclusively a bodily experience.

The mental excess energy takes the form of overthinking: ruminating, seemingly inescapable thinking. When mood is negative, this ruminating focuses on negative experiences and interpretations and can drastically worsen depression. Trying to use typical cognitive-behavioral techniques in this state is very difficult: these thoughts are much less amenable to cross-examination and searching for thinking errors.

When mood is positive, the overthinking is creative and intense and unremitting. But notice what happens when mood is about mid-range. Thoughts can be scattered, "one thousand at once". But they can also be intensely focused, singular, "obsessive". This can easily look like Obsessive-Compulsive Disorder (OCD) because the patient's mind just won't let go of a particular concept or concern or image, and drives thinking about the idea at a rapid, intense rate. But unlike OCD, there is little "pathologic doubting". There may be intense wondering and re-thinking and re-doing, but checking is limited to one or two repetitions, not 10's of times as in pure OCD. One mother described her son's overenergized thinking as "Mission Mode": he could not be satisfied until the focus of his thoughts had been pursued as much as physically possible at the time. For example, if he decided he wanted to have an ice cream cone, he would become completely dedicated to making that happen, regardless of the impact on the rest of his family. This was a distinct, cyclically recurrent energy state, not his otherwise normal polite self.

I've offered these descriptions of mixed states because to demonstrate the utility of a *spectrum* approach to mixed states, and the need for it, we're about to review DSM-5 criteria. Keep in mind a vision of an unequivocally overenergized body and mind, because some of the DSM changes involve subtle aspects of the experience that can obscure the very important mixed-state concept.

Mixed States in the DSM-5

The latest DSM edition has made important changes in the diagnosis of mixed states.

1. Broaden the range of mixed states to include subthreshold manic symptoms. In the DSM-IV, a bipolar mixed state could only be invoked if full criteria for mania were met, along with full criteria for Major Depression. A patient with Major Depression and several significant manic symptoms was simply *depressed* if those manic symptoms fell short of full mania. For patients with a prior diagnosis of bipolar disorder, such subthreshold manic symptoms during a depressed phase might signal an informed clinician to avoid antidepressants, as discussed in Chapter 12.

But a patient with a prior diagnosis of Major Depression, now in another episode but with these subthreshold manic symptoms, by DSM-IV would still be diagnosed with Major Depression. The manic symptoms simply disappear, in terms of her formal diagnosis. This leaves no caution, at least in her diagnosis, against using antidepressants. Yet as several research groups have shown, the presence of even one manic-side symptom during an episode of depression predicts a greater likelihood of adverse reactions to antidepressants (Frye et al., 2009; Goldberg et al., 2009).

For example, consider Mr. Patel, who presents to your clinic with clear and severe depression. If he also has racing thoughts, increased though not useful activity, and impulsive risk-taking, he could not have been diagnosed by the DSM-IV criteria as having bipolar mixed state, because he only had three (not four) manic symptoms, as required with irritability. The DSM-5 would allow Mr. Patel to be diagnosed as having a mixed state, using the new "Mixed State specifier." The specifier requires that in addition to depression, at least three of the following criteria are present:

1. Elated or expansive mood (not irritability)
2. Decreased need for sleep (not insomnia)
3. Increased self-esteem
4. Flight of ideas
5. Increased activity
6. Pressured speech
7. Increased risk-taking (not distractibility)

This obviously broadens the range of a bipolar mixed state relative to the DSM-IV. But a second DSM-5 change has even greater implications.

2. *Allow the Mixed State specifier to be used in Major Depression.*
A patient with unipolar depression can have manic symptoms? Indeed, that is just what Cassano and colleagues (2004) demonstrated over 10 years ago: as patients' symptom intensity increased, so did their experience of manic symptoms—regardless of whether they had unipolar or bipolar disorder. As though in acknowledgment of that finding, with the advent of the DSM-5 changes, one need no longer invoke "bipolar disorder" to acknowledge the presence of manic symptoms.

This is major shift in the structure of the DSM. Bipolarity is no longer a yes/no, present-or-absent phenomenon. It can be present across the entire range of mood disorders from purely unipolar to full Bipolar I. This change *almost* creates a mood spectrum, at least for mixed states. A patient can be slightly mixed or very mixed, and unipolar mixed or bipolar mixed. But there is a cutoff: at least three manic symptoms are required. Fewer than that still falls into diagnostic oblivion, as it did in the DSM-IV. Moreover, some crucial symptoms are missing.

3. *Disallow overlapping symptoms: implications for mid-spectrum presentations.* Three manic symptoms do not appear on the DSM-5 Mixed State specifier list:

- irritability
- distractibility
- insomnia (decreased sleep with dysphoria about it, one might say)

The DSM-5 committee called these "overlapping" symptoms, as they are also found in Major Depression. Yet in the STEP-BD data, the most common mixed-state symptom was distractibility: 50 percent of patients with mixed symptoms endorsed it (Goldberg et al., 2009).

In the STEP-BD study, flight of ideas was endorsed by 30 percent. There's one of the allowed DSM-5 mixed state symptoms. But remaining allowed, nonoverlapping symptoms—increased activity, increased risk taking, decreased need for sleep, increased self-esteem—were all infrequent, around 10 percent, with increased speech at 15 percent. Broadening a mixed-state category yet restricting it to the nonoverlapping symptoms has not created as broad a spectrum as it might appear.

By contrast, using Koukopoulous's more clinically defined criteria for mixed states (Faedda et al., 2015; Sani et al., 2014b), Dr. Ghaemi's group found the following symptoms were prominent: psychic agitation or inner tension, 97 percent; absence of retardation, 82 percent; dramatic description of suffering or weeping spells, 53 percent; talkativeness, 49 percent; and racing or crowded thoughts, 48 percent (Sani et al., 2014a).

To their list I would add extreme insomnia (e.g., a net of three to four hours of sleep per night for days at a time, usually broken) as an additional mixed-state marker. Patients in these states are intensely dysphoric. They long for sleep as a form of relief. They try over-the-counter medications for sleep, and when those don't work they ask us for help: benzodiazepines, Z-drugs, trazodone. They are lying awake with racing negative ruminations. This is not "decreased need for sleep" (no wonder they don't endorse that).

The great debate about which symptoms should count (overlapping, nonoverlapping, agitation) is just beginning as of this writing. One way to escape the debate is to look at which symptoms predict doing badly on antidepressants: not just developing manic symptoms but experiencing lower quality of life and lower likelihood of long-term positive response to mood stabilizers. What manic symptoms, if present during depression, might predict these outcomes on antidepressants?

In my experience the most important markers for those outcomes in a patient currently depressed are irritability, distractibility, agitation, and extreme insomnia. Ironically, none of these are on the DSM-5 list (for further comment on this irony, see Koukopoulos et al., 2013. For a contrasting view, see Goldberg's lament on this subject: "A farewell to differential diagnosis?"; 2015).

Fortunately there are alternatives to antidepressants with as much evidence for efficacy in bipolar depression, none of which make bipolar disorder worse. Rather than stressing over whether a patient with bipolarity is truly mixed, and therefore should receive an antidepressant or not, one can turn to these alternatives first. There are at least nine, discussed in Chapter 12.

In summary, a spectrum approach to mixity provides a more flexible and subtle view of mixed states than the DSM (even with the advances in the DSM-5). Is there a risk of overdiagnosis of mixed states, with this broader view? Certainly. Some patients, through the spectrum lens, could be regarded as mixed who would not be mixed through the DSM's categorical lens. The main impact of the mixed-state label at this point seems to be on whether to use an antidepressant in a depressed patient. High-energy symptoms of irritability, distractibility, insomnia, and agitation are useful markers. Anxiety is another.

Anxiety as a Bipolar Symptom

Is anxiety a symptom of bipolar disorder? Not in the DSM, not in the minds of most practitioners, and certainly not in most patients' understanding of bipolarity. Yet a review article on mixed states by a committee from the International Society for Bipolar Disorders (ISBD) describes anxiety as a "core symptom" of this version of bipolar disorder (Swann et al., 2013). How did we get from bipolar to anxiety?

Your patients' experience may explain the connection. The ISBD article calls out the following symptoms in particular as part of the experience of mixed states:

- General hyperarousal
- Inner tension
- Irritability/impatience
- Agitation
- "Frantically anxious"

You've seen patients with these symptoms, of course, often with depression. Not all of those patients have bipolar disorder—but some do, according to the ISBD team.

Hopefully you're ahead of me at this point, thinking, "Anxious depression can be bipolar? Serious problem." Because how do we usually treat anxiety, let alone anxious depression not recognized as bipolar? Right: With an antidepressant, unless the patient is fortunate enough to have access to psychotherapy and a practitioner who puts it high on the list of treatment options. Of course this is ironic, because antidepressants can induce mixed states, as emphasized by the ISBD authors. Once again the very medication to which the patient is led if bipolarity is missed can make things worse, in this case inducing the very symptoms it is sometimes used to treat.

The risk for antidepressants inducing mixed states in patients with bipolarity also works in reverse for patients who are already on an antidepressant. Suppose you are asked to see Mr. Cheng, who originally came in for treatment of depression and was given an antidepressant. Now his depression is better, but his anxiety is worse. Is this a transient anxiety such as some patients experience when starting antidepressants, or is this the development of a bipolar mixed state? You didn't get to see Mr. Cheng before his primary care provider started the antidepressant, so interpreting his current anxiety is difficult.

All this starts to make psychotherapy look like a good option. First, psychotherapy won't make undetected bipolarity worse. Second, it affords time for a diagnostic appraisal over multiple sessions, even while delivering treatment. Third, it has been shown effective in randomized trials for all of the anxiety disorders and even the most severe forms of depression. Why doesn't everyone just start there? You know the answers: access, cost, stigma relative to pills one can take at home, having to search for a good therapist who doesn't have a waiting list. By comparison, a pill prescription is so simple, so much more societally sanctioned, so immediate. To make the choice between therapy and antidepressant medication on an even playing field, the therapist would have to be very closely co-located, preferably on site, hopefully available for a warm hand-off. Moreover, well-trained therapists can handle complex differential diagnoses: for example, is this anxiety alone or anxiety *and* bipolarity?

Generalized Anxiety Disorder: Overlapping Criteria and How to Handle Them

As the ISBD review of mixed states says, "not all agitated depressed states are bipolar." Some patients, perhaps the majority, just have anxiety. On the other hand, look at the criteria for generalized anxiety disorder (GAD) in Table 3.1 and compare their overlap with bipolar criteria. I've organized the DSM GAD criteria to facilitate this comparison, but not added or omitted anything; and have used plain language description of bipolar experience, all within the DSM criteria.

Table 3.1. **Comparison of GAD and bipolar disorder criteria**

Generalized Anxiety Disorder (DSM)	Bipolar Disorders (Patient Experience)
Cognitive	*Cognitive*
• worry	• anxiety, agitation (in mixed states)
• difficulty concentrating	• distractibility
Energy	*Energy*
• keyed up, on edge	• motor agitation
• restlessness, tension	• restlessness
• easily fatigued	• extreme fatigue (depressed phases)
• difficulty falling/staying asleep	• extreme insomnia (manic/mixed phases)
Mood	*Mood*
• irritability	• dysphoria, irritability

   Some would quibble with "insomnia." In the DSM version of bipolar disorder, insomnia does not count, only "decreased need for sleep." Surely you've seen patients in a dysphoric stage of hypomania who are desperate to get to sleep: they ask for zolpidem, trazodone, benzodiazepines, anything to help them get out of the state they're in, which they know from experience will diminish if they can just get some sleep. This is bipolar disorder, but this is not "decreased need for sleep."

Otherwise, isn't this a virtual 100 percent overlap? Obviously the DSM committees do not confer and say, "oh, you have that on your list? We have that on ours, too!" Distinguishing GAD from bipolarity using the foregoing criteria looks impossible. A Bipolarity Index might tip the scales. But if not, a difficult decision arises. The standard medication approach for GAD is an antidepressant. But antidepressants can make bipolar disorders worse.

Psychotherapy to the rescue! With this approach, one need not be certain about which of these highly overlapping descriptions best fits the patient. Instead, one can start treatment and continue to observe. But some evidence suggests that at least for GAD, medications work better—for example, a recent meta-analysis of 234 randomized GAD trials (Bandelow et al., 2015). Relying on psychotherapy alone might undertreat a serious problem.

On the other hand, efficacy is only one side of the coin in risk/benefit judgments. All medications for GAD carry significant risks. All are associated with weight gain, for example (all antidepressants except bupropion; Blumenthal et al., 2014), and most cause sexual dysfunction in a large percentage of patients. There are also rarer risks. Finally, there is the risk of inducing more anxiety if the patient has enough bipolarity to enter a mixed state. How do we choose?

A Case Example: GAD or Bipolarity?

Consider again Mr. Cheng, whom you encountered as he came in with anxiety, after originally having sought care for depression and received an antidepressant. When you later referred him to me for consultation he presented with hyperarousal, inner tension, irritability, impatience, and agitation—and a history of episodes of depression. He was 50 years old, with a history of serious physical assault and PTSD symptoms from that. His PHQ-9 depression scale was 21 (very high) and his GAD-7 anxiety scale was 19 (extremely high; maximum is 21). But his history also suggested fairly clear cyclic changes in mood and energy. So, in addition to his likely PTSD, does he also have bipolarity? Or might his inner tension, outward agitation, and irritability be GAD? Or could this be PTSD alone?

For questions like this, to which there are no clear answers, I recruit the patient's help (shared decision making, discussed further in Chapter 5). Mr. Cheng was educated about the GAD/bipolar overlap. His Bipolarity Index was quite high. We found what looked like subtle hypomanic phases, lasting only a day or two. PTSD was clearly present, so we considered whether he also had enough bipolarity to guide treatment. He understood the bipolarity issue, endorsed that interpretation, and we started lamotrigine. At five weeks he increased to 75 mg daily. Returning at six weeks, his PHQ-9, which had been 21, was now 5. *Five:* that's just what we were hoping for. But here's the surprise: despite his known PTSD, his GAD-7 score, which had been 19, was now 3—almost no anxiety at all.

Is the moral of Mr. Cheng's story: "sometimes lamotrigine can treat anxiety, too"? No. The moral is that bipolarity, including below DSM thresholds, can cause mixed states with severe anxiety. Even in the face of another condition that also causes anxiety (e.g., PTSD), treating the bipolar component can lead to tremendous reductions in anxiety. The other moral of Mr. Cheng's story is that when a patient presents with anxiety, a practitioner should get a full Bipolarity Index assessment. (Use the MoodCheck tool from Chapter 2, for example). If an antidepressant is considered, the Bipolarity Index becomes mandatory if the diagnosis is ambiguous or uncertain.

What If the Patient Is Already on an Antidepressant?

If your patient is doing well, and an antidepressant is not causing too much trouble, obviously one option is to continue it. But if she is not doing well, before turning around and prescribing another antidepressant or a benzodiazepine, conduct a full Bipolarity Index assessment. (As they still teach in medical schools, "when your treatment is not working, question your diagnosis.")

How many antidepressant trials should a patient with GAD have before turning to a different strategy, for example, consideration of a mood stabilizer (on the presumption of a possible mixed state)? The logic is the same as for antidepressants in depression across the mood spectrum, discussed in the previous chapter: the higher the bipolarity, the fewer the trials. For a patient whose Bipolarity Index is extremely low, by the time he's had three antidepressants and is still not doing well, he should have at least had a course of psychotherapy, perhaps two. If he's still not doing well after all that, once again, question the diagnosis: maybe he has an attachment disorder or borderlinity; or consider the possibility of some trauma yet to be discussed. Finally, at that point, I'd likely compare low-dose lithium when discussing the inevitable consideration of atypical antipsychotics (quetiapine, for example, clearly has antianxiety effects, but also carries significant metabolic risks). (More on these choices in the treatment chapters.)

Explaining Mixed States to Patients

Before closing this chapter, you might find useful some clinical experience with patient education about mixity. The goal here is to make the concept clear and "sticky" (memorable and persistent; Heath and Heath, 2007), while patients are assimilating a lot of other information. Thus some literal waving of hands is warranted (forgive my pedantry in describing the motions).

Just after introducing bipolarity, you may have to explain another very counterintuitive idea: manic and depressive symptoms can occur at the same time. Here's my brief explanation. First, extend the thumb and little finger of the right hand away from one another, thumb pointing straight up, saying "bipolar disorder, it's like the north and south pole," getting your patient on board, nodding along. Now gently explain "actually, it's more like a graph, with a manic side and a depression side" as you hold your thumb and forefinger at right angles, thumb pointing to your left (this creates a graph window oriented properly for your patient). With your left hand now label the axes, manic and depressed, and then, waving around in the middle of the graph, you complete the story: "Manic and depressed symptoms can actually happen at the same time, and any mixture of them seems possible. At one time these 'mixed states' were confined to the upper corner of the graph [pointing accordingly, up and to your left] but now many mood experts regard the entire territory of this graph as a mixed state."

That may go flying by in the middle of a busy session, little of which is well remembered by patients. Hopefully the handwaving helps (is it sticking on you?). Some patients will benefit from being directed to the Internet, but of course it's best to steer them to resources you are confident will accord with your handwaving. I use PsychEducation.org (concordance with my explanations is nearly guaranteed, since I wrote it). The search function allows for quick access to relevant pages—or just search for "PsychEducation.org mixed state". The mixed-state page presents many of the ideas and references you've seen here, in 10th grade English.

Chapter 4

Bipolar or Borderline (or PTSD or ADHD)?
Managing Difficult Distinctions and Comorbidities

Bipolar disorders are in the differential for nearly every psychiatric presentation, from psychosis to depression to obsessive thinking to substance use. Three conditions present the most difficult differential diagnostic challenges relative to bipolar disorders because of the extensive overlap in diagnostic criteria and overall phenomenology: borderline personality disorder, post-traumatic stress disorder (PTSD), and attention deficit disorder (ADD). Worse, these conditions are commonly comorbid with bipolar disorders. Thus the diagnostic question is often not "this, or that?" but "this, that, or both?"

The bottom lines of this chapter are:

- admit the tremendous overlap in diagnostic criteria (resistance is futile)
- focus on treatment options; it takes the pressure off of difficult diagnostic distinctions
- think iteratively—start with low-risk options and adjust treatment as you go, keeping an open mind about diagnoses that might be escaping you.

These principles will emerge in consideration of the three diagnoses, relative to bipolarity.

Borderlinity, not Borderline Personality Disorder

Borderline personality disorder (BPD)—what an unfortunate choice of terms. We in psychiatry who are so normal (ahem) shall deem a patient to have a "personality disorder." Great public relations.

Nevertheless, there is a real phenomenon this label is intended to describe. Contrary to Akiskal and others, who suggested incorporating borderlinity into the bipolar spectrum (Akiskal et al., 2006), most recent data suggest that borderlinity is a different phenomenon than "bipolarity" (Ghaemi et al., 2014). The classic presentations of BPD (e.g., behaviors reflecting attachment problems, from overvaluation/devaluation to abandonment distress) are clearly different from the classic forms of Bipolar I (e.g., sustained euphoric mood, with pressured speech after two nights with no need for sleep). But as clinicians well know, there are many variations of borderlinity, often hesitatingly referred to in a diagnostic assessment as "borderline traits."

Many authors have written about differentiating BPD and bipolar disorders. For example, Joel Paris and Donald Black (2015) emphasize getting the right treatment to the right patient, particularly psychotherapy for BPD instead of medications. Even though I disagree with their emphasis on DSM criteria to differentiate BPD from bipolar disorders, I completely agree with their emphasis on psychotherapy and avoidance of atypical antipsychotics.

In any case, controversy reigns in this area. Should you need an example, see the recent exchange between the BRIDGE team (Perugi et al., 2013) and Joel Paris (2013). Therefore, lest it be misunderstood: in the following analysis, I am *not* saying that some phenomenon which the "borderline" term attempts to capture does not exist. I am not saying it is a version of bipolar disorder. As the very controversy here attests, there is overlap and uncertainty about the boundaries of these two conditions. So while some research teams continue to work on distinguishing them (e.g., Coulston et al., 2012), we need some means of coping with the middle ground, where borderline traits overlap with bipolar traits.

The Overlap Problem: Borderline and Bipolar

In Brown University reports of bipolar "overdiagnosis", the most common diagnosis from the Structured Clinical Interview for DSM Disorders (SCID) for patients misdiagnosed as bipolar was Major Depression (Zimmerman et al., 2010b). This makes sense: clinicians had detected depression but also found something suggesting bipolarity, perhaps a finding from the wedge of hypomania that they thought sufficient to invoke bipolar disorder. During the SCID, however, that finding did not reach the DSM threshold, whereas depression was confirmed: voila, "unipolar."

But in their data, the other common SCID diagnosis for the patients misdiagnosed as bipolar was BPD (Zimmerman et al., 2010a). The Brown University team found that positives on the Mood Disorders Questionnaire—a tool designed to detect bipolarity—were actually more likely to warrant a *borderline* diagnosis than a bipolar diagnosis when the SCID was used as the gold standard.

Using the SCID as the arbiter of what illness the patient "really" carries is of course problematic: we lack lab tests and other objective means of establishing the "true" diagnosis, and resort to the SCID instead. (Colleagues in surgery and internal medicine sometimes offer sympathy over this, sometimes derision.) Think of how a SCID is performed: a research assistant—in this case two well-trained graduate students—asks the patient a series of questions, following a strict written guide. For this kind of work, some standard is required and the SCID is accepted in research circles as the best for this purpose. Indeed, this convention is so routine that it might appear, if we do not pause to think about it, as though our field has accepted the idea that a graduate student following a question guide is somehow closer to "truth," whatever that is in this case, than clinicians who may have seen the patient over many visits.

Nevertheless, the Brown University reports underscore what clinicians encounter all the time: BPD and bipolarity swirl around one another. As one thoughtful review concluded, bipolar and borderline disorders "are often indistinguishable given the core characteristics of emotional dysregulation and impulsivity that feature in both" (Coulston et al., 2012).

Table 4.1 lists DSM criteria for the two conditions, emphasizing this overlap. The borderline criteria are straight from the DSM. The bipolar column lists well-accepted clinical features of bipolar disorders.

Table 4.1. **Criteria for borderline and bipolar disorders**

Domain	Borderline	Bipolar
Stable/ unstable	Unstable sense of self Transient paranoia or dissociation Affective instability	Unstable mood Transient paranoia Affective instability
Anger	Intense anger	Intense anger
Relationships	Unstable intense relationships	Unstable relationships
Suicidality	Recurrent suicidal behavior	Suicidal ideation or attempts
Impulsivity	Impulsive spending, sex, drug use, risky behaviors	Impulsive spending, sex, drug use, risky behaviors
Attachment	Abandonment fear Chronic emptiness	Normal attachment range, at least prior to onset
Symptom duration	Hours to a day	Technically >4 days

Because of the extensive overlap, differentiating these conditions by DSM criteria places tremendous weight on the last two domains. But symptom duration for hypomanic symptoms is strongly debated. For example, Parker and colleagues found that the four-day requirement excluded 315 of 501 patients (63 percent) who otherwise met Bipolar II criteria (Parker et al., 2014). Those with briefer hypomanic symptoms did not differ from those with standard hypomania duration in age of onset of symptoms or family history of bipolar disorder (suggesting that the two groups did not differ biologically, despite one meeting DSM criteria for Bipolar II and the other not).

If one discards the duration criterion as unsupported by research data, differentiating bipolar from borderline comes down to the attachment criteria alone. Experienced clinicians can recognize the attachment disturbance within minutes in a first interview: the transference energy is often intense, early, and trends toward rapidly overvaluing or devaluing providers. I would not expect structured interviews by graduate students to capture this phenomenon, and thus do not find the studies by Zimmerman et al. compelling, regarding their emphasis on borderlinity over bipolarity, given the overlap between all the remaining criteria (Zimmerman, 2015).

The point here is not to declare the two conditions indistinguishable but to emphasize that DSM criteria alone do not discriminate them well. Fortunately, however, other features not found in the DSM (nor the SCID) do differentiate the two conditions somewhat (see Table 4.2).

Table 4.2. **Other features of borderline and bipolar disorders**

Domain	Borderline	Bipolar
Age of onset	Childhood; disturbances should be noted even before puberty and strongly shortly thereafter	18–24 with relatively normal premorbid mood, relationships, function
Family history	Substance use and trauma	Bipolar or very high-functioning relatives
Episode precipitants	Common, usually interpersonal, with rapid symptom onset thereafter	Largely independent of psychosocial events

Recognize the Bipolarity Index elements here? (They are italicized in the table.) Their ability to help differentiate borderlinity from bipolarity underscores their importance in initial histories. None of these three factors are as powerful as the attachment factor, in my opinion, but they can be useful, particularly when findings align, for example, childhood onset, family history negative for bipolar disorder, and episodes commonly associated with interpersonal events are all found together. Unfortunately, trauma is so prevalent in both borderline and bipolar conditions, PTSD is often a given. The diagnostic question is whether there is bipolarity *underneath* that often more obvious trauma. Let's look at PTSD in the same way, comparing diagnostic criteria with bipolar disorder. Then will come an examination of the impact of all this overlap on treatment choices.

The Overlap Problem: PTSD and Bipolar

Table 4.3 is constructed in the same fashion as the earlier one, with DSM criteria for PTSD (not all of them) compared with common bipolar symptoms. The borderline column is copied from the previous table for three-way comparison.

Table 4.3. **Comparison of PTSD, bipolar disorder, and borderline disorder**

Domain	PTSD	Bipolar	Borderline
Stable/ unstable	Unstable experience Transient paranoia or dissociation Affective instability	Unstable mood Transient paranoia Affective instability	Unstable sense of self Transient paranoia or dissociation Affective instability
Anger	Intense anger	Intense anger	Intense anger
Relationships	Unstable relationships	Unstable relationships	Unstable intense relationships
Suicidality	Suicide risk	Suicidal ideation or attempts	Recurrent suicidal behavior
Impulsivity	Substance use, impulsive avoidance	Impulsive spending, sex, drug use, risk behaviors	Impulsive spending, sex, drug use, risky behaviors
Attachment	Normal attachment range, at least prior to trauma	Normal attachment range, at least prior to onset	Abandonment fear Chronic emptiness
Onset	After trauma	After mood changes	Interpersonal
Symptom duration	Hours to a day with each intrusive recall	Technically >4 days	Hours to a day

Again, the point is to illustrate the overlap between these conditions. If there is an obvious trauma with an obvious date of occurrence, that helps; but of course, the trauma is often an entire childhood's experience, and then there is no specific trauma date nor easy pre/post comparison possible.

Hopefully these tables have made clear the problem with which clinicians are all too familiar: these three conditions are sometimes extremely difficult to differentiate. Moreover, each is itself a spectrum.

A Spectrum View of Trauma and Borderlinity

"Trauma" is obviously a continuum from extreme events involving life or death to moderate events of misfortune. Moreover, there is a spectrum of responses to the same event: some people have experienced terrible trauma and yet seem relatively unaffected (bottle that); whereas others are debilitated by much more minor but to them very trying experiences.

Likewise, borderlinity also makes more sense as a continuum than as a yes/no phenomenon. Consider: Borderline specialist Marsha Linehan characterizes BPD as arising from an "emotionally invalidating environment" in childhood (Linehan, 1993). Family environments surely sort into a continuum from highly emotionally attuned to utter empathetic failure; children range from emotionally thick-skinned and unperturbable to easily injured and extremely sensitive. Interactions among these varying emotional environments and a given child's temperament create the myriad combinations we see clinically, where establishing a cutoff for the presence or absence of BPD is difficult. Just how much avoidance of abandonment constitutes "frantic," for example?

So we have *three* continua, when the mood spectrum is added to the borderline spectrum and the trauma spectrum. Not only do their criteria overlap, these three conditions can cause or adversely affect the others. Indeed, by their nature, they are likely to do so. For example, in a family with a parent with poorly controlled Bipolar I, the children carry genetic risk for bipolar disorder but are more likely than peers to experience physical and sexual trauma and more likely to experience an invalidating emotional environment. No wonder people are struggling to distinguish these conditions. They can be so woven together that teasing them apart is clinically impossible. What to do?

Getting Out of the Woods: Focus on Treatment

Treatment options for these three problems (borderlinity, trauma, and bipolarity) differ in only a few crucial respects. So why not focus on the treatment implications of those differences (or lack thereof), instead of gnashing teeth about diagnoses with broadly overlapping criteria and frequent comorbidity? Look at what one must consider to decide between psychotherapy, mood stabilizers, and antidepressants.

1. Dialectic Behavioral Therapy (DBT). At present, DBT is the most widely accepted treatment for BPD, though other therapies have randomized trial evidence for efficacy, notably the STEPPS program from Iowa (Blum et al., 2008) and the Mentalization approach from Bateman and Fonagy (2009). What if the patient really has bipolar disorder, not BPD, and mistakenly gets DBT? This is not much of a problem (except perhaps for inefficient use of a limited resource): most patients with a mood or anxiety disorder would benefit from the skills component of this treatment, or the support, and perhaps even the safety focus. At least DBT is not likely to do harm in a patient with bipolar disorder. Indeed, multiple studies have tried mindfulness as a treatment for bipolar disorders, including an online approach (Murray et al., 2015).

2. Mood stabilizers. Diagnosticians fret about distinguishing unipolar from bipolar disorder because they fear the latter will lead to use of atypical antipsychotics, and many fear that calling BPD "bipolar" will run the same risk. But what about lithium and lamotrigine? What do they do in BPD? What medications are most effective for BPD?

In a thoughtful commentary, Kenneth Silk outlines the medication approaches for BPD (2015). His bottom line: nothing is great, all might help some, antidepressants are not clearly better than mood stabilizers (indeed, the latter may be somewhat better for some symptoms), and psychotherapy is the mainstay instead. A Cochrane review places similar slight emphasis on mood stabilizers while concluding that none are particularly effective overall (Stoffers, 2010).

At minimum it seems fair to say that antidepressants have not been shown to be clearly *superior* to any other medication class. Therefore, consider the scenario in which a patient with BPD is mistakenly diagnosed as having bipolar disorder. If the emphasis is therefore on mood stabilizers and avoiding antidepressants, this will not lead pharmacotherapy in a wrong direction. It may not help much. Too vigorous an attempt to control symptoms with medications could expose the patient to undue side effects and risks. Hopefully the clinician will remember the medical school dictum: "when your treatment is not working, question your diagnosis." Don't *cling* to a presumption of bipolar disorder; keep thinking and reevaluating. As treatment proceeds, the patient should be understanding more about bipolarity and become progressively more able to assist with the differential diagnosis (including contradicting an inaccurate bipolar interpretation).

An inaccurate bipolar diagnosis, where borderlinity would have been more accurate, will not lead to "wrong medicines," although it can lead to many medication trials with little benefit and toward medications with more risks than antidepressants.

Again, I emphasize: if the patient has tempestuous interpersonal relationships, impulsive self-harm, and dramatic mood swings, a good clinician will keep borderlinity high in the differential, including in ongoing diagnostic revisions. Perhaps even more important, if chronic emptiness and abandonment fear are prominent in the history, regardless of how much bipolarity was detected, a borderline-focused psychotherapy should be strongly considered, independent of medication strategy. Thus a spectrum approach to bipolarity does not preclude good clinical approaches to borderlinity of any degree (assuming psychotherapy resources such as DBT are locally available, a separate and sometimes significant problem).

3. Antidepressants. Here we come to the single element in treatment that goes in two opposite directions depending on the diagnosis. With BPD, antidepressants may be tried and may help somewhat. But in bipolar disorders, antidepressants can cause a worsening in several ways (discussed in Chapter 12): not just inducing a manic episode but more perniciously by inducing mixed states with agitation, irritability, and suicidal ideation. Perhaps even worse, as described in Chapter 12, antidepressants can—according to some—induce a long course of subtle worsening that can take years to detect and many months to reverse. In a patient with significant borderlinity, a persistent dysphoria is likely to be attributed to the illness (or should I say to the patient?) rather than to an antidepressant. When the system of care shuffles patients from one provider to another, the opportunity to detect that antidepressants might be contributing to (rather than relieving) suffering is often lost. There is no alternative but to keep wondering if the antidepressant might be part of the problem. This is difficult when the patient is significantly depressed—how can one consider removing a medication whose very name suggests it is the solution? On the other hand, when the patient has been experiencing severe depressive symptoms, often for years, *while taking* an antidepressant, one can consider the possibility that it is ineffective at a minimum. At that point, strong consideration should be given to a trial of antidepressant discontinuation (guidelines for the process in Chapter 12).

Likewise, before an antidepressant is used, it is crucial—*primum non nocere*—to make sure the patient does not have significant bipolarity, perhaps underneath BPD (knowing that the two are frequent co-travelers). If the patient is already on an antidepressant and experiencing agitation, irritability, and suicidal ideation, one must consider the possibility that the antidepressant is the culprit (to some degree), not just the borderlinity.

All the arguments above apply in PTSD as well:

- The differential is difficult, it is frequently hard to be certain.
- One is often looking for bipolarity underneath trauma (complicating the search).
- Psychotherapy is the preferred approach.
- Medications help, but none particularly well.
- Antidepressants are commonly used.
- Before antidepressants are used, make sure that a thorough search for bipolarity has been conducted.
- If the patient is on an antidepressant and experiencing agitation, irritability, and suicidal ideation, consider antidepressant-induced mixed states from undetected bipolarity.

Attention Deficit Disorders

Here again there is overlap in diagnostic criteria, and again the way out of the woods is to focus on treatment options and maintain vigilance for being inaccurate with one's first diagnosis. As a psychiatrist for adults, I've not often had to face the difficult differential diagnosis of a youngster who presents with distractibility, irritability, and hyperactivity. ADD is included in this chapter primarily to draw a parallel with the foregoing disorders: the criteria overlap and so do the conditions. I found the following a useful guide, from a children's bipolar specialist and his team (Sala et al., 2014). They encourage thinking about bipolarity when ADHD symptoms:

- appear for the first time later in life.
- appear abruptly in an otherwise healthy child.
- were responding to stimulants and now are not.
- come and go and tend to occur with mood changes.

Other markers that should prompt consideration of bipolarity from the outset, regardless of ADHD symptoms, include when a child:

- begins to have mood symptoms, less sleep, or hypersexuality.
- has recurrent severe mood swings, temper, rage.
- has hallucinations or delusions.
- has strong family history of bipolar disorder and is not medication-responsive.

Stimulants appear surprisingly unlikely to exacerbate bipolar disorder when added to an optimized mood stabilizer, although data for this assertion are limited. Three randomized trials in adolescents on adequate mood stabilizers showed no increase in mood instability when stimulants were added to prior adequate bipolar treatment (reviewed in Peruzzolo et al., 2013). Nevertheless, before considering stimulant medications, the same cautions reviewed above for borderlinity and PTSD apply here:

1. The differential is difficult; it is frequently hard to be certain.
2. One is often looking for bipolarity underneath ADD, complicating the search.
3. Psychotherapy is the preferred approach, at least initially.
4. Make sure before medications are used that a thorough search for bipolarity has been conducted.

5. If the patient is on a stimulant or antidepressant, and experiencing agitation, irritability, and suicidal ideation, consider medication exacerbation of undetected bipolarity.

These general cautions apply for all of the difficult differential diagnoses relative to bipolarity.

Chapter 5

Getting Ready for Treatment:
Principles, Practices, and Problems

For patients in the middle of the mood spectrum, the emphasis in treatment need not be on anti-manic prophylaxis and management of high-risk psychotic relapse, because by definition mid-spectrum patients are not at risk of full manic episodes. Patients with Bipolar II, properly diagnosed, do not often progress to Bipolar I. In my experience, mid-spectrum patients do not tend to progress to more prominent hypomania either (few data exist on this because the group has not been recognized until relatively recently).

Therefore the emphasis in treatment in the middle of the mood spectrum is on helping patients with a current depressive episode, as this is when they routinely appear for help. But one should do so with prevention of *subsequent* depressions in mind. As Harvard's Gary Sachs cautioned years ago: "Don't treat the mood du jour. Treat the cycling." He overstated for emphasis, as of course you want to address the mood du jour, most likely depression. But his point was to avoid approaches for the current mood that will make subsequent mood episodes more likely, if you have alternatives. Seems obvious, right? This end goal drives all the intermediate goals and steps.

Three General Principles

The core ingredients of bipolar treatment are:

1. Maximize non-medication approaches
2. Rely on mood stabilizer medications
3. Avoid antidepressants

We'll look at each of these principles in turn, then consider some basic facets of mood disorder treatment.

1. Non-medication approaches. What can patients take charge of that might reduce the need for pills? Beginning treatment with an emphasis on what they can do is often well received by mid-spectrum patients who are afraid that "bipolarity" leads to lithium and other medications that will make them feel "like a zombie." True, the discussion of options does come around to lithium (and the good news, no zombies), but the more that can be done without medications, the fewer of them may be required, and doses needed may be lower.

Holly Swartz and her colleagues tested a bipolar-specific psychotherapy alone versus quetiapine for Bipolar II (Swartz et al., 2012). Results: equal improvement in both groups. But this was a small pilot study, only 25 patients total, so we can't conclude the treatments themselves are equal, because the study was admittedly not sufficiently powered to find a small difference. We *can* say that in an initial examination of relative treatment efficacy, psychotherapy as monotherapy for bipolar disorder held its own. Well, almost: there was considerably more lorazepam use in the therapy group—not significant, but again with the small sample size, little was likely to reach that threshold.

The therapy pioneered by the Interpersonal and Social Rhythm Therapy (IPTSRT) team, of which Dr. Swartz is an energetic member, is the focus of the next chapter on psychotherapy. That chapter will also detail "dark therapy," an intriguing approach that appeals strongly to patients: intuitive and simple, nearly free, but difficult to fully implement.

Emphasizing non-medication approaches helps draw patients toward the central ingredient in bipolar treatment: self-management. Particular behavioral changes are outlined later in this chapter and detailed in Appendix C.

2. *Rely on mood stabilizers.* This might seem so obvious as to require little emphasis. But to my continued astonishment, many expert reviews emphasize treatment with "FDA-approved medications," which generally means going straight to atypical antipsychotics. Here's a recent example. In their summary of bipolar depression treatment, three well-known mood specialists emphasized: "Only three medications are currently approved in the U.S. for acute bipolar depression: two atypical antipsychotics and a combination atypical antipsychotic-selective serotonin reuptake inhibitor" (McIntyre et al., 2015). They clearly implied that because these are the FDA-approved medications, one should start with them.

Thus description of an opposite approach is warranted, namely that antipsychotics are *not required for most forms of bipolar disorder*. They may be needed for patients with Bipolar I during manic phases, to speed recovery (usually the driver is the pressure to shorten hospitalizations, even if it means starting multiple medications at once, which otherwise we generally avoid). Some patients will not improve enough on mood stabilizers and will have to consider adding an atypical later. But we should not be led by FDA indications (this goes for children as well as adults), because:

- to market a medication requires a specific FDA "indication" for a specific diagnosis.
- to obtain an FDA indication requires two randomized trials with relatively pure populations of patients warranting that diagnosis.
- conducting large randomized trials of a medication versus placebo takes a large research team, requiring very large sums of money.
- generic medications, such as lithium, do not generate profits sufficient to support large randomized trials.
- therefore the only medications that are likely to earn an FDA indication are new, expensive, brand-name medications.

If one begins with the idea that treatment should be guided by FDA indications, one is led directly into the hands of the pharmaceutical industry.

By contrast, in national and international guidelines, lithium and lamotrigine are the most commonly suggested medications for the monotherapy of bipolar depression, as shown in Table 5.1.

Table 5.1. **Suggested medications for bipolar depression (as monotherapies)**

	Lithium	Lamotrigine	Quetiapine
2004 Australian/NZ College of Psychiatry	✓	✓	—
2005 American Psychiatric Association	✓	✓	✓
2005 TMAP (Texas)	✓	✓	✓
2013 CANMAT (Canada)	✓	✓	✓
2014 NICE (European)	✓	✓	✓

Source: Updated and adapted from Malhi et al. (2009).

These three medications in particular represent the main medication options for mid-spectrum bipolarity, where the main problem is depression. Protection against an episode of mania is not generally required. Granted, some Bipolar II hypomania can be destructive to finances and relationships, but in theory, if these episodes are extreme enough to reach such proportions it should be called Bipolar I mania. Of course this is a spectrum of severity. Some patients with Bipolar II may require anti-manic prophylaxis. But for the majority of patients with bipolarity (Bipolar II and south on the spectrum), the target is either a current depression or prevention of the next depression.

Not just depression: the target in the mid-spectrum is *cyclic* depression. Stop the cycling, and you'll stop the depressive episodes. You don't even really need antidepressant efficacy, in theory: any mood stabilizer will do, because if you can prevent the next cycle, you prevent symptoms of all kinds, including depression.

But patients almost always arrive in a depressed or mixed state, so a mood stabilizer with antidepressant effects would be preferable. Quetiapine makes the list on this basis, but its metabolic consequences are so concerning that in my opinion it's a distant third choice. This is not unanimous among psychiatrists; some would place quetiapine and lurasidone much higher.

3. Avoid antidepressants. Few controversies in psychiatry are as overt and sometimes heated as this one. So let's put it this way: avoid antidepressants for the treatment of bipolar depressions, *almost always*. At least start with a determination to avoid turning to them if at all possible. I'd even use quetiapine before an antidepressant in almost all cases, despite my concerns about its metabolic effects.

Chapter 12 details this controversy, which remains contentious because of the difficulty of establishing just how problematic antidepressants really are. Some psychiatrists (like me) fear antidepressants greatly for patients with bipolarity; others use them with much less hesitation. Sometimes these differences in opinion suggest more about the psychiatrists than about antidepressants themselves. For example, how often do antidepressants, given to a patient without a mood stabilizer on board, cause a "switch" into mania? Different studies have found rates varying from 4 percent to 30 percent! Providers choose the study that matches their views.

With such a range, camps on opposite sides of this issue can sit back and lob data at one another with little resultant change in opinion or practice. For example, at an international meeting in 2013, two experts squared off in a debate about antidepressants. Afterward, one well-known researcher called for "more blood on the stage" (as in Phelps, 2014b). He was joking, but reflecting the common knowledge that this issue is often heated. Often the debate appears more like discussions of politics and religion. Appendix A presents a possible explanation for that resemblance. Frankly I think the model presented there explains more of the controversy than do the data over which the arguments are taking place.

The simple solution to this debate is to focus on *nine* alternatives to antidepressants for patients with significant bipolarity. These alternatives have as much evidence for efficacy in bipolar depression as antidepressants (at least in Bipolar I) and do not generally make bipolar disorder worse, as can antidepressants. They are presented in Chapter 12, along with a handy way to remember them and present them to patients.

For now, suffice to say that antidepressants must be considered very carefully for patients with bipolarity. Choosing to whom to offer an antidepressant, which antidepressant to use, what doses to consider, and how long to keep it in place if the patient improves—these are all tricky enough for patients with clearly established bipolar disorder. For midspectrum patients, these questions become even more complex, more of a judgment call based on the fundamental question: "How bipolar is he?"

To review, three principles guide treatment of bipolarity: (1) maximize non-medication approaches, (2) rely on mood stabilizer medications, and (3) avoid antidepressants. But even before initiating treatment of any kind, a crucial step is establishing "concordance": does the patient understand and accept the diagnosis offered?

Step Zero: Establishing Concordance

Bipolar I mania is hard to miss. Some patients can recognize it even during a manic phase. Most can recognize it after the episode is over. For these patients, labeling a subsequent mood downturn as "bipolar depression" is not a surprise.

But for nearly everyone else with bipolarity, depression is the problem that brings them in for help. Only rarely will they understand that bipolar disorder is not just a manic-depressive illness but a spectrum of conditions, most of which resemble depression, not mania. Very few know of a mood variation called hypomania or the related diagnosis called Bipolar II.

Of course a famous actress appearing on the cover of *People* magazine and announcing that she has Bipolar II helped a great deal. Upon receiving the diagnosis at age 41, Catherine Zeta-Jones said, "This is a disorder that affects millions of people and I am one of them" (Cotliar and Tauber, 2011).

Similarly, a primary care physician wrote an essay for the *Journal of the American Medical Association* titled "Normal Is a Place I Visit," describing her experience with Bipolar II. She noted that: "Upon my graduation I was the recipient of an award given to the graduate who demonstrated outstanding dedication to studies and clinical work and compassion for patients. I was chief resident of my prestigious residency program. My professional record is excellent and unblemished." She also notes, "I have lived in fear that one day I will be unable to continue the pretense of being normal and will be 'found out.'" She threw that fear aside and wrote an essay about her experience of bipolarity (Fiala, 2004). How courageous. Like Kay Jamison (1995) before them, Ms. Zeta-Jones and Dr. Fiala used their position in life to fight stigma. Their efforts have surely helped advance understanding of bipolar disorders.

Yet meanwhile, the idea that mood disorders exist on a spectrum from unipolar to Bipolar I and the corollary concept of bipolarity are still far from general knowledge. This leads to the familiar conundrum most readers will have faced: a Mr. Roberts comes in for depression and is told that he has a variation of bipolar disorder called Bipolar II. His first reaction is likely to be "Oh no, I know what bipolar is. I know I don't have that."

Of course he is thinking of Bipolar I and of mania, about which he may know rather little other than to be afraid of it. Or he might know a lot about it because he has a relative with Bipolar I and has always worried that he might somehow get it too. In any case, for most people, the word *bipolar* has very negative connotations. We can all be thankful to well-known celebrities and thought leaders for using their positions to enlarge the public's understanding of bipolar disorder and change some of those negative connotations. Nevertheless, while depression has become something many people can admit to and accept, bipolar disorder remains more stigmatized.

Thus the soundtrack from Chapter 1: Do not tell Ms. Arguello that she has "bipolar disorder," lest you lose her right there. Instead, tell her she does *not* have Bipolar I, manic-depressive illness, that's clear. But she has more than plain depression, that's clear as well, because she has (insert all the relevant non-manic markers from your Bipolarity Index inquiry, like family history, response to antidepressants, postpartum onset; and all the applicable hypomanic symptoms from DIGFAST). Same approach for Mr. Roberts.

Now the crucial step, for concordance: how is the patient handling this? Is it making sense, is she accepting your explanation, your diagnostic framework? If not, avoid the "Righting Reflex," as the old motivational interviewing texts used to call it: that is, the natural tendency to want to explain it again. That's about the last thing you would want to do at this point (although I'm sure I've done it, probably many times).

Instead, by carefully reading his face as you were initially explaining your diagnostic interpretation, you should have a good idea of how this information is affecting Mr. Roberts. The next step, the crucial one, is fortunately simple: pause and reflect your observations, for example, "it looks like this is making some sense to you" or "something about this is bothering you" or "that wasn't what you wanted to hear." Then another crucial step: listen diligently and watch closely for the real answer he provides. His nodding assent may be just social grace in the face of a professional's assessment ("What do I know?", he asks himself, still very shaken by the diagnosis, for example). Or he may cover what he really feels because he hasn't figured it out yet, but it's our job to be able to detect that kind of hesitation, that mismatch.

The point: do not proceed to explain treatment for a condition that he does not think he has. You would both be better off to back up, review, and perhaps send him off to do some further learning about all this. I use PsychEducation.org, which starts with a page on diagnosis of bipolarity and a page on its treatment. More detailed information is available on the many linked pages.

Patients like Ms. Arguello and Mr. Roberts usually come back from the website with one of two reactions: either "Wow, I had no idea, that describes me very well" or "Interesting, but I don't think it really applies to me." They have often read about treatment options as well: how their position on the mood spectrum determines the role of antidepressants, how much can be done without medications, and basic information on the risks and roles of lamotrigine and lithium.

With all this information in hand, patients may well have reached their own conclusions about their position on the mood spectrum—the crucial step before initiating treatment. If not, at least you'll have saved a lot of time explaining things. (Of course, many will not have done so, for myriad reasons and you'll have to use session time for this process).

Once the patient is sufficiently in accord with the diagnostic framework you've provided, you can turn to treatment options. The recently popularized shared decision making model is a good basic approach at this stage for most patients, so we'll review that first, as it applies here.

Shared Decision Making

Though certainly not new, bringing patients and their loved ones into the process of medical decision making has experienced an exponential growth in the literature over the past decade (Blanc et al., 2014). For readers who have not encountered this literature yet, in brief: shared decision making (SDM) is "a collaborative process that allows patients and their providers to make health care decisions together, taking into account the best scientific evidence available, as well as the patient's values and preferences." This quote comes from the Informed Medical Decisions Foundation (informedmedicaldecisions.org).

SDM itself is a spectrum phenomenon: collaboration in medical decision making runs the gamut from a clinician who simply tells the patient what her treatment will be to one who carefully positions herself alongside the patient and provides information, but does not lead or strongly influence the patient's choice of treatment. The latter clinician is considered in the following discussion.

How does SDM apply to the spectrum of mood disorders? First, it reinforces the importance of diagnostic concordance. Obviously patients will not be able to participate fully in deciding how to treat a condition they do not think they have. More directly, SDM reinforces buy-in for treatment, through eliciting the patient's current beliefs and fears: first about diagnosis, as above, and then about treatment. Then comes psychoeducation addressing misconceptions and, if necessary, more exploration of the apprehensions about treatment. For example, on hearing that one patient in a thousand develops a serious allergic skin reaction from taking lamotrigine, some dismiss that risk, whereas other patients immediately think "Oh, I'd be that one patient." Describing how uncommon "one in a thousand" really is, compared with other treatment risks, might be sufficient to address that thought; or for some, a cognitive-therapy reframing of risk appraisal might be more effective.

The key is to elicit the patient's health beliefs. Otherwise, the procedures, alternatives, and risks (PAR) review, which is medicolegally required, is just a rote monologue. Some texts call this a PARQ, adding "questions," but a better option would be PARL, adding "listening." Obviously this applies to most patients, not just those with mood disorders, the possible exception being those patients whose mental status does not allow for a true discussion of diagnostic subtleties and treatment details, but even there, family and significant others may want to participate in an SDM process.

What does SDM look like? Two processes run almost simultaneously: laying out options and facilitating choice. As clinicians know, patients arrive with preferences about treatments they will consider and treatments they definitely want to avoid. Sometimes these preferences are quite extreme: flatly dismissing psychotherapy, for example, or wanting to start with something "natural," even if the evidence for its efficacy is slim or absent. As you've likely learned, if you think that fluoxetine is clearly the right choice for a patient's Major Depression, you're foolish to simply announce that. First you need to find out if the patient's Aunt Carmen had a terrible reaction to fluoxetine!

Instead, the first step is to present the treatment options you think are most reasonable, by virtue of their risk/benefit ratios for this particular patient, selecting your top three. That number can vary, of course, but for most patients and circumstances, three is sort of a Goldilocks number: Two does not create a broad sense of choice, and four is too many to assimilate. Emphasize that all of them have sufficient advantages to make this list, so you'll mostly be comparing cons.

Watch your patient's face as you present these options. By the time you're done, you should know the patient's order of preference. Thus the second element of SDM, facilitating choice, proceeds almost simultaneously with presenting options. In most cases, you should not have to spend additional time exploring the patient's values—they are usually sufficiently evident, as you go through options.

For example, for a mid-spectrum mood disorder, you might compare a non-medication approach versus lamotrigine, versus low-dose lithium (or another antidepressant trial; odds are the patient will already have had one or two antidepressants at least). Obviously you can spin these options so as to make one sound far preferable to the others. This is one of the reasons I so love my work, because this step is truly an art: how much spin will you apply? Some patients truly prefer to be told: "here's what we're going to do." No big preamble, no extensive psychoeducation, just get on with it. They don't want to know about options, they want to know what you the professional think is best, and they're ready to do that. For these patients, you might say, "you've never had an antidepressant, but I think you're far enough along the mood spectrum that it would be best to start with this stuff called lamotrigine. I'll tell you the main things you need to know, and of course you can go read about it or ask me for more information."

At the other end of the spectrum of engagement are patients who don't want your input on the choice at all. For example, they might generally mistrust the medical profession and prefer to have seen someone who would focus on nontraditional means of healing. They want to research, in their own fashion, any options you lay out and may discount anything you say as potentially having been biased by your allopathic myopia, professional alliances, or your inclination to stay within a "standard of care" they inherently reject.

For the latter group of patients, you will likely need to take a motivational interviewing stance: emphasize their autonomy, empathize with their hesitation to look at lamotrigine, and acknowledge that lithium in this case may have some advantage because it is "natural." You might capitalize on that by noting that lithium is found in public water supplies in various parts of the world and that most studies have found lower suicide rates in those areas—suggesting that even tiny amounts of lithium can be psychoactive—and therefore a very low dose might be enough to see some benefit in their case. Whatever openings you're given will probably be small, and the trick is to avoid pressing forward toward a treatment. You may have diagnostic concordance, but you don't have treatment concordance—for anything. A patient like this needs time to do his own research. You can support and encourage that. You may even be able to suggest some criteria by which he evaluates treatment options: for example, exploring what kinds of evidence he is inclined to trust (very possibly not the same as yours). With caution, so as not to appear to be leading the way, you might suggest particular resources to consider. Emphasizing non-medication approaches can help.

Important Non-Medication Ingredients in Treatment

Mid-spectrum mood episodes can be severe. They do not constitute "a milder form of bipolar disorder," as they are often mistakenly characterized. The suicide rate in Bipolar II is as high as in Bipolar I, for example (Novick et al., 2010). Anxiety, discussed in Chapter 3 as a symptom of mixed states, can dramatically lower quality of life. Nevertheless, for people with mid-spectrum mood disorders, mania or the risk of its recurrence is not a threat, lowering the need for aggressive, rapid treatments. Often patients can begin with less risky, less side effect–prone treatments. Some will be hesitant to even consider medications, particularly those with significant risks, even if those risks are relatively rare. Many patients want to know about everything they can do to manage symptoms without turning to medications.

Maximizing non-medication approaches is a good idea even if medications will also be required. Several studies have shown that adding non-medication approaches to treatment as usual (e.g., medications and routine clinical management) produces better outcomes. These interventions range from basic lifestyle changes to fish oil supplements to a variety of psychotherapies. So whether the goal is to avoid medications entirely or simply minimize them, begin consideration of treatment options with non-medication approaches.

Though core ingredients in good outcomes, the following elements are so well known I've relegated discussion of them to Appendix C. Please see that material for the full consideration these important ideas deserve.

1. Abstinence from street drugs (except marijuana in some forms for some patients)
2. Regular, sufficient sleep in a darkened environment
3. Healthy diet, low in refined carbohydrates, but perhaps also low in gluten
4. Regular physical activity (though in hypomanic phases, perhaps *less* exercise!)
5. Smoking cessation, except when emphasis on this erodes therapeutic alliance
6. Stress reduction—many approaches, including community connection

Appendix C also considers widely used over-the-counter options such as vitamin D, and non-pill approaches like light therapy, that patients may ask about but that are not routine in treatment of mid-spectrum mood disorders.

Duration of Treatment and Relapse Prevention

Even in the first discussion of mood stabilizers, a common question from patients is "How long will I have to take this stuff?" For most patients with any kind of bipolar disorder, one should not answer "for the rest of your life." Even if that was true—and it is not, for some patients—it's a poor way of introducing the topic.

Instead, I suggest that when the patient asks "How long?", you respond with something like: "How about we get you out of this episode first and then we'll come back to that question? It might look different then, for one thing. I'll admit, because you've had these symptoms for a long time [as most patients have], we might be looking at a long time for treatment as well. But that's an issue best examined when you're feeling well."

This may satisfy the patient for the short term, particularly if his current symptoms are intense. If not, and certainly soon in any case, another conversation is needed. (Granted, these discussions take time, which is often limited. We are looking at the ideal here, and the reality may be quite curtailed by comparison). The important follow-up conversation is based on acknowledging that the patient is in charge. Unless she's on a mandated injectable antipsychotic, the choice to continue treatment is hers, and she must exert that choice every day. Someday she's going to wonder "Why am I still taking this stuff? I feel fine." Hopefully you'll have had a chance for the follow-up conversation before that day. It should occur near the start of the first full recovery from symptoms.

You might begin thus: "Nearly everyone will wonder at some point if they have to keep taking this stuff. Your symptoms might return if you stop. Most people are tempted to find out. I'll just ask that before you do that, you talk to me. If you're determined to try it, I'll work out a plan with you to taper off the medications. The key will be to make a plan for what to do if your symptoms begin to return. We should have that all worked out before you stop."

Then begins a discussion of a relapse detection plan. You want to have this discussion in any case, regardless of the patient's long-term plan for medication adherence, as it can dramatically improve outcomes. For example, in a mental health center in England, a plucky "research psychologist with little clinical experience" demonstrated a remarkable reduction in relapse frequency in a few meetings with patients (median 9 sessions, range 1–12; Perry et al., 1999). She and her clients focused on the prodromal symptoms patients had before their last mood episode. She asked them to recall what happened as they began to become depressed or manic. They wrote down three early changes that could signal a time to watch closely, and three later symptoms, signaling time to take action. Relevant actions were also specified, for example, call a friend or call the mental health center. All this was placed on a laminated card patients were invited to carry with them. The results were quite striking: a 30 percent reduction in manic relapse (these were patients with Bipolar I). Unfortunately there was no reduction in depressive relapse. Whether the outcomes would be different in mid-spectrum patients is not known, but one would think it should help, with depression as the primary focus in that group. Depression can be insidious, beginning subtly then spiraling rapidly as thoughts and behaviors shift. Early recognition and response could abort an entire episode, obviously the intent of this relapse detection process.

For the patient who is contemplating discontinuing her medications, consider whether she should include significant others or a good friend in the decision making. Should they know what's going on? Should they be invited into the discussion as to whether tapering off is a good idea? In any case, patients should have someone they trust helping them monitor how things are going.

After working out the detection plan, the patient needs to determine how she'll respond to worsening. This is particularly important as a medication is tapered: go back up, go back on? Or switch to a different medication? The latter might be preferable if the medication wasn't working well enough or fully tolerable enough.

Throughout this entire collaborative discussion, you are in a position to convey your concerns, perhaps even your hesitations and doubts. But this is classic motivational interviewing: most important is to maintain an empathic connection to the patient if you can (not always possible, I admit). If that connection is lost, you lose your ability to help your patient adhere to a plan of any kind: he's on his own. Nearly all patients will want to try going off medications, and often do so all at once. If you can instead create a systematic reduction, tapering one medication at a time, you've created the opportunity for an early recognition that perhaps this isn't such a good idea after all before symptoms return.

Mood Charting

Mood tracking, using some sort of chart, is routinely emphasized by bipolar specialists, particularly academics. But in my experience, few patients can sustain regular mood charting for more than a month or two. They often begin with enthusiasm but tire of it. The chart, like taking medications, is a daily reminder of an illness or condition that nearly all patients wish they did not have. They may track symptoms for a while out of curiosity or to have an objective record of what they're going through. If they can sustain it even briefly, mood charting can be very helpful when medication changes are being made, to track outcomes. But daily questions tantamount to "How sick were you today?" are inherently dysphoric for many. For this and other reasons, including trouble keeping track of the chart itself (where should it live? when will they record?), adherence to daily charting is difficult.

Asking patients to do difficult things, particularly on a regular basis, is a recipe for nonadherence at minimum and potential rupture of the treatment relationship at worst. So I do not emphasize mood charting, but I have the luxury of seeing patients for follow-up as soon as the most recent change we've made is likely to have shown itself as beneficial or not. This can be just a week or two sometimes, though other times it might be several months. If I was stuck—as some colleagues are—with an "every three months" return schedule, I might consider asking a staff member to assist patients with routine charting at weekly or bimonthly intervals.

You may be aware of the many smartphone or tablet apps for mood tracking. Some are quite good. (I do not list them here because any ranking or review would be out of date well before publication). All are subject to the same limitations already given.

Several research groups are working on passive tracking using cell phones to gather data on patient activities (with their consent). Phones have accelerometers that can be programmed to track activity and sleep (or lack thereof); the rate of calls and texts serves as another indicator of energy, motivation, and social interaction. Some such systems can automatically transfer this information to the patient's medical record and alert the care team when he is trending toward an extreme.

When these are available at low expense, some mid-spectrum patients will definitely benefit from using them—for example, those who can quickly become so depressed that they lose the motivation to contact their care team or a significant other. Such tracking could also be a useful alternative to monthly questionnaires. While these could be spectacularly useful in Bipolar I, their role in the management of a mid-spectrum patient is less clear. Of course someone will try to use these in lieu of actual visits with a psychiatrist or therapist. If the outcomes are as good, is that okay? The answer depends entirely on having outcome measures that track what really matters. Low PHQ-9 scores are not equivalent to improved prognosis or quality of life. Suffice to say that mood charting and tracking are complex issues which should be considered carefully and planned individually, not simply endorsed for all patients.

PMS, PMDD, or Bipolarity? Treatment Considerations

Women have additional factors to consider in managing mood, relative to men: perimenstrual, and perimenopausal mood shifts; and pregnancy. Perimenopausal depressions are so poorly studied, indeed not at all in mid-spectrum patients to my knowledge, that I focus here on the other two experiences.

Premenstrual Dysphoric Disorder (PMDD) is obviously a mood cycling of sorts, with repeated experiences of:

- Sadness or hopelessness
- Extreme moodiness
- Anxiety or tension
- Marked irritability or anger

That sounds like bipolarity, right? Depression symptoms, mood shifting, anxiety (as in mixed states; per Chapter 3), and irritability are all shared. How can one distinguish PMDD—or the less severe version known as premenstrual syndrome (PMS)—from bipolarity?

First, for the diagnosis of PMDD, a woman is asked to record her symptoms prospectively. For a woman who wonders if she is having symptoms through the month or only perimenstrually, this prospective tracking is obviously necessary. The treatment approach depends on her results. If her symptoms occur throughout the month, she would be regarded as having a primary mood disorder.

By contrast, if her symptoms routinely begin just seven days prior to menses, and remit with the onset of menstruation, then almost by definition she is experiencing PMDD. If a medication approach is selected (as opposed to exercise, calcium, chasteberry, etc.; University of Washington Department of Family Medicine, 2012), it will be a serotonergic antidepressant. Since these can make bipolar disorders worse, it is crucial to distinguish PMDD and PMS from bipolarity. Can bipolarity produce symptoms that occur consistently just prior to menses?

The answer is yes. When women of reproductive age have been having mood symptoms throughout their monthly cycle, and then get better on a mood stabilizer regimen, they often still have perimenstrual symptoms. Whereas prior to treatment any perimenstrual worsening may have been difficult to detect in the context of continuous symptoms, now she may have symptoms that look like PMS. Indeed, these *are* symptoms that clearly associate with menstrual stage. But the solution for a perimenstrual exacerbation of an underlying mood disorder with significant bipolarity is *not* an antidepressant. That could induce mixed states and more pronounced cycling. Instead, in my experience the best way to handle these perimenstrual worsenings is to slightly increase the mood stabilizer that has already improved her symptoms. If that is already at its highest tolerable dose, then after consideration of exercise and sleep quality and the rest of the important non-medication approaches, and checking thyroid status (Chapter 10), first consider omega-3s (Chapter 9) and then addition of another mood stabilizer.

Once again careful assessment of bipolarity is warranted—this time, when a woman appears to be experiencing even relatively obvious PMDD. Perimenstrual symptoms could be the obvious ones while through the rest of the month there are additional symptoms she may not see or be troubled by. Those less obvious symptoms could suggest that an antidepressant for PMDD would be precisely the wrong approach.

Hopefully by now the spectrum perspective on mood disorders is becoming somewhat reflexive for you and you already understand: menstrually related mood symptoms span a continuum from none to mild to moderate (PMS) to severe (PMDD), as shown on the vertical axis in Figure 5.1. Of course bipolarity spans a continuum from none to Bipolar I, as on the horizontal axis.

The resulting graph maps the space created by these two continua. Although treatment approaches are clear at the four corners, they are not clear in between. For example, at some point along the top of the graph, one would have to switch strategies from antidepressants to mood stabilizers. Note that there is no obvious cutoff at which to make that switch. Clinical judgment is required, followed by close monitoring to see if the

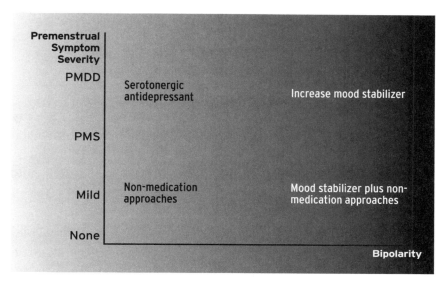

Figure 5.1 **A spectrum of approaches to perimenstrual symptoms**

first strategy selected is working, with an open mind to switch strategies if not.

Interestingly, a research team at Stanford showed that women with bipolar disorder who were taking lamotrigine had *less* fluctuation in mood within and across menstrual cycle phases than women with bipolar disorder on other medications (Robakis et al., 2015). So lamotrigine, which is usually the preferable medication strategy for mid-spectrum mood disorders (Chapter 7), may have some additional specific value in women with menstrually related mood symptoms.

Pregnancy

My home state of Oregon has developed a clinical initiative called *One Key Question* (http://www.onekeyquestion.org/why-is-this-important/), which encourages practitioners to ask "Are you considering becoming pregnant in the coming year?", noting that:

- The average American woman desires two children, but she is fertile for about 39 years.

- Most women spend more than 30 years of their lives trying to prevent an unintended pregnancy every month.
- They spend the remainder of those years trying to have as healthy a pregnancy as possible.

For women with bipolarity, managing reproduction is particularly important. Many aspects of the experience will have an impact on mood stability, from sleep deprivation to social stress to hormonal changes. And of course the management of medications before and during pregnancy and after delivery is important for mother's and baby's safety and health.

Most psychotropic medications are teratogenic (causing abnormalities in the developing fetus) to some degree. According to general teaching, the only reliably safe medications during pregnancy are the first-generation antipsychotics. Establishing the safety of a medication during pregnancy requires a registry of women who were taking that medication before conception, with no others, who were followed through pregnancy and delivery. These registries must be very large to have the necessary statistical power to detect even a doubling of risk, since the baseline risk is so low. As of this writing, lamotrigine registries (there are several around the world) are just becoming large enough to rely on—and lamotrigine has been in widespread use for over 15 years. The safety in pregnancy of newer medications will take many more years to establish in this slow process.

Thus for women of reproductive age, if a psychotropic medication is part of treatment, then a contraception plan should also be considered if she is sexually active with men or may become so. All women of reproductive age should be asked Oregon's One Key Question early in the management of their mood disorder.

Managing medications through pregnancy begins before conception. For example, divalproex is often singled out as "contraindicated in women of reproductive age" because it is 10 times more teratogenic than lithium. It carries a 1/100 risk of neural tube defects (Jentink et al., 2010) versus lithium's 1/1,000 risk of cardiac malformations (Cohen et al., 1994). In addition, a Cochrane review strongly suggests that children exposed to valproate in utero have lower intelligence where no other anticonvulsants were thus implicated (Bromley et al., 2014). Yet a 1/1,000 risk with lithium, although lower, is still significant. Even lamotrigine has not been entirely exonerated: a North American registry found an increased risk of cleft lip and cleft palate, although the UK registry did not (Grover and Avasthi, 2015). Most references at this writing appear to have concluded that lamotrigine does not carry this or any other risk of major malformations, but these are all moving targets. I have to search PubMed every time the question arises to find the latest thinking for any medication's safety during pregnancy or breastfeeding.

In any case, singling out divalproex doesn't make much sense to me. All these medications carry potential risk, including unknown risks, except perhaps the typical antipsychotics. Every medication requires planning regarding a possible subsequent pregnancy. With effective planning, even teratogenic medications may be used in women of reproductive age. We don't have much choice in some cases. Such planning involves highly reliable contraception until a pregnancy is intended, and a discussion of the multiple steps involved when a pregnancy is desired.

At a minimum, good mood control prior to pregnancy is almost a requirement. If she's not doing well beforehand, your patient is not likely to be doing well during a pregnancy, when a new life depends on her choices and will soon depend on her ability to parent. Indeed, the very decision to undertake a pregnancy should ideally be made when mood is stable. During such a period of wellness should come much discussion, including:

- how much risk does she face in going off medications during conception and first trimester;
- will she accept the need to go back on medications if significant symptoms return, and will she require help detecting this need;
- will she go back on her previous medications, or perhaps use a first-generation antipsychotic during the first trimester (perhaps even switching to one before conception, if medications are needed throughout this process);
- how her medications are affected by different stages of a pregnancy (lamotrigine and lithium, for example);

- how her medications will be managed just prior to delivery and just afterward;
- whether she is planning on breastfeeding her child and what medications might be safe in that context; and
- how the high risk of postpartum depression will be managed.

Unfortunately more than half of all pregnancies are not intended (Finer and Zolna, 2014). Thus the wisdom of Oregon's One Key Question: "Are you considering becoming pregnant in the coming year?" If the answer is no, a discussion of the need for highly effective contraception can take place.

Most psychiatrists will not frequently manage patients through pregnancy. If available, one could consider consultation with a subspecialist for help in creating a detailed plan. Unfortunately, finding such a specialist will be difficult in many areas. One resource that has been tremendously helpful in this realm for those of us without such access is the Massachusetts General Hospital's Center for Women's Mental Health (http://womensmentalhealth.org). Their Reproductive Psychiatry Resource and Information Center has a searchable library of essays on everything from PMS and PMDD to the multiple issues of pregnancy to menopausal symptoms.

Chapter 6

Psychotherapy for the Mid-Spectrum Patient
Selling Social Rhythm Therapy with Virtual Darkness

Multiple bipolar-specific psychotherapies have been shown in randomized trials to produce better outcomes than control treatments. Medications alone are not sufficient management for most patients. But one particular therapy is especially appropriate for patients in the middle of the mood spectrum: Social Rhythm Therapy. This chapter focuses on that technique after a brief review of the other therapies and their common ingredients.

Bipolar-Specific Psychotherapies

Starting around 2000, randomized trials of bipolar-specific therapies began to be reported. Prior to this there was little evidence to support a role for psychotherapy in the treatment of bipolar disorders. But rather suddenly, the evidence was at hand and it was clear: these therapies are essential in a full treatment plan.

Therapists who see patients with bipolar disorder should be aware of these approaches. Table 6.1 provides basic information.

Table 6.1. **Psychotherapies for bipolar disorder**

Therapy	Focus	Rx Manual	Reference
Prodrome detection	Prevention	(n/a; see below)	Perry et al., 1999
Psychoeducation	Prevention	*Psychoeducation Manual for Bipolar Disorders*	Colom et al., 2006
Bipolar-specific cognitive-behavioral therapy (CBT)	Prevention/ treatment	*CBT for Bipolar Disorder* *Managing Bipolar Disorder: A CBT program*	Basco and Rush, 2005 Otto et al., 2008
Interpersonal and social rhythm therapy (IPTSRT)	Prevention/ treatment	*Treating Bipolar Disorder: A Clinician's Guide to IPTSRT*	Frank, 2007
Family-focused therapy	Prevention/ treatment	*Bipolar Disorder: A Family-Focused Approach*	Miklowitz, 2007

1. Prodrome detection has been incorporated into all the later, more comprehensive treatments but is a remarkable study unto itself. It was described in the previous chapter, the proactive discussion of relapse prevention and planning, because it strongly informs the process of long-term management of mood.

2. Psychoeducation is a 21-session program offered in groups. The experimental group received extensive education about bipolar disorders. The control groups were support groups, with no psychoeducation (interestingly, run by the same two therapists who provided the extensive psychoeducation therapy, Drs. Vieta and Colom. Imagine the challenge of shifting gears between groups!). Over two years, relapse rates for the control group reached 90 percent versus 60 percent for the psychoeducation group participants (Colom et al., 2003). Even at five years, a significant difference between relapse rates for the two groups could still be seen (80 percent versus 100 percent for the controls; Colom et al., 2009). Granted, the relapse rates are quite high, but the lower rate in the psychoeducation group is a clinically very meaningful difference: even five years after the 20-week intervention, one patient in five is still doing well, because of the psychotherapy, when all the others have relapsed.

3. Bipolar-specific CBT has been developed by multiple authors, only some of whom are listed in Table 6.1. Though there are variations (e.g., emphasizing mindfulness, Ives-Deliperi et al., 2013; or a dialectic behavioral approach, Van Dijk and Segal, 2009), a relatively pure CBT approach was used in the large randomized trial with the STEP-BD research program, along with IPTSRT and Family-focused therapy. It includes extensive emphasis on prodrome detection and treatment contracts around that aim; psychoeducation; and many of the standard elements of depression-specific CBT. All three of the STEP-BD psycho-therapies, including bipolar-specific CBT, proved superior to treatment as usual (medications plus a moderately enhanced clinical management program) for recovery from a symptomatic phase (not just prevention of a later phase; Miklowitz et al., 2007).

4. Interpersonal and social rhythm therapy is a variation of inter-personal therapy (IPT) developed specifically for bipolar disorders. The social rhythm therapy (SRT) component is examined in detail later. IPT itself, like CBT alone, has years of randomized trials demonstrating effi-cacy (Markowitz and Weissman, 2004). The primary test of IPTSRT was the STEP-BD therapy study. In this case the developers of IPTSRT at the University of Pittsburgh formed the study team. Again the specialized treatment was an adjunct to medications and their clinical management, and it proved to be superior in recovery rates to that control treatment (Miklowitz et al., 2007).

5. Family-focused therapy for bipolar disorders followed the treat-ment developed by David Miklowitz and his team in Colorado. This program focuses on family psychoeducation, reductions in levels of expressed emotion in the household, and making sure the family is working as an effective team around the management of symptoms. In the STEP-BD this therapy yielded results comparable to bipolar-specific CBT, and IPTSRT (Miklowitz et al., 2007). A replication in adolescents did not show benefit relative to pharmacotherapy and brief psychoedu-cation alone (Miklowitz et al., 2014), but another program added CBT elements and did show benefit relative to a control psychotherapy as adjuncts to pharmacotherapy (West et al., 2014).

Finally, note that the Barcelona group that developed the psychoeducation intervention has also been working on a program that targets functional improvement, not just symptom control. They bravely tested this approach against their own psychoeducation groups as well as against a treatment-as-usual control group. Their newer *functional remediation therapy* was superior to control (Torrent et al., 2013), including in Bipolar II specifically (Solé et al., 2015). Interestingly, psychoeducation alone, which in this study was also superior to the control treatment, worked as well as functional remediation therapy on their measure of functional recovery (statistically, though a trend favored the remediation therapy in each study).

Common Ingredients in Bipolar-Specific Psychotherapies

Most current iterations of these treatments *combine* elements from these trial-proven therapies. Common ingredients include:

- early detection of symptoms
- stress management
- some direct treatments for depression
- medication adherence boosters
- handling of comorbid conditions like substance use problems or anxiety disorders
- some degree of bipolar psychoeducation

But most of these psychotherapies, and their respective descriptions and treatment manuals, have generally lumped together all the different forms of bipolar disorder and inevitably place a focus on detection, management, and prevention of *mania*. Mid-spectrum patients do not need this focus and can be put off by a manual that seems to be written for someone else.

One notable exception is a workbook approach developed specifically for Bipolar II by a trio from the Massachusetts General Hospital Bipolar Clinic and Research Program. Their *Bipolar II Disorder Workbook* is an excellent tool (Roberts et al., 2014). Another comprehensive workbook that can be mined selectively for elements appropriate to mid-spectrum patients was developed by Amy Kilbourne and Mark Bauer (Bauer et al., 2009). The breadth of this workbook is so large that one cannot simply assign the whole thing to patients, but its format allows specific tools to be handpicked.

None of these tools have been studied for patients whose bipolarity is less than Bipolar II but more than Major Depression—the middle of the mood spectrum. One approach seems to have particular applicability: SRT.

Social Rhythm Therapy

SRT is a very simple intervention, but I find it challenging to implement. Patients are reluctant to change the often very late bedtimes they have evolved. They stay up late hoping to become so exhausted that when they finally get in bed, they'll fall asleep quickly and not have to listen to their depressed, negative train of thought (loud, repetitive, incessant). Their reluctance led to me to evolve an approach to teaching SRT that differs significantly from the original. Of course, varying a treatment from the original raises the risk that my version loses some essential ingredient and may thus lose efficacy. On the other hand, if by varying the original it becomes easier to promote and for patients to adopt, loss of fidelity may be a justified risk.

First, look briefly at SRT in its original form. Think about this: what time did you:

- wake up
- get out of bed
- eat breakfast
- see your first other human
- first listen to the radio or TV or use the Internet
- leave home
- begin work, school, or other activity
- get some physical activity
- eat lunch
- stop school, work, or other activity

- take a nap
- eat dinner
- read a book, play a game with family, or other evening leisure activity
- watch TV or use the Internet in the evening
- get in bed
- go to sleep

These are social rhythms. If you give your patient a handout that lists these activities, with a space to note the times of each for a full week, you have administered a social rhythm inventory. (Such forms, called the social rhythm metric, are available at http://www.iptsrt.org with registration or with an Internet search for same; or simply by making a quick version by hand for your patient.) If your patient actually completed it for the week, imagine what it would look like for someone with poorly regulated bipolarity. At least moderate chaos, right?

SRT helps patients develop regular rhythms for all these activities. As you might imagine, this often requires some serious motivational interviewing: patients are likely in precontemplation for at least some of the suggested changes, such as a regular bedtime. Which of these social rhythms would you expect patients have the most difficulty making into a fixed-schedule routine?

A related question: which of these activities do you think have the most impact on circadian rhythm? An obvious presumption of this therapy is that bipolarity is a disturbance of circadian rhythm—a well-justified assumption for many patients. Likewise the therapy assumes that creating a more stable social rhythm can foster a more stable mood. Note that even if this latter assumption proves wrong, the "toxicity" of this treatment is almost nil: there is little harm in having a regular bedtime for a few weeks, for example. Thus it makes sense for nearly anyone with mood instability to try it.

But thence the rub: many patients are reluctant to change the very elements that have the most impact on circadian rhythm. Each of the activities on the list affect our biological clock, but sleep and darkness are the most powerful of all (Monk, 2010). Yet those are the ones patients are most reluctant to give up, particularly their evening television and Internet use. Rather than engage in a possibly lengthy process of motivational interviewing around setting regular bed- and rise times and limiting late-night television and Internet use, I've found the following approach much easier and surprisingly effective. (No data to report, regrettably. Consider and try it.)

What follows may seem like a long story, though it's a fun one. It revolves around a single case report, not our usual modus operandi. The point of the story is not to advocate using the treatment this one fellow underwent, but to suggest an easier approach, one that will move toward the same goal: a regular bedtime well before midnight, and a regular rise time, relatively close to sunrise.

The story comes in three parts, which at first appear unrelated: first the story of dark therapy, then the story about the primacy of blue light, and finally how these can be combined to offer a treatment that promotes SRT.

Dark Therapy

If antidepressants can make bipolar disorders worse (which is true) and if light is an antidepressant (which is true for many, though not all patients), then might the opposite also be true? Might *darkness* be a mood *stabilizer*?

Consider the experience of one patient who was treated at the National Institute of Mental Health (NIMH) for severe rapid cycling bipolar disorder (Wehr et al., 1998b). (Granted, this is just one patient, but you'll see what they were able to do *with no medications at all*.) Look at the graph of his mood, over time, in Figure 6.1, which presents years of his experience in schematic form.

The graph shows three years of severe rapid cycling, with no well intervals. Treatments tried at the time, if any, were clearly not working. Then the team began an intervention at the time marked with the gray line. The next cycle was less pronounced, and the patient fairly quickly moved to a more stable mood, doing particularly well in the latter part of that year and the following one.

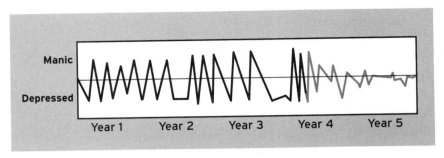

Figure 6.1 **Treatment of rapid cycling with no medications**

How did they do this? The team put him in a dark room at 6 p.m., every night, until 8 a.m. the following morning. No light, no television. He got so much better so fast that they backed off to a more sustainable regimen within a few weeks: 10 p.m. to 8 a.m., in "enforced darkness." This kept him well, with no medications.

When patients hear this story, the almost universal reaction is "Wow!" Then quickly comes the second reaction: "but I can't do that, I have to . . . (take care of children, work, study, etc.)." In my experience, patients are usually thinking about watching television. In any case, once I've elicited the "Wow!" reaction, I relieve their anxiety by noting that there may be another way to get the same benefit without enforced darkness. We use a workaround to create "virtual darkness."

But before learning about virtual darkness, you might want to know: is there further research support for the efficacy of darkness as a mood stabilizer? Admittedly, not much so far. There is a second case report, similar to the one in the NIMH study (Wirz-Justice et al., 1999). There is also a small trial in patients admitted to hospital with mania who were randomized to treatment as usual, or the same plus dark therapy (14 hours of enforced darkness for three nights). In this brief inpatient stay, patients receiving dark therapy lowered their Young Mania Rating Scale scores more quickly than those receiving treatment as usual and were discharged earlier on lower doses of anti-manic medications. (Interestingly, this result was confined to patients who had been admitted within two weeks of the onset of their mania, as though illness episodes can have a critical period for responding to a simple therapy; Barbini et al.,

2005). Another randomized trial of dark therapy is nearly complete as of this writing.

Why is there so little research on such an interesting idea with such powerful results? The lead investigator on the older inpatient study explained: "no money." Darkness is free. No profits will be generated advocating that patients treat themselves with a readily available resource.

However, getting complete darkness, particularly in an urban environment, can be quite difficult. Streetlights and urban nocturnal glare can make bedrooms quite light. Of course the biggest culprits are televisions, computers, and handheld electronic devices (lit screens). Patients are very reluctant to give up use of these bright-light-emitting sources, especially if the stopping point is early, say, 6 p.m. I have not had much luck negotiating away their use. Often the best I can do is arrange for patients to turn them off by 10–11 p.m.

Fortunately, there is another way to sell the idea of regular sleep in the dark. This requires another story.

Amber Lenses for Virtual Darkness

In 2000 a new photoreceptor in the human eye was discovered. This photoreceptor is not a rod or a cone (Brainard et al., 2001). Its fibers connect not to the visual cortex but to the suprachiasmatic nucleus of the hypothalamus, where the main biological clock is found. Thus these cells have been dubbed "circadian photoreceptors."

This receptor was quickly found to react almost exclusively to a narrow range of color, from blue-green to violet. Basically these cells are blue-light receptors (Brainard et al., 2001). Yellow, orange, and red wavelengths do not activate these cells under most conditions. Furthermore, it was found that these photoreceptors are the primary source for the brain's understanding of biological time: when is day, and when is night? Rods and cones have little impact by comparison.

Thus circadian rhythm is determined largely by blue light, absence of which is equivalent to *darkness*, from a circadian standpoint. This effect was confirmed in humans by using lenses tinted a particular shade of amber that filters out blue light entirely but transmits the rest of the light spectrum. In the form of wrap-around safety glasses, these lenses can prevent almost 100 percent of blue light from reaching subjects' retinas, yet allow sufficient light for reading and other activities.

The key experiment to demonstrate that these lenses do indeed create a circadian "virtual darkness" was performed by Kayumov and colleagues (2005). In their sleep lab, volunteers were first invited to spend the night—lights out at 9 p.m.—with their melatonin levels sampled hourly. They were allowed to sleep when they wished in the beds provided. Later the subjects returned to the lab overnight again, but this time the lights were left on and tasks simulating shift work (paper and pencil exercises) were performed all night. Again their melatonin production was sampled hourly. With this regimen, melatonin was found to be completely suppressed through the night. On a later third night of study, lights again were left on and again the shift-work tasks were required, but this time the subjects wore the amber safety glasses all night. Their melatonin production was almost identical to that of the first, lights-out night. This study has since been replicated in several variations.

Thus amber lenses have been shown to create circadian darkness in lit environments. But can these lenses—which can be purchased for as little as $7—be used to create a virtual darkness that would allow a trial of dark therapy without the enforced darkness protocol of the NIMH? Could patients have their darkness and eat it, too?

In an initial clinical test of this idea, I gave research-grade amber lenses to 20 consecutive patients with bipolar disorders after explaining the rationale. I asked my patients to wear the lenses for two hours before going to bed. Once in bed, in real darkness, they could remove the glasses. Of these 20 patients, 10 reported a notable reduction in sleep latency, as though they had been in the dark for several hours before bed. The other half, interestingly, reported no impact (Phelps, 2008). The lenses either worked, rather remarkably in many cases, or they did nothing at all.

But of course the true test of this approach would be a randomized trial of amber lenses versus a control lens, with participants blind to the hypothesis and investigators blind to treatment condition. The first pilot study was done by an undergraduate student for her senior thesis (Burkhardt and Phelps, 2009). It too showed a sleep improving effect from the amber lenses. A much more definitive study is under way in Norway, where Tone Henriksen and her colleagues are replicating the inpatient study of dark therapy for patients admitted with mania, this time using amber lenses for virtual darkness. A case report of a patient's experience during this trial describes a rapid and sustained decline in manic symptoms after amber lenses were initiated (Henriksen et al., 2014). Dr. Henriksen and colleagues also noted a markedly increased regularity of his sleep intervals, as had been seen just before the improvement experienced by the NIMH patient. Notably, the Norwegian patient's hospital stay was 20 days shorter than his average for numerous previous hospitalizations for mania.

At this writing, many of us with an interest in this area are anxiously awaiting publication of the full Norwegian study. After all, these lenses cost around $7 and pose little risk of harm (except for wearing them while driving home after work and falling asleep at the wheel, which may warrant a warning but is easily avoided; perhaps on an inpatient unit they could be broken into sharp pieces and used for cutting). If this virtual darkness approach really does act as a mood stabilizer, then there is little to prevent its rapid adoption. The pair of lenses that fits over corrective lenses does look a little odd (safety glasses, at home?), but other models are more stylish (or so I insist to reluctant patients). Interestingly, among patients who have experienced benefit from wearing them, none have continued to use them regularly, but they resume use when sleep regularity becomes problematic.

Selling Regular Sleep

Dark therapy holds some promise as an inexpensive, low-risk mood stabilizer option. But telling this whole story—or referring patients to my website version to reinforce a brief in-office explanation (http://psycheducation.org/treatment/bipolar-disorder-light-and-darkness/dark-therapy; including where to buy amber lenses)—has another benefit. The NIMH case of severe symptoms that came under control with no medications almost always grabs patients' attention, even the skeptical or reluctant. It helps a psychiatrist's credibility to be suggesting a non-medication approach, and the blue light/amber lenses story is fascinating unto itself. But the most important "sell" in all this is the value of regular sleep.

That value is nicely illustrated in the NIMH case (Wehr et al., 1998b). Figure 6.2 shows an additional record (schematic, adapted from the original) from the later years of their study, data on his sleep. A wristwatch accelerometer, like the modern Fitbit, was used to create a record of movement. Continued for weeks, the running record creates light areas of activity and a dark band of inactivity that represents sleep. Note that such a dark band becomes apparent just after dark therapy is initiated. Prior to that, the patient's sleep was so chaotic and irregular there was no discernible pattern.

Most importantly, note that the regular pattern of sleep that begins just after dark therapy is initiated *precedes* most of his mood improvement. Thus it appears that the active ingredient in the NIMH's regimen of enforced darkness was regularity of sleep. Darkness simply facilitated that regularity. Based on this result, one could suspect that other means of developing sleep regularity should also have a mood stabilizer effect. This has been demonstrated in the SRT research.

Therefore I explain to patients that sleep regularity, however it is achieved, is the goal. Having generated firm attention and an open mind with the dark therapy story and the amber lenses work-around story, I

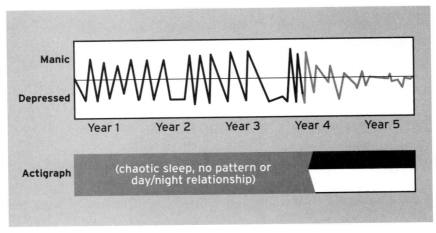

Figure 6.2. **Wristwatch actigraphy illustrates sleep response**

let them off the hook with an option to simply strive for a regular bed-time and a regular rise time. If they are enthused about the lenses, we sell pairs at cost in our front office to facilitate a trial.

As you can gather from my enthusiastic account of this approach, it has worked very well to promote adoption of earlier and regular bed-times. The key is to develop a willingness to give up late-night light. Think about it: darkness is as natural as oxygen. Evolutionarily, nearly a third of our time should be spent in the dark, or at least nothing more than firelight. But electricity and the many devices it powers allow us to steal time from darkness. For some people, and for many with bipolar disorders, this violation of the natural order can dramatically decrease sleep. Decreased sleep decreases mood stability. How do we help patients get more regular sleep?

Answer: the story of dark therapy and virtual darkness is highly engaging for patients, demonstrating the importance of a regular pat-tern of sleep in the dark. The stories make the whole endeavor seem more essential—which of course it is. The key is regularity, however it is achieved. But as we shall now see, physiology conspires against us.

The Asymmetry of the Biological Clock

Unlike the sun, humans' biological clocks do not run on a 24-hour cycle. Most individuals' clocks run slightly longer, 24.2 to 24.5 hours depend-ing on the study (following the pioneering cave experiments of Michael Siffre; e.g., Foer and Siffre, 2008). A regular pattern of light and dark exposure is necessary to set the biological clock to a 24-hour day/night cycle. But the human clock is not symmetric—that is, it is not equally adjustable in both directions. Because it runs slightly longer than 24 hours, it more easily drifts toward staying up later, and getting up later, than the reverse direction. Ubiquitous electric light promotes this drift by extending "day," suppressing the natural signal to bring our activities to a close and prepare for sleep (darkness). Some individuals are more susceptible to this drift than others. Indeed, bipolarity is associated with a tendency to want to stay up late, an "evening chronotype" (Etain et al., 2014; Jeong Jeong et al., 2015).

Use of electronic devices at night exacerbates this drift. Televisions, computers, tablets, and cell phones are worse than electric light alone, because light intensity varies inversely with the square of distance: a hand-held tablet two feet away is more than twice as bright as a laptop screen of the same size three feet away (for a point source this is true; less so for a large screen, but still quite true for a source as small as a phone).

Whether or not you work the math, the conclusion is clear: a cell phone one foot away is a very bright light because of its proximity. Patients expose themselves to the circadian equivalent of high noon with large TVs, close computers, or very close tablets or phones, and then wonder why they have difficulty falling asleep. Surely you've had the experience of becoming drowsy at 9 p.m., then finding yourself wide awake at 10 p.m. after saying to yourself "I'll just have a look at my email."

Worse yet, late-night light exposure drives the biological clock toward a later set point, with a matching delay in the hour of biological waking (a "phase delay"). For example, my late-night light exposure writing this book makes tonight's sleep slower to arrive, by moving my circadian rhythm of sleep to a later hour. The next morning, I'm slower to wake because my biological clock is not telling me to do so. If a patient does not have a job or other morning responsibilities, and stays in bed trying to "catch up on sleep," this further promotes a circadian phase delay. Ironically, even though it may be more difficult to get up at my regular hour, I am *protected* by my work schedule.

Unfortunately, in the absence of that protection, you've probably seen phase delays driven by late-night light and absence of a regular rise time become quite extreme. Patients can be awake at 3 a.m. or later (usually watching television, compounding the problem) and not get out of bed until noon. They cannot fall asleep earlier because their circadian rhythm is no longer in sync with the day/night cycle. They do not want to go to bed earlier, as SRT calls for, because they will lie awake—listening to their thoughts, which are often highly negative, creating another disincentive for going to bed early.

Worse yet, many patients with a PTSD component are understandably dark-phobic and will leave a light or TV on, sometimes all night, further blurring the distinction between day and night and promoting phase delay. They can basically lose all track of physiologic time: they have no systematic circadian drive to sleep. With the additional physiologic arousal of an underlying PTSD, they can have a terrible time getting any regular sleep at all—even without any bipolarity (seriously complicating our diagnostic efforts).

Once a patient is seriously phase-delayed or has lost track of physiologic time entirely, it can be extremely difficult for him to get to sleep earlier. He will lie there and curse your social rhythm therapy instructions to go to bed by 10:30 p.m.

As you may have prescribed for patients, a more acceptable solution to this problem is to suggest an alarm clock set for 15 minutes earlier every *morning*. Patients will still find this difficult, often hitting the snooze button repeatedly or just turning the whole thing off. If necessary, suggest a *series* of alarm clocks, each slightly farther away so that staying out of bed becomes more practical than returning to it. Or there's Clocky, an alarm clock that leaps off the bedstand and rolls around the room beeping! Indeed, demonstrating the ubiquity and severity of this problem, a YouTube video describes 20 different alarm clock variations from a fly-away propeller that must be reattached to the clock to turn it off, to a dumbbell that must be bicep-curled 30 times (see https://www.youtube.com/watch?v=albGoar3P0I). The most physiologic of these devices is called a dawn simulator. They are so simple, inexpensive, and easy to use that they can be the main driver of circadian rhythm change, and then one of the main tools to maintain a regular schedule.

Corollary to Amber Lenses: Dawn Simulators

Just as the onset of darkness signals the end of circadian day, the arrival of light in the morning signals the next day's start. But many patients, especially in urban environments, have to use dark curtains (or even aluminum foil over the windows) to create a truly dark bedroom. Now they have no dawn signal. Others may have to rise well before dawn for work. Many patients experience a dramatic mood swing in the fall, exacerbated by the shift from daylight savings time. In all these cases, a "dawn simulator" can provide a strong force to move and maintain circadian rhythm by providing a signal that says "pssst, it's morning."

These gizmos are simply a rheostat and a timer. The device turns on a light gradually over about 30 minutes, from zero to full intensity. There are smartphone apps as well. Though not yet formally tested, most of these apps are free, so for smartphone owners they're easy to try out.

These devices are easily tested: the light should wake the user from sleep (translucent eyelids allow the signal to reach the brain even with eyes closed). If she wakes too early, she can move the light across the room or use a dimmer bulb. If she does not awaken with the light, move it closer or use a brighter bulb. Any white light will do, as it contains plenty of blue light, the active ingredient.

Dawn simulators have been shown in a randomized trial to have an antidepressant effect in seasonal affective disorder (Terman and Terman, 2006). Although little further research has been done with these devices, we have a tool that is potentially mood-stabilizing through its effect on circadian rhythm and antidepressant. It is also cheap and harmless. How many other treatments do we have that meet this description? Moreover, even if it doesn't work, patients might still appreciate it: why wake to an alarm? Why not wake up to a gradually increasing light, with the alarm as only a backup? All this is achievable without any risk of exacerbating bipolarity (to my knowledge, no hypomania has ever been reported due to a dawn simulator).

How should dawn simulators be used? In the summer, they may not be necessary, unless patients have had to black out their bedroom. But in early September as the morning sun signal arrives later and later, they should set the device to reach a maximal dawn signal when they need to be waking up for work or school. Patients with no such obligations can use a dawn simulator to bookend their sleep with a natural circadian signal that facilitates staying on schedule and getting out of bed at a regular hour (e.g., no later than 8:30 a.m., preferably earlier to stay in synchrony with the sun as much as possible).

The dawn simulator is the physiologic corollary to amber lenses. Both tools strengthen natural determinants of circadian rhythm, light and darkness. For most patients, if it makes sense to use one, it makes sense to use the other.

Excess Sleep Carries Risk, Too

Mania often gets more attention than depression, despite the latter's greater prevalence, because mania is more dramatic. Similarly, precipitation of manic episodes from sleep deprivation also gets more attention than the risk of excess sleep. Yet the latter appears to make some depressions worse. Just as a little mania makes people sleep less, and thus get more manic, a little sleep excess, at least in some patients, can make depression worse, which makes people sleep more, and so on into a spiraling depression.

For example, one of my patients commutes to another city during the week for work, requiring that he get out of bed at 5:30 a.m. Monday through Friday. He came in and said, "You know, on Saturdays, my mood is worse, and on Sundays it's much worse. Then Monday, it's a little better. By Wednesday I'm fine again." On weekends, he was sleeping in until 8 a.m. or so, as much as 2.5 additional hours of sleep. When he accepted the idea that on weekends he would need to be out of bed no later than 7 a.m., preferably 6:30, and implemented that schedule, his fluctuations stopped.

The most dramatic evidence for a relationship between excess sleep and depression comes from the overnight sleep-deprivation studies (now euphemistically called "wake therapy"). One night without sleep has long been recognized to dramatically improve a depressed patient's mood, regardless of their position on the mood spectrum (Berger et al., 1997; Colombo et al., 2000). But with the next night's full sleep, patients would again become depressed. However, several regimens have now been devised that preserve the mood improvement. Some of these, which combine light therapy and precisely timed sleep phase shifts, are referred to as "triple chronotherapy" (Benedetti, 2012). As one sleep/mood specialist summarized:

> There are a fair number of studies now showing that that combination actually works really well for some people and helps sustain the antidepressant effect of sleep deprivation. In the US, I don't think anyone really does this routinely in clinical practice because no insurance company is going to pay to have people in the lab to

do this. There are a couple of groups in Europe who do this more routinely. . . . It's a shame it's not part of more routine clinical care because it does work so well. (Philip Gehrman, quoted in Brooks, 2015; more on this technique in Appendix C)

Chronotherapy's effectiveness underscores the central importance of sleep, including total sleep duration and especially its timing.

Summary

Regular bedtimes and regular rise times are the central ingredients in SRT. For many patients, if they do not have a regular sleep pattern, they will not respond to even aggressive medication approaches. Excitingly, for many patients, aggressively pursuing a regular pattern of sleep can have dramatic mood-stabilizing effects. More research in this area would be very helpful.

Helping patients understand the principles behind dark therapy, amber lenses, and dawn simulators is useful even if those techniques are not used, because they shift the emphasis away from passive medication treatments toward personal management of mood. In theory this shift can help lower the amount and number of medications required.

Although the psychotherapies referenced in this chapter are all important, and any one of them could be particularly important for a given patient, in my experience SRT is one of the most central ingredients in all of these therapies, for all points on the mood spectrum. I hope my descriptions will help you implement it with your patients. In the next chapter, we turn to a medication approach for mid-spectrum patients.

Chapter 7

Efficacy versus Tolerability:
Why Lamotrigine Is the #1 Medication Option for Mid-Spectrum Mood Disorders

Medication chapters in this book will not repeat basic information found in standard resources like *Up-To-Date*. Here we will focus instead on factors that drive choices between treatments, as well as details not commonly discussed, and potentially confusing issues.

A note about pharmaceutical company influence: for about five years I accepted speaking honoraria from manufacturers of lamotrigine and quetiapine, but I stopped in early 2009 when they required me to give their scripted talk, not mine. I used their payments to subsidize the care of patients who could not afford treatment, as well as for time to create my website, never making more money than I did seeing patients full-time. Discussion of lamotrigine and other medications in this book is not influenced by having accepted those honoraria, as far as I can discern. For example, in this chapter you will find discussion of some lamotrigine risks that do not appear in most reviews. But judge my neutrality for yourself. Additional information about my experiences with pharmaceutical company honoraria are presented on my website (in the About section; http://psycheducation.org).

Lamotrigine's Positives

Lamotrigine is nearly the ideal medication for mid-spectrum mood disorders. It has an antidepressant effect, which is the top priority for a medication in this niche. It cannot be relied on for prevention of manic episodes (a generally accepted truism; see Bowden and Singh, 2012, for example). But as noted previously, mid-spectrum patients by definition do not require anti-manic protection. Instead, lamotrigine offers multiple other advantages over other medications for bipolarity.

1. Weight-neutral. Lamotrigine has not been associated with weight gain, as have many other psychotropics. Of course some patients will gain weight while taking it, but in general, they'll gain no more than those on placebo or taking nothing.

2. Few side effects. Most people experience no side effects at all. Many have said "It doesn't feel like I'm taking anything." They have to remind themselves what life was like before lamotrigine, else be tempted to conclude that it is "not doing anything."

3. No significant long-term risks. Lamotrigine has been around for over 20 years and as of this writing has yet to show any significant risks associated with its long-term use. The rash risk (Stevens-Johnson syndrome and other allergic reactions, handling of which is discussed below) is confined almost entirely to the first six to eight weeks of use. A slight risk persists, barely above population norms.

4. Low toxicity. Too high a dose causes side effects that are generally mild and remit quickly when the dose is lowered. These include subtle cognitive impairment and balance problems, both of which often require direct query to detect, because patients may not have recognized them as problems or as related to lamotrigine.

And yet, as though brushing these advantages aside, academic discussions about lamotrigine focus on the problems with its evidence for efficacy.

The Efficacy Debate

Almost everything we know about lamotrigine effectiveness for depression derives from studies of Bipolar I and Bipolar II. Indeed, this is unfortunately the case for all the medications in this book. Why no data on mid-spectrum patients? Because the DSM does not recognize these patients separately—they are lumped with Major Depression. Only with the advent of "mixed depression" (Chapter 4) have any studies focused on patients with subthreshold manic symptoms. For mid-spectrum patients we are forced to extrapolate down the spectrum from experience with medications at the bipolar end.

At what point might a patient's bipolarity be so minimal that an antidepressant, rather than lamotrigine, becomes an appropriate strategy? For patients with little evidence for bipolarity, antidepressants are a logical choice if psychotherapy is not available, practical, acceptable, or effective. Nearer the other end of the spectrum, when patients meet DSM criteria for Bipolar II, lamotrigine is an obvious starting place, as I'll suggest shortly. In between, it's a judgment call to be made by the clinician and the patient, weighing the evidence for risk and benefit for both lamotrigine and antidepressants. Thus, information on lamotrigine's efficacy, which might seem somewhat belabored here, is crucial in this mid-spectrum decision. Likewise, information on antidepressant efficacy and risk—extrapolated to the middle of the mood spectrum—is also essential in this decision (presented in Chapter 12).

To begin: has lamotrigine been demonstrated to be better than a placebo in bipolar depression? Surprisingly, given the number of treatment guidelines in which it is a first-line monotherapy, several analyses found evidence for lamotrigine's efficacy lacking (Calabrese et al., 2008; Ghaemi et al., 2008b; Taylor et al., 2014). On the other hand, Calabrese participated in another meta-analysis published a year later which arrived at the opposite conclusion: lamotrigine is indeed better than placebo, at least for patients whose initial depression is quite severe (Geddes et al., 2009). Interestingly, the latter review specified a minimum Hamilton Depression Scale (HAM-D) score of 24 as the cutoff for apparent efficacy: patients whose depression was less severe than 24 on that scale did not show benefit. This is almost exactly the same cutoff identified for *antidepressant* efficacy studies, in an important analysis of these commonly prescribed medications (Fournier et al., 2010): below HAM-D scores around 24, antidepressants were no better than placebo. Thus one could say that lamotrigine has just as much evidence for efficacy as do the far more studied antidepressants: when depression is severe, they both work. When depression is mild to moderate, improvement on lamotrigine, or antidepressants, is as likely with a placebo.

One of the problems with the lamotrigine reviews is that there aren't many studies to analyze: less than half as many for lamotrigine than for quetiapine, for example (Taylor et al., 2014). Those we do have are subject to publication bias: negative studies go unpublished while positive studies reach print, circulation, and discussion (Ghaemi, 2009; and multiple analyses by Eric Turner and colleagues, beginning with his seminal analysis of unpublished antidepressant studies in the *New England Journal of Medicine*, 2008).

In this context, clinical experience becomes all the more relevant in interpreting the efficacy data.

Randomized Trials versus Clinical Experience

An old saw, frequently invoked but of unknown attribution, says there may be "nothing worse than a little clinical experience." Too small a clinical sample can suggest spurious associations (sampling bias). Another old saying: "when a new drug shows up, use it quickly before it stops working." In other words, initial enthusiasm over a new treatment can lead us to see patient improvement that is not replicable later when the excitement has diminished (a positive expectation bias). If one believes strongly in a particular treatment, one can miss, downplay, or explain away the times it doesn't work while crediting the treatment for every success (confirmation bias). Likewise, strong beliefs can influence which patients' experience is remembered and which forgotten (recall bias). If a practitioner reserves a favored treatment for patients likely to improve and turns to alternative treatments for patients with more complex and intermixed problems (selection bias), that can skew her impression of how often her favored treatment actually works relative to other options.

Thus medicine has come to value the randomized clinical trial, which removes many sources of bias and controls for others. Conversely, clinical experience—observations of patient outcomes—is generally downplayed as a source of information about what treatments are truly effective. But with regard to mid-spectrum bipolarity, I believe we've swung that pendulum too far. For example, we can declare lamotrigine ineffective and posit olanzapine/fluoxetine combination (with vastly greater risks) as a first choice for bipolar depression, if we are looking only at randomized trial data (e.g., Taylor et al., 2014).

Yet clinicians who see many patients and have time to really listen to those patients' experience can often quickly identify a new medication that is truly effective. When olanzapine first came out, for example, within a few months my colleagues and I could see: "Oh, now this stuff, this really works." Unfortunately, just a month or two later, we could also see: "Oh, this stuff causes weight gain like we've never seen except with clozapine." We did not need randomized trials for this.

One more example, then back to lamotrigine: when ziprasidone first came out and was touted as unlikely to cause weight gain, we all began trying it, in hope. Within a few months it seemed we had all figured out it was far less reliable than other medications and rife with side effects, though it was true that it did not seem to cause weight gain. But it just wasn't working, except for a rare patient who would seem to do beautifully on it (we still puzzle over how to identify those few patients!). The point: we did not need randomized trials to prove this to us. When a drug's efficacy is very large or nearly absent, clinical experience can reliably and rather quickly identify this.

Of course all this presumes that medical culture and pharmaceutical marketing are not exerting their extremely strong influences. Bleeding with incisions and leeches remained a treatment for decades when medical culture supported it, against manifest evidence of inefficacy and harm. Guarding against tacit assumptions is extremely important. Likewise the expensive spectacles staged by pharmaceutical companies at national meetings, their frequent representative visits, free samples, and the obvious gifts disguised as education (fine dining remains among these after the trips and golf were banned)—all of these can strongly affect clinical observation, not just judgment. Often one can have difficulty identifying when these influences are at work, making one's own experience worth questioning.

Nevertheless, and heretical as it may sound to many academics, I think we've placed randomized trials on too high an altar, and in the process downgraded the value of extensive clinical experience. Clinicians who see patients all day, every day, and have time to really listen to their experience and query for subtle changes, can see things that randomized trials may not detect.

Lamotrigine may be one of the best examples of this. For example, meetings of the International Society for Bipolar Disorders have largely been dominated by academic researchers (with some recent change welcomed by the organization). However, over the past decade of meetings, a small band of clinicians has grown, and we confer with one another while the scholars relate their most recent findings. In our subgroup, lamotrigine is generally regarded as the obvious first choice in treatment of bipolar depression in patients with Bipolar II or further down the mood spectrum. Of course that observation on my part is also subject to the biases outlined already. But even with my best efforts to self-police, I think this observation stands. How is it that clinicians are so far from the academics on this issue? That is the subject of the section below on efficacy versus tolerability. First, one more brief question about efficacy in unipolar depression.

What about Lamotrigine in Unipolar Depression?

If lamotrigine also showed at least *some* evidence for efficacy at the unipolar end of the mood spectrum, that would help establish a role for its use in mid-spectrum patients. Unfortunately, there are few full trials of lamotrigine in unipolar depression, and among those, the evidence for benefit is equivocal: not quite zero but close, one might say. It simply cannot be relied on as a treatment for major depression. Among residents and primary care providers in cases where I'm consulting, I frequently see lamotrigine used as an adjunct in treatment-resistant depression. Perhaps that practice reflects a recognition of the very low risk of this medication relative to atypical antipsychotics, but there are few data to support this practice.

On the other hand (and this observation *does* accord with my experience), one review of lamotrigine found that patients with more treatment resistance, comorbid anxiety, and borderline personality disorder traits may be more able to benefit than those with pure unipolar depression (Zavodnik and Ali, 2012). Of course one could wonder whether those patients might have had some degree of bipolarity. As per the logic of Chapters 3 and 4, this question of bipolarity is better addressed through trials of treatment than through diagnostic head-scratching. But which treatment? Here lamotrigine returns to the fore among medication options, because medication choice is based on evidence for efficacy *but also evidence for harm*. Let's look at that balance for lamotrigine in mid-spectrum patients.

Efficacy versus Tolerability

The list of lamotrigine's positives that begins this chapter is really an accounting of its relatively high tolerability: weight-neutral, few side effects, no long-term risks known, low toxicity risk. When patients are invited into a shared decision-making process (as described in Chapter 5), they frequently place great weight on the tolerability side of the benefit/risks see-saw. They generally give far less weight—especially compared to the academics' meta-analyses—to the evidence for efficacy side.

This strong weighting of tolerability over efficacy is even more pronounced among mid-spectrum patients where the risk of a recurrent manic episode does not loom in the past, a specter of potential social disaster that must be prevented even if the costs are relatively high. Instead, there is often a very long history of depression—such that saving a month or two by picking a high-efficacy agent first is often not a priority for patients. Instead, they recognize that if they find a medication that works, they're likely to be on it for an extended period of time. So starting with a medication that carries no known risk if continued for years is very appealing. (Some vigilance about rashes is still required with lamotrigine: the risk returns almost to baseline after arriving at a steady dose, but it never quite reaches zero).

Not being associated with weight gain is a very strong factor in favor of lamotrigine for most patients. The idea of having no side effects at all ("I don't feel like I'm taking anything") is also appealing. By contrast, despite quetiapine's significantly better evidence for efficacy, its significant potential for causing diabetes and increased cardiovascular risk leaves the see-saw tilted far toward lamotrigine for most patients I see.

Yet some mood specialists rank olanzapine/fluoxetine combination (Taylor et al., 2014) or quetiapine (Nierenberg et al., 2015) at the top of the list for bipolar depression. Among the most recent treatment guidelines, the European NICE (National Institute for Health and Care Excellence) offers lamotrigine "if the patient prefers" after olanzapine/fluoxetine and quetiapine (NICE, 2014b). I am astounded by this rank ordering, but other mood specialists seem to split roughly 50/50 on whether lamotrigine should be among the first-line options (e.g., Ketter et al., 2014; Malhi et al., 2009; Parker and McCraw, 2015; Selle et al., 2014; Vieta and Valentí, 2013).

Worsening on Lamotrigine

Reviews of lamotrigine's benefits and risks always include a discussion of the rash, but most do not mention the possibility of increasing agitation, anxiety, irritability, and difficulty sleeping. I did not attribute this collection of symptoms to lamotrigine even after prescribing it for several years. But over time I've had some patients in whom these symptoms developed just after lamotrigine was initiated, with few life events to obscure causality; remission of these symptoms immediately followed discontinuation, further implicating lamotrigine. Once I knew to look for this, I started seeing it more often.

Right about the same time, I had the good fortune to refresh an old connection with a smart and skilled psychiatrist, Kurt Mueller. Like the ISBD clinicians noted earlier, he had independently developed a high regard for lamotrigine for mid-spectrum patients, and we compared notes. Without any lead-up I asked him, "how often do you think lamotrigine makes people worse, like an antidepressant?" He answered without hesitation: "Oh, about one person in 20 or 30." That was the same frequency estimate I'd come up with.

We're not the only ones. An Israeli team (Raskin et al., 2006) has reported three cases of lamotrigine-associated hypomania or mania, but all were receiving complex regimens to which lamotrigine was added very rapidly (a practice which in my view is almost never warranted). Their case series cites a previous single case report by Margolese et al. (2003) that describes what I've seen very well: A 23-year-old woman with no history of bipolar disorder had only a partial response to psychotherapy plus 400 mg bupropion. Somehow her team decided to add lamotrigine. They observed: "After 1 week of 25 mg, Ms. A reported an improved mood. After another week at 50 mg, she noted a further improved mood, decreased anxiety, and increased energy."

Similar initial improvement has occurred in nearly every patient of mine who subsequently worsened, very similar to what can be seen with antidepressants in patients with bipolar disorder, who can report very rapid improvement. (Gary Sachs joked at a conference years ago: "When your patient calls up on Day 2 to report that he's not felt this good in years, maybe ever, your response should be 'Great, let's celebrate: let's lower the dose of your antidepressant.'").

The Margolese case report continues: "Two weeks later her lamotrigine dose was increased to 75 mg. One week thereafter she reported decreased sleep (2-4 hours per night), increased energy, distractibility, mood lability, and increased spending." They diagnosed hypomania and lowered her dose to 50 mg, and these symptoms were diminished at a two-week follow-up. She apparently stayed on the 50 mg dose and did well for over a year (what happened with the bupropion dose is not stated). More recently a Japanese team reported two cases of "murderous impulses" associated with lamotrigine: one at 125 mg, with symptoms diminishing after a dose reduction to 75 mg, and one at 25 mg, with symptoms remitting on discontinuation of lamotrigine (Saito et al., 2014).

Randomized trials of lamotrigine have reported no such findings in their aggregate data or in individual adverse event reporting. Thus Dr. Mueller and I would appear to be overestimating the frequency of these responses. Or perhaps we are detecting more subtle worsening that would not have come to the attention of investigators conducting a randomized trial.

The Rash: Incidence

Lamotrigine is just one of numerous medications that can cause Stevens-Johnson syndrome (SJS) and related severe rashes such as toxic epidermal necrolysis (all often lumped as SJS). Sulfonamides (e.g., the antibiotic trimethoprim-sulfamethoxazole) and anticonvulsants are the main culprits but penicillin and nonsteroidals can also cause SJS. Even benzodiazepines have been implicated, though at a rate of about four in a million (Martín-Merino et al., 2015).

Estimates of the frequency of SJS and related severe rashes range from the often cited 1/1,000 to 1/3,000 (Mockenhaupt et al., 2005—the definitive reference, in my opinion), and occasionally 1/5,000 (e.g., *Bipolar Network News*, from Dr. Robert Post). Even though these rates vary fivefold, for patients they boil down to somewhere between "extremely uncommon" and "rare." Of course they also often announce (and more may think) "I'll be that one patient in a thousand," particularly on hearing that I've yet to see a full case of SJS after prescribing lamotrigine often for well over a decade. Of course my experience is not surprising as I'm likely only just now approaching 1,000 new prescriptions.

In any case, for a severe reaction that occurs in only 1/1,000 new patients, or perhaps three to five times *less* often, lamotrigine-induced rash gets an inordinate amount of attention in risk/benefit analyses. On the other hand, when it occurs, it can be awful and dangerous. One certainly would not want to downplay this risk, because patients can find photographs of frightening cases online. Given the controversy over evidence for efficacy, we are not in a good position to soft-pedal risk even if statistically warranted.

Unfortunately lamotrigine also causes a benign rash at a rate closer to 1/10 (Wang et al., 2015). So after hearing about SJS, patients may be alarmed if they experience a typical drug reaction, small red bumps on arms, trunk or legs ("morbilliform rash") . Clinicians who use lamotrigine must have a routine for handling this event.

Handling a Rash without Stopping Medication

Most references suggest that if any skin rash occurs, lamotrigine should be stopped. For example, the prestigious Black Dog Institute in Australia recommends stopping and waiting for six months before considering a cautious rechallenge, after a benign rash (see http://www.blackdoginsti tute.org.au/docs/Lamotrigineassociatedrash.pdf).

However, years ago a neurology colleague explained to me how he handles what appear to be benign drug reactions. First, be familiar with the signs that indicate possible SJS:

1. Any rash that is accompanied by fever, flu-like symptoms, or lack of appetite.
2. Any rash that involves the membranes lining the eyes, lips, mouth, nostrils, genitals, or anal area.
3. Any rash that is prominent on the neck and upper trunk.
4. Merging, widespread red swollen rashes (wheals or hives) some-times with round red target-like spots.
5. A rash comprising purplish, small spots or larger areas of skin.
6. Discolorations that, when pressed with the finger, do not go white as other rashes do, and are tender to the touch.
7. Skin swelling and redness all over the body, with or without widespread shedding of the skin. (Black Dog Institute)

If any of these are present, stop lamotrigine without taper. But if the rash is morbilliform, on arms, trunk, and/or legs; if it itches and becomes more uncomfortable in the shower; and most important, if it lacks any of the 7 features above, there is another way to handle it.

First, if you have a good relationship with a dermatologist who is nearby, exploit it. I'm told dermatologists would love to see SJS because they don't get the chance very often, but check that assumption. On seeing a rash about which you're worried, which may be *any* rash when you are first using lamotrigine, send the patient to your dermatologist colleague, if she can see the patient within a day or two before the rash subsides and becomes harder to interpret.

If you don't have access to such services, you can always just stop lamotrigine and later conduct a rechallenge, described below (perhaps as soon as four weeks after the rash is gone, not six months, though the longer one waits, the lower the risk; Aiken and Orr, 2010).

My neurology colleague, who has over 20 years of experience using multiple rash-inducing medications (e.g., carbamazepine, divalproex, and phenytoin, not just lamotrigine), said if the rash appears very likely benign he simply lowers the dose one step and watches very closely until the rash is clearly gone. Then he waits at least a week and resumes the titration with smaller increments and more slowly (benign rashes and SJS almost always occur during titration, not once the dose is stable, so titration rates are a controllable risk factor).

"Watch very closely" in my practice means that the patient must call me every day and describe the rash, relative to its appearance on the previous days. If it is clearly not worse, then he is authorized to take another of the one-step-lower doses. I have found phone descriptions of the rash to be adequate for assessing items 1–7 on the Black Dog Institute list above, but if there was any question about the benignity of the rash, I would have the patient come in so I could examine it. (Multiple online dermatology programs routinely use a photograph taken by the patient, but handling these on your own in proper HIPAA fashion is tricky). We continue this ritual one day at a time, with no further doses to be taken until authorized by me after hearing the new rash description. The ritual continues until the rash is clearly diminishing, which has generally required only two to three days.

Remember, the vast majority of rashes are benign: 1 in 1,000 patients starting lamotrigine will have SJS but 1/10, or 100 patients, will have a benign rash. Thus of 100 rashes, 99 will be benign. Granted, the remaining 1 of the 100 may have a dangerous condition, warranting caution here. But 99 trials of lamotrigine will be interrupted unnecessarily if one follows the standard dictum for 1,000 patients. Often I've heard colleagues lament "and the patient was doing really well on it, too!" Which brings us to the idea of rechallenging patients who've had a rash and then stopped lamotrigine.

Lamotrigine Rechallenge after Rash

The foregoing procedure would be more worrisome were it not for a remarkable case series and literature review by Aiken and Orr (2010). Dr. Aiken describes multiple cases in which the initial rash was far more worrisome than a typical morbilliform drug eruption, yet the patients were successfully restarted on lamotrigine with no recurrence of a rash of any kind. Granted, the restart was extremely cautious: starting with 5 mg (the pediatric dose) and increasing by that amount every two weeks. Note some of the descriptions of patients' rashes who were treated successfully thus:

- vesicles on tongue
- wheals on arms and tongue
- pruritic macules on face and neck
- blistering papules on knuckles
- wheals and macules on lips, tongue, and arms; edema of legs
- diffuse petechial rash, including face; with lymphadenopathy

and so on. Note that *all* of these cases have signs that suggest SJS according to the Black Dog list of features.

Dr. Aiken and I agree that one should almost never begin lamotrigine more quickly than the standard titration of 25 mg for two weeks, 50 mg for two weeks, and so on. One of the most important reasons for this restraint, even in patients who have severe depression and for whom one would wish to see a very rapid response, is to avoid the *benign* rash. If one goes too quickly and a rash occurs, even if benign, it can completely derail or at least significantly slow the lamotrigine trial. Which brings us to another issue: how slow *is* lamotrigine?

Lamotrigine Is Not Slow

Lamotrigine has a reputation for being very slow to produce results. This is often used as a reason to choose some other agent, to which response is thought to be faster. On some psychiatric inpatient units, for example, lamotrigine is often not considered for bipolar depression. This is ironic because lamotrigine is probably not slower to produce benefit than antidepressants: after all, most clinicians would agree that once started, before an antidepressant can be pronounced ineffective, the trial should go at least four weeks (even with no evident benefit all that time; many would say six weeks, and some would say eight or more).

Yet a randomized trial suggests that lamotrigine is not slow to produce benefit, even with the (important) slow titration (Brown et al., 2006).

Indeed, twisting the irony further, the study was sponsored by Eli Lilly, makers of the olanzapine/fluoxetine combination. This was a head-to-head comparison of lamotrigine versus their combination pill. Given the sponsor, one would expect that if anything, somehow the deck would be stacked against lamotrigine. For example, the study was set to last only seven weeks. Lamotrigine, per standard titration, was being gradually increased for the first six weeks, whereas olanzapine/fluoxetine was rapidly introduced.

In this study lamotrigine was never as good as the combination pill. That result is often cited in the efficacy debates already described. But lamotrigine was not slow. As shown schematically in Figure 7.1, the depression scores (CGI scale; a clinical measure) improved in parallel.

Lamotrigine was always a little less effective, but response (as evident in the slope of the rising curve of CGI scores) was just as fast as to the combination pill. This supports my observations that lamotrigine often seems to be doing something positive within the first week of 50 mg (i.e., week 3) and sometimes even at 25 mg.

Thus if it makes sense to start an antidepressant on an inpatient psychiatric unit, it makes sense to start lamotrigine. I would grant that for a case of severe bipolar depression, where the patient's life is at

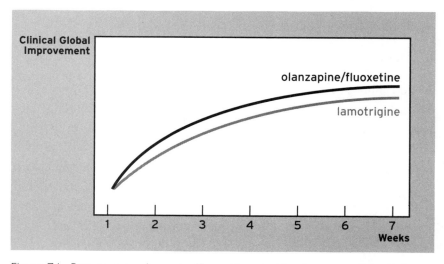

Figure 7.1. **Response to olanzapine/fluoxetine combination versus lamotrigine in bipolar depression**

stake, using a treatment with robust evidence for efficacy instead of lamotrigine could make sense: electroconvulsive therapy (ECT), for example, or perhaps quetiapine; maybe olanzapine/fluoxetine combination. Patients in the middle of the mood spectrum can certainly have depressions this severe.

But those patients will likely have had those depressions many times before. They face the likely prospect of having them again, unless a treatment is found to prevent recurrences (a "maintenance" agent). So unless the depression is immediately dangerous, it does not make sense to me to hurry toward a treatment with significant side effects (e.g., risk of memory impairment with ECT) or long-term risks (e.g., developing diabetes with quetiapine or olanzapine) and skip over a treatment with few side effects and no established long-term risks. Most patients in my practice prefer to work their way through options starting with those that, if they work, will be most tolerable in the long run, even if likelihood of response is lower. If lamotrigine doesn't work in six weeks (reaching at least 100 mg), we move on.

Clinically Relevant Drug Interactions

Two drug interactions with lamotrigine must be managed carefully, although if handled properly they are not dangerous and should not affect medication selection. One other interaction does not require management but it gets inaccurate press coverage, so is included here.

1. Valproate/divalproex. As you probably know, valproate (generally administered as an enteric coated pill, e.g., divalproex) inhibits the metabolism of lamotrigine. You may not know that lamotrigine is not metabolized through the P450 liver cytochrome system but by a liver glucuronidase. Valproate inhibits glucuronidase almost immediately on its introduction (unlike the slow induction of enzymes associated with carbamazepine). The effect begins with very low doses: a 30 percent reduction in lamotrigine clearance at 125 mg of divalproex, and the maximal effect, 50 percent reduction, at 250 mg of divalproex and up (Kanner, 2004).

Thus adding divalproex to lamotrigine is neither tricky nor dangerous. Simply cut the dose of lamotrigine that the patient is taking in half as divalproex is added. Lamotrigine levels should stay roughly the same.

But adding lamotrigine to divalproex is a different story. Typical instructions suggest starting lamotrigine at 25 mg every other day instead of every day. Why not just cut the pill in half and start at 12.5 mg daily—wouldn't that be lower exposure and smoother? To be even more cautious, one could start with a 5 mg pediatric dose and increase every week, staying just below the total doses in the general guidelines but starting with a much lower dose and smoothing the increase yet further.

Since the severe and the benign rashes are related to the rate at which the medication is introduced, it seems logical to keep the initial doses as low as possible (if practical) when adding lamotrigine to divalproex. Doing so does not add much additional titration time. Perhaps cutting the pill in half to 12.5 mg prevents 1 in 100 benign rashes. As long as patients don't give up because I've made the titration too complex (a risk one can reduce by watching the patient's face as the plan is explained, reverting to a simpler regimen if warranted), perhaps this enables one or two more patients to get on lamotrigine without any rash.

2. Carbamazepine. Carbamazepine (CBZ) induces the metabolism of medications that are cleared via the gluronidase system as well as the P450 oxidases. So it will lower lamotrigine levels just as it lowers other medications metabolized in the liver.

Clinically this interaction is relatively straightforward as long as one remembers to account for it. Adding CBZ to lamotrigine will gradually lower lamotrigine to roughly half its prior level or even lower (Perucca 2006). However, if depression increases, first make sure that CBZ itself is not inducing that mood shift. I've seen numerous patients become acutely depressed within the first two weeks of starting CBZ.

Compare the increase in depression one might expect from lowering lamotrigine levels: the time course is quite different. CBZ enzyme induction is a gradual process over the first several weeks (how long depends on the half-life of the enzyme turnover; in general this is three to four days, so maximal induction takes about two weeks to ramp up; Brodie et al., 2003). A patient who becomes depressed in the first week after starting CBZ has not done so because her lamotrigine level went down; it is more likely a CBZ direct effect, and the medication should be stopped. By contrast, a more gradual onset of increasing depression starting more than a week after CBZ was introduced could be from falling lamotrigine levels, and one should consider increasing the lamotrigine dose.

The other way around—adding lamotrigine to carbamazepine—is even more straightforward. Initial lamotrigine levels will be lower because carbamazepine enzyme induction is already in place. Theoretically one can start lamotrigine at higher doses, say, 50 mg for two weeks, instead of 25 mg. I simply use the induction to allow a lower/smoother start: 25 mg to start with *weekly* increases to 100 mg.

When carbamazepine is stopped, how long will it take before enzyme induction is diminishing and it will be time to lower lamotrigine doses? Pharmacokinetic modeling following discontinuation of carbamazepine suggests a deinduction half-life of approximately four days (Schaffler et al., 1994). Though the entire process will take just over two weeks, significant changes will have happened within days, so consider lowering lamotrigine well before carbamazepine is fully tapered off.

3. Oral contraceptives. Birth control pills lower lamotrigine levels roughly 50 percent (Christensen et al., 2007; Wegner et al., 2009). If a woman goes on oral contraceptives and becomes depressed, that could be from the contraceptive itself (steroid hormones can make bipolar disorders worse by causing depression, mixed states, or manic symptoms). But it could also be from a reduction in lamotrigine, if she was taking that before starting the oral contraceptives.

Conversely one might recommend that a woman not *stop* her oral contraceptive while titrating up on lamotrigine, as the doubling effect could compound a dose increase and raise the risk of severe rashes. Finally, lamotrigine side effects could increase during the hormone-free week (in theory). I've not seen this but may have been missing it, as they are subtle (per above).

But a more alarming interaction is the possibility that lamotrigine could interfere with an oral contraceptive and lower its efficacy, allowing conception to occur. This is stated outright as a risk on WebMD: "If you are taking an oral contraceptive, it may not work as well to prevent pregnancy" (Lamictal Interactions, http://www.webmd.com/drugs/2/

drug-8486-7217/lamictal/lamotrigine-oral/details/list-interaction-details
/dmid-1396/dmtitle-lamotrigine-hormonal%20contraceptives/intrtype-
drug). That certainly sounds alarming. However, the references cited
by WebMD all refer to the reduction in *lamotrigine* when an oral contraceptive is added, except one, which speaks to the issue of potential
contraceptive failure. That reference concludes: "A modest decrease in
the plasma concentration of levonorgestrel was also observed but there
was *no corresponding hormonal evidence of ovulation*" (Sidhu et al., 2006;
emphasis mine).

Could that "modest decrease" still leave a woman at risk? One would
think that in nearly two decades of lamotrigine use, reversal of contraception would have emerged in at least one case report. Searching
PubMed for "lamotrigine oral contraceptives pregnancy" yielded reviews
but no such reports.

Lamotrigine During and After Pregnancy

One of my patients, who had done well with lamotrigine but had a few
mild mood shifts while on it (suggesting that lamotrigine at 150 mg was
just barely enough to give her good mood stability), planned a pregnancy. She chose to stay on lamotrigine through the first trimester. In
the early second trimester, her depression returned. What to do?

Don't add low-dose lithium, as I did. Wait: what's wrong with that?
It worked, her mood recovered. The problem is that it was *unnecessary.*
Lamotrigine levels decline with increasing estrogen concentrations (thus
the effect of birth control pills described above). By the second trimester
lamotrigine levels can be 50 percent lower than before pregnancy (Pennell et al., 2004). All I had to do was increase her dose.

Fortunately, the Reproductive Psychiatry Resource and Information
Center at the MGH Center for Women's Health lets me off the hook on
this one (Nonacs, 2015). Dr. Nonacs reports that "our group typically
does not increase the dose of lamotrigine prophylactically in women
with bipolar disorder" and quotes Verinder Sharma's group (another
authoritative source) who found that "no evidence in [their] small case
series to indicate that lower blood levels of lamotrigine were associated
with relapse."

In my patient's case, it should have been obvious: she had done well on lamotrigine but was probably at the edge of sufficient blood levels. I rarely get a lamotrigine level: if it's not working, turn it up, what difference does it make what the level is? When you run into a side effect, turn it down until that's gone; it still makes no difference what the level is. If you get to 400 mg with no side effects and insufficient benefit—a rare outcome—then okay, maybe get a level, or you could still just turn it up until you run into a side effect or 500–600 mg daily, which is not without precedent. But in this case a blood level before or very early in pregnancy would have helped me. Dr. Nonac's group at Harvard recommends getting a level before pregnancy for comparison later if needed.

I should have increased my patient's lamotrigine, not added lithium. When my error somehow dawned on me (it's not every day I manage mood during a pregnancy), we turned up the lamotrigine and turned off the lithium, and she stayed well through the rest of pregnancy and postpartum as well.

The bonus is that she was able to breastfeed. The MGH group notes that lamotrigine has increasingly been used during breastfeeding and found no reports of adverse events in the baby from this practice (Nonacs, 2010), nor significant concerns in a 2014 update (Cohen, 2013).

In summary, lamotrigine is an obvious candidate for treating mid-spectrum depressions. Its fewer side effects and lower risks put it at the top of my list for a patient who has never had a mood medication but who has enough bipolarity to skip past antidepressants. More common is the arrival of patient in your practice who is already on an antidepressant and not doing well. When mid-spectrum bipolarity is suspected in that context, low-dose lithium augmentation is another strong treatment option (examined next).

Chapter 8

Low-Dose Lithium Is a Different Drug and Better Than Antipsychotics for Mid-Spectrum Patients

As noted previously, mid-spectrum patients from Bipolar II on down to subthreshold bipolarity and bipolar spectrum disorders do not have manic episodes. Thus they do not need the anti-manic effects of full-dose lithium. For these patients, obtaining a therapeutic blood level is not necessary. Sometimes as little as 150 mg of lithium can have a substantial impact on mood, anxiety, and sleep.

Used in this way, low-dose lithium (e.g. blood levels of 0.7 mEq/L and lower) is essentially a different drug than full-dose lithium. Lower doses generally have few side effects (often none) and much lower risks. Unfortunately, the name of this new tool is still "lithium."

Low-dose lithium is not new. Lithium has been used in unipolar depression for years as an augmentation agent (adding it to an antidepressant already underway). In a meta-analysis of trials of adjunctive lithium in treatment-resistant depression, lithium was better than a placebo in 5 of 9 studies. Taken together, 45 percent of patients improved on adjunctive lithium versus 18 percent on placebo ($p < 0.001$; Bschor et al., 2003). That's nearly one in every two patients improving, in treatment-resistant cases. In my experience, the response rate has seemed to be even higher, though as noted in the last chapter, using one's personal experience to appraise the frequency of outcomes is fraught with potential bias. A few good outcomes in a row could skew one's impression.

Yet low-dose lithium has been extremely useful in my practice, beyond what it seems could be explained by biased accounting. For example, one of our residents began her full-time outpatient clinic with a string of patients with treatment-resistant depression whom she treated with low-dose lithium augmentation. After the fifth responder in a row, she was becoming quite convinced of lithium's value: these were treatment-resistant patients, after all, referred to a specialty mental health program after failure to improve. The string of successes continued. We were both laughing at the extent of this run when she presented what we estimated to be her tenth responder in a row, all in the first month of her rotation.

(Those kinds of results can have more impact on our beliefs than reading the meta-analysis by Bschor and colleagues, even though they shouldn't. For example, one case of Stevens-Johnson syndrome should not change one's lamotrigine prescribing, but I know that when it finally causes a horrendous rash I'll hesitate with the next patient for whom lamotrigine would have been my first choice. Our resident's experience is described here because for some readers it will have more meaning than a meta-analysis. Watching that string of lithium responders continue to lengthen strengthened my belief in adjunctive lithium, I admit. Patient experience is a powerful teacher—to be evaluated with caution).

Lithium, a Feared Drug

Experienced clinicians learn not to spring their recommended treatment on a patient without first finding out how it is likely to be received. For example, if I think sertraline is the best antidepressant option for Ms. Heath, rather than declaring so, I might first ask "Now, thinking about antidepressants, there are quite a few. Have you heard about some of them, good or bad?" Perhaps her close neighbor had a terrible reaction to sertraline that really scared Ms. Heath; it helps to know this before I suggest it. A different agent may be a better option simply because the "valence" of sertraline is so negative for Ms. Heath.

One can generally assume a negative valence around lithium. True, some patients think of lithium as natural because after all, it is an element, it comes out of the ground. But most people associate lithium with severe mental illness. Mid-spectrum patients are often frightened to discover that their depression is on a continuum with other versions of bipolar disorder that can cause "mania," as in "maniac." Lithium is for those people, they think. They do not want to be like that, and anything suggesting they might be is bad. This attitude can be less than conscious.

Three Reverse Spins

Therefore one needs to have a schtick, a story for lithium, to give it a different spin early on, and give it an appropriate fair chance among other options. Here are three that have worked for me. The first is given roughly as I explain it to patients. Notice the admission right away that lithium can cause trouble. Patients will recognize excessive spin, so presenting negatives helps demonstrate that the information is not a whitewash.

1. Low-dose lithium is like a different drug. True, about 1 person in 10 simply cannot tolerate lithium, even at low doses: they get flat, dull, and "blah." Forget it, give up, that doesn't get better with time. But nearly everyone else can take low doses with no side effects or very few (you might get some dry mouth, but you won't get a tremor—that's a full-dose lithium thing). "Low-dose" means as little as 150 or 300 mg, whereas a full dose is more like 900–1,200 mg. We do have to do a blood test to check some things, but we don't need "therapeutic levels"—that's for Bipolar I, the full manic-depressive version.

2. Lithium in the water. In at least five studies from countries where lithium is found in small concentrations in public water supplies, investigators have found an inverse correlation with suicide rates. In a Japanese study of this phenomenon the correlation was very striking: the higher the lithium concentration in the public water supply, the lower the suicide rate, in 18 communities (Ohgami et al., 2009). That study was criticized for lack of epidemiologic sophistication (Huthwaite and Stanley, 2010) but seems to have been accepted as an important finding worth follow-up (see an invited commentary: Young, 2009). Similar findings have been reported as far back as 1972 (per Schrauzer and Shreshtha, 2010). For a review, see Vita et al., 2015; one exception is a negative report from Britain (Kabacs et al., 2011), but there lithium levels in the water were quite low compared with other reports.

The important point to convey to patients is not that lithium may lower suicide risk, although indeed that appears to be true, but rather that *very low concentrations may be psychoactive.*

3. Alzheimer's dementia. Lithium has been shown to promote neuronal survival in the face of atrophic factors (a neurotrophic effect). Because of this effect, it has been studied in several neurodegenerative conditions (Forlenza et al., 2014). Recent data suggest that lithium could potentially prevent progression to Alzheimer's dementia, described shortly. At this writing these are preliminary results, as I emphasize to patients. But if this proves to be true, given that we still have no other means of preventing such a terrible illness, lithium's reputation will surely improve. However, this entire tale must be told with caution, as preliminary positive results using lithium for amyotrophic lateral sclerosis were not borne out, leading to significant disappointment (Gamez et al., 2013).

Several population studies have found that patients with bipolar disorder who used lithium, as opposed to other mood stabilizers, have lower rates of dementia (Gerhard et al., 2015; Kessing et al., 2008). Animal models have shown that lithium can lower tau protein concentrations through its effect on an enzyme called GSK-3B, which has been strongly linked to Alzheimer's. Unfortunately, a 10-week randomized trial did not show this tau reduction in humans (Hampel et al., 2009). This study included repeat cognitive assessments as a secondary measure; these also showed no change, albeit over a brief period of lithium. Dosing was designed to produce a blood level between 0.5 and 0.8 mmol/L.

But perhaps these studies failed because they began too late, after Alzheimer's dementia was already established? Following that logic, Forlenza and colleagues (2011) studied patients with amnestic minimal cognitive impairment, that is, patients who by definition were at high risk for progression to Alzheimer's but still possessed relatively good cognitive function. The investigators used a low dose of lithium (blood level 0.25–0.5 mmol/L) and a long study duration (12 months). Although the final sample was small (40 patients total), the lithium group did end up with significantly lower tau protein levels in cerebrospinal fluid than did controls. Preservation of cognitive function was better in the lithium group but did not reach statistical significance in this small sample. Among the subset of patients who did progress to a diagnosis of Alzheimer's, cognitive function was significantly better in the lithium group (i.e., in this subgroup, lithium did not prevent the progression but did reduce the degree of loss).

A more recent study (Nunes et al., 2013) used an even lower lithium dose, only 300 *micrograms*, for a longer period of time (15 months). This dose is much closer to the water-supply doses described above, truly a microdose. In this study, the lithium group showed no decrease in performance on the Mini-Mental Status Exam, whereas the control group showed statistically significant losses. If this study is replicated, it should be recognized as having contributed to a tremendous medical advance.

These data have already been made widely known through a *New York Times* article touting low-dose effects, including both the antisuicide correlation and the anti-Alzheimer's research (Fels, 2014). Even though the enthusiasm in the article goes beyond what data currently support, it prompts a question. Severe mood disorders themselves are a risk factor for Alzheimer's disease (Zilkens et al., 2014), so should older patients with a family history of Alzheimer's be given low-dose lithium as a preventive agent (if other factors such as creatinine level, thyroid status, and additional medications do not contraindicate it)? In my opinion, based on the data now at hand, high-risk patients should indeed be given the option of taking 150 mg of lithium, at least once they're over 60, perhaps much earlier. The risks of this dose are extremely low if contraindications are absent. If it is perfectly tolerated, that is, no side effects at all, why *not* use it? At this point, we have nothing else to offer for the prevention of Alzheimer's (besides prudent life-style changes that anyone is wise to make: regular physical activity, rational diet, stress reduction including meditative or spiritual practices, and community engagement). Hopefully more data in support of lithium in this role, or an alternative strategy, will emerge soon.

Underutilized: Seven Insufficient Reasons

Among U.S. psychiatric residents, 25 percent did not prescribe lithium even *once* in an entire year (Rakofsky and Dunlop, 2013). How can that be? Perhaps an explanation lies here: In an online forum at Studentdoctor.net, one resident said, "I am increasingly hesitant to prescribe lithium to anyone due to its vast collection of serious side effects—endocrine, cns, derm, renal, cardia, etc." So let's look at these organ systems in turn, and evaluate the basis for hesitation in using lithium. And let's start with weight gain, which for many patients is the biggest concern of all.

1. Weight gain. This is not generally emphasized as a lithium risk, though it should be. Weight gain is prevalent in modern society, particularly in the United States. Bipolar disorder itself is associated with weight gain, at least in a subset of patients (Mansur et al., 2015). Avoiding medications that can exacerbate this problem is obviously prudent, wherever possible. Lithium can cause 4–6 kg of weight gain, primarily in the first two years of use, in at least 20–30 percent of patients (Printz et al., 2003).

Without doubt this is a serious risk. But it does not differentiate lithium from alternative medication treatments, all of which have the same problem (except lamotrigine and carbamazepine). Compared to most medication-induced weight gain, lithium's is probably one of the smallest and has not been associated with metabolic syndrome. Nevertheless, this is still a significant issue, not to be downplayed.

2. Endocrine. Induction of hypothyroidism is often given an incidence of 10 percent in texts, but that is a low estimate. One study found emerging hypothyroidism on lithium in 36 percent of patients (Fagiolini et al., 2006). Women are at much greater risk for this than are men (Kirova et al., 2005), especially women with a family history of hypothyroidism and those with elevated antithyroid antibodies (Kibirige et al., 2013). Indeed, the risk is so high among women I don't generally add the expense of obtaining antithyroid antibody levels—I just emphasize the very high likelihood of inducing hypothyroidism with lithium when considering it for a woman with a family history of thyroid problems. Think about it: if the overall rate is one in three (Fagiolini et al., 2006), and women are at much greater risk than men, then for a woman with a positive family history, the likelihood is well over 50 percent. One should just plan on probable hypothyroidism in such patients, clearly include this risk in the comparison of treatment options, monitor closely, and be happily surprised if it does not occur.

Thinking further: if the likelihood of having to add thyroid replacement is very high, then perhaps it makes sense to consider thyroid hormone as a treatment itself, first, before adding lithium. After all, levothyroxine has been used as an adjunctive treatment for years for unipolar and bipolar depression. Lab results, usually in hand at this point, could tip the balance: What is the patient's thyroid-stimulating hormone (TSH) level at the time of considering lithium?

If the TSH is already over 3.5 (mIU/L) the likelihood that lithium will cause overt hypothyroidism is even greater than if the TSH is around 1.0–1.5 (Bocchetta and Loviselli, 2006). This makes sense: A high TSH is often associated with antithyroid antibodies, the presence of which is correlated with lithium-induced hypothyroidism. So a high TSH portends a need for levothyroxine. Thus we should ask: How much help might thyroid hormone alone provide, for mood? The short answer is: possibly some benefit, though data for T4 are sparse. See more on the use of T4/levothyroxine in this role in Chapter 10.

Before leaving the endocrine realm, two other hormonal abnormalities are associated with lithium, though at far lower rates: hyperparathyroidism and hyperthyroidism. Incidence of each is so low, 1 percent or less, that it should not guide treatment selection. Monitoring for these requires no more than the standard TSH and basic chemistry tests one is already routinely obtaining to follow thyroid and renal function; just watch the calcium levels as well.

3. Renal. How common is renal failure when taking lithium? How fast does it develop? Can you see it coming, and transition off lithium while renal function is still in the normal range? I find the answers to these questions very reassuring and presume that one of the reasons practitioners worry about prescribing lithium is because they don't know this information. I keep checking it, figuring I must be wrong, they must know something I don't; but at each revisit in the past decade, the story comes out the same.

How common is renal failure on lithium? A recent study focused on this question found: "About one-third of the patients who had taken lithium for *10–29 years* had evidence of chronic renal failure but only 5% were in the severe or very severe category" (Aiff et al., 2015; emphasis mine). Common, all right—almost one in three, but most of these patients were on full-dose lithium. How fast? The authors note that even in the first year of treatment, looking at an aggregate of nearly 5,000 patients, they could detect an increase in median creatinine levels. Of course two-thirds of the patients do not experience renal compromise, so the median in this study must be driven by one-third of patients' creatinines increasing more steeply.

This means that one can identify patients at risk by watching their creatinine levels over time. If the levels are going up, one must taper off lithium in favor of something else. With this approach, the patient may enjoy the benefits of lithium (which he is presumably experiencing, else there's no point in continuing it) then step off before he loses too much renal function. We should not be cavalier about reducing renal function, of course. Causing a decrease now may endanger the patient later even if lithium is stopped when creatinine is still 1.1 (mg/dL).

How far up should one allow the patient's creatinine to rise before switching off lithium? Surprisingly, I've seen no guidelines on this. Perhaps that is not so surprising, as this is purely a judgment call, weighing "the devil you know"—lithium and further renal damage—versus the "devil you don't know": Will an alternative agent actually work to prevent another manic episode? There is no way to know for sure except to wait and see if such an episode occurs, which is nerve-racking. But notice this is largely an issue in Bipolar I, regarding prevention of manic episodes with sustained high lithium levels (e.g. 0.9–1.1). It is far less relevant in mid-spectrum patients, who do not require mania prevention, and who are less vulnerable in the first place for not having required high blood levels for years. So for mid-spectrum patients, concern about deteriorating renal function is a low-level concern, though still important: One *must* follow creatinine levels in every patient taking lithium. (My threshold for discontinuing lithium is the first time creatinine reaches 1.1 mg/dL. Once that is seen, we start planning an alternative. At the first 1.2 value, we begin a slow switch-over process. Most often, alternative treatments for prevention of mania do work. Why further endanger renal function when you know you'll have to switch later anyway?)

What about nephrogenic diabetes insipidus (NDI)? Like climbing creatinine, NDI is also associated with dose and duration of lithium (Rej et al., 2014). It is far more reversible with lithium discontinuation. In the absence of lithium toxicity, NDI is not inherently dangerous, but polyuria and nocturia can be bothersome (Movig et al., 2003). These symptoms warrant dose reduction and search for alternative agents.

The bottom line is that lithium-induced renal dysfunction:

a. is limited to a subgroup of patients (about one third of patients taking high dose lithium);
b. takes years to develop;
c. can be identified "in progress" by watching creatinine, and a plan for transitioning to another agent developed, all over months if not years; and
d. is dose related, such that low-dose lithium is in a different category of risk.

4. Cardiac. Causing cardiac risk really raises prescriber anxieties: after all, unlike kidneys, we only have one heart. What *are* the cardiac risks of lithium? My conclusion from the following literature review is that we may have made a mountain out of a molehill. Be your own judge. This is tricky territory, as risk appraisals involve not only data but fear: fear of overtreating but also undertreating, underdetection as well as the hassle/expense of overdetection, and legal liability.

Lithium *toxicity* is associated with dangerous conduction changes. But properly managed lithium, especially using low doses, runs a very low risk of lithium toxicity. What cardiac risk do therapeutic or sub-therapeutic levels carry?

Surprisingly few references are available on this subject. Nearly all articles point to a single review in 1982, which describes sinus node dysfunction, atrial flutter, atrioventricular block, right bundle branch block, left anterior hemiblock, ventricular tachycardia, ventricular fibrillation, and QT segment prolongation (Mitchell and Mackenzie, 1982). Sounds bad, but of course the question is, "How often to these occur and how much trouble do they cause?"

Case reports of sinoatrial node dysfunction at therapeutic doses exist. Bipolar specialists described three cases in 1979 (Roose et al., 1979); another case was reported in 1984 (Montalescot et al., 1984). In these cases, the authors' point was to demonstrate that lithium is a potential culprit when a patient is experiencing an arrhythmia. These were not cardiac deaths or severe complications.

Similarly, consider QT prolongation. Readers are familiar with the concern about numerous psychotropics lengthening the QT interval enough to produce torsades de pointe, a fatal ventricular arrhythmia. The most recent alarms surrounded citalopram (FDA Drug Safety Communication, http://www.fda.gov/Drugs/DrugSafety/ucm297391.htm). In a 2015 review of the literature on this issue, 18 cases of QT prolongation associated with citalopram were identified; 10 developed torsades. The majority of the torsades cases were in overdoses (Tampi et al., 2015). Another case, unfortunately fatal, was later reported in a "massive" overdose (Kraai and Seifert, 2015). (Tidbit: escitalopram causes less QT prolongation than citalopram at equivalent doses, e.g., 10 mg escitalopram relative to 20 mg citalopram. Even at 30 mg of escitalopram, the effect is less than caused by 40 mg of citalopram; Lam, 2013).

Now compare lithium. As of a 2010 review, it had not been associated with torsades (Alvarez and Pahissa, 2010). A PubMed search at the time of this writing, using the terms "lithium torsades," found no additional references. Why so much attention, then, to lithium's cardiac effects? Granted, it is important to know that these effects occur, particularly when a primary care provider or cardiologist is trying to determine the root cause of an arrhythmia. At that point, a pre-lithium electrocardiogram (ECG) would be great to have. Lacking it complicates the search but does not endanger the patient, at least not directly. It just complicates the analysis. Consider: does this potential later conundrum (lacking a baseline ECG when trying to sort out an arrhythmia) justify calling for an ECG for every patient over 45 years old, prior to lithium? I do not think so, yet that is a standard recommendation.

In that light, here is a brief but pertinent tangent: where do these recommendations come from? For example, Georgia's Department of Juvenile Justice has a medication monitoring program for lithium that includes a pretreatment ECG and repeat ECGs every two years (see http://www.djj.state.ga.us/Policies/DJJPolicies/Chapter12/Attachments/ DJJ12.24AttachmentC.pdf). And that's in young people! Consider how these recommendations can promulgate. Once a particular protocol is established, *removing* a recommendation would require a respected and outspoken committee of experts. Protocols thus become like one-way valves: expansion is permitted, even reinforced, because more stringent recommendations reflect even greater care for patient safety. Let no risk go undetected! But shrinking these lists rarely occurs, even when experts recommend it.

For example, after monitoring ECGs during lithium therapy in 53 consecutive patients, a team of specialists recommended: "In the absence of symptoms or signs of heart disease, routine monitoring of ECG is not necessary during lithium treatment" (Bucht et al., 1984). Note the date on that reference. Perhaps I've missed something in the ensuing three decades. However, a PubMed search for articles related to that 1984 study yielded no more relevant references among 108 citations. It did turn up another old (1980) review, which concluded that "lithium does not adversely affect cardiac function as measured by exercise tolerance tests and it is held that there is no contraindication for lithium even in patients with heart disease when there are clear psychiatric indications for its use" (Rao and Hariharasubramanian, 1980).

Bringing my tangent to a close, I conclude that recommendations for ECG monitoring for patients on lithium reflect the gradual accretion of more and more stringent monitoring recommendations by well-meaning groups—but not the arrival of additional data warranting more careful use of lithium or ECG monitoring. I have never routinely ordered ECGs for patients I'm starting on lithium, regardless of age. I think the rationale is insufficient, even without factoring in cost to the medical system and the patient. This may worry some providers, but let any debate be cast in references, not opinion. Of course one should always be open to new data (or those one has missed).

5. Skin. Lithium can cause or exacerbate psoriasis, but how often this occurs is not clear (was it a latent psoriasis, triggered; or de novo?) Resolution with lithium discontinuation has been observed in about 60 percent of cases (Wolf and Ruocco, 1999). But lithium can exacerbate an existing psoriasis, so inquiring about it prior to initiating treatment with lithium is warranted.

Acne is very commonly caused or worsened by lithium. At least this is more reliably observable than psoriasis, both before and during lithium treatment. Dose reduction or discontinuation are usually necessary, as the treatments for acne carry their own risks, and failure to control it has personal consequences that can also be quite costly to patients.

6. Neurologic. A recent thorough review of lithium risks found that "a number of rare, potentially serious neurological adverse effects have been reported, including extrapyramidal symptoms, 'pseudotumour cerebri' or occasionally cerebellar symptoms" but concludes that severe neurologic effects from lithium are rare (Grandjean and Aubry, 2009). Tremor is common; and in conjunction with other medications, lithium can produce myoclonus that interferes with function. Both of these motor disturbances warrant dose reduction; or if lithium's benefits are significant and necessary, consider suppression with a beta-blocker.

By comparison, cognitive effects from lithium are common. Controlled studies do show a statistically significant negative effect of lithium on memory, vigilance, reaction time, and tracking (Grandjean and Aubry, 2009). Yet all are usually dose-related effects. Because mid-spectrum patients do not require "therapeutic" blood levels, one can simply lower the dose until these cognitive side effects are fully manageable or absent. Few patients will tolerate them as an ongoing burden unless the search for alternative treatments has already been exhaustive.

Finally, lithium *toxicity* deserves a place on lists of lithium risks. It is far more likely to occur when lithium levels are high-therapeutic, for example, 1.0–1.1 mEq/L (McKnight et al., 2012). Close monitoring is required at such levels. But for low-dose lithium—e.g., blood levels of 0.7 or lower—even the inadvertent addition of an antihypertensive or nonsteroidal anti-inflammatory is unlikely to lead to toxicity levels.

Blood monitoring is still warranted when using low-dose lithium, but the main purpose is to follow TSH and creatinine, not lithium levels.

Of course, taking the opportunity to obtain a lithium level while the blood sample is available is prudent, just to stay confident the level is low. But patients may need some help understanding that the laboratory report's "therapeutic range" does not apply to lithium used in this fashion. The lower threshold refers to Bipolar I: Is the level sufficient to prevent the next manic episode? Low-dose lithium is determined not by blood level but by efficacy and tolerability: targeting 100 percent symptom control but zero, or close to zero, side effects.

Blood tests should be done at least yearly once all is stable, primarily to watch creatinine, but much more often during initiation of treatment. How often? The main question here is: "How quickly can hypothyroidism develop in a patient who has just started lithium?" A published case suggested routine screening at *six weeks* after providing an example of a man whose TSH went from normal to 7.6 in that interval (Joffe, 2002). Is six weeks too late, then? How many patients are we allowing to become hypothyroid, knowing they are at risk, because we don't check a TSH until the more commonly recommended three-month interval? On the other hand, we certainly can't wait even six weeks for a follow-up lithium level: even with low-dose lithium, that should be done within a few days of reaching steady-state levels.

Unfortunately, this means at least two blood draws in the first few months of treatment (and a third if baseline TSH and creatinine are not already available). The literature also documents *transient* increases in TSH after lithium is initiated, so an increase may not warrant immediate prescription of levothyroxine. Obviously some clinical judgment is required here; just don't wait too long for that first follow-up TSH.

Comparison with Antipsychotics

Bipolar disorders are often managed with antipsychotics. Sometimes these are warranted for acute mania, but in the long run even in Bipolar I monotherapy with a mood stabilizer is the goal. For mid-spectrum patients, however, antipsychotics are overkill. Two mood stabilizers, the first titrated to maximal tolerable doses before another is added, are preferable to even a single antipsychotic in most patients, in my opinion.

Why such adamant avoidance of antipsychotics? Not because of the risk of tardive dyskinesia, though certainly that is a consideration. Rather, because most patients on antipsychotics can tell they're "taking something." With lamotrigine and low-dose lithium, and even carbamazepine and divalproex (discussed in the next chapter), many patients can feel normal—as though they're taking nothing. This is an extremely important goal for a treatment that often goes on for years.

In my experience, many patients—if not most—strongly dislike the effects of taking an antipsychotic. These medications differ somewhat from each other, but as a class, they function as "don't think so much" medications. Patients can feel this. One of my residency colleagues decided that because we often prescribed antipsychotics, we ought to know what it was like to take one. So he hiked into the woods with his tent and took risperidone for two days. His summary: "What a waste of a weekend. I just sat there."

So in general, I try to engineer antipsychotics out of the picture. In the long run, the tardive dyskinesia risk is justification enough for this practice. But when one adds the metabolic risks of the most commonly used antipsychotics, on top of tardive dyskinesia and adverse cognitive/motivational effects, the risks of lithium begin to look preferable. So it has been with most patients I've tried to help understand these relative risks, using the shared decision-making approach described in Chapter 5.

But what about evidence for *efficacy* for lithium? Does it really have the antidepressant effects a mid-spectrum patient needs? Obviously none of the foregoing considerations are necessary if lithium does not actually work in this role.

Contrasting Evidence for Efficacy

The bottom line on lithium's efficacy is very much like that for lamotrigine. Evidence seems to fall short of what many people have witnessed, in patient after patient, for years. Even though the data are not entirely supportive, lithium remains among the first-line interventions for bipolar disorder of all forms. See my diatribe about clinical observation versus randomized trials in the previous chapter on lamotrigine: the same logic applies here.

For the literature-oriented, examination of a few studies will illustrate the mixed nature of research trial data. The recent LiTMUS trial directly examined the use of low-dose lithium, just as outlined here (Nierenberg et al., 2013). Over six months, lithium at blood levels ranging from low (<0.04) to high (up to 0.9) did not improve mood outcomes. True, those in the lithium group ended up with similar outcomes with 25 percent less use of antipsychotics, and that's an achievement. But otherwise lithium was not impressive.

However, one of the investigators later concluded that it would be inaccurate to say "lithium doesn't work" (J. Calabrese, quoted in Gever, 2011). The LiTMUS paper (Nierenberg et al., 2013) cites several factors that could account for outcome observed:

1. The sample was unusually broad and inclusive (Bipolar I and Bipolar II; few limits regarding comborbid conditions) and treatment options other than lithium were wide open.
2. Only about one fourth of patients reached remission regardless of treatment group, suggesting that the patient population was relatively treatment resistant.
3. Open treatment could have allowed biases about lithium to affect outcomes.
4. Insufficient statistical power to see a difference between the lithium-added group and the treatment as usual group.
5. A baseline difference in illness episodes preceded the initiation of the trial (randomization failure).

At a minimum, the LiTMUS study leaves the value of low-dose lithium quite uncertain. Another well-known study with mixed results suggested that high blood levels are necessary (Gelenberg et al., 1989), but a later reanalysis showed that patients who were taking low levels of lithium during the prerandomization phase and were then randomly selected to *continue* with low levels stayed well (Perlis et al., 2002).

In a review of adjunctive lithium in unipolar depression, other authors conclude:

To date, this treatment approach called lithium augmentation is the best-documented approach in the treatment of refractory depression. In international treatment guidelines and algorithms, lithium augmentation is considered a first-line treatment strategy for patients with a major depressive episode who do not adequately respond to standard antidepressant treatment. (Bschor et al., 2003)

Expert consensus can be widespread yet still be wrong. Adding more opinions in favor of lithium's efficacy does not constitute evidence. But it is somewhat reassuring. As this group of well-respected investigators summarized: "Lithium is a safe and effective agent that should, whenever indicated, be used first-line for the treatment of bipolar disorder . . . Its use in bipolar disorder is under-appreciated, particularly as it has the best evidence for prophylaxis, qualifying it perhaps as the only true mood stabilizer currently available" (Malhi et al., 2012).

Chapter 9

Before Antipsychotics, More Options to Consider

The previous chapter offers a summary of reasons why antipsychotics should generally be avoided in the treatment of mid-spectrum patients: tardive dyskinesia, metabolic syndrome, and above all, the cognitive/motivational effects.

Recall that metabolic syndrome is not just weight gain and dyslipidemia, but also includes a progressive insulin resistance that is a precursor to diabetes. Insulin resistance is a common comorbidity in bipolar disorders independent of treatment. Indeed, the two conditions may share some mechanisms and thus exacerbate one another (as one worsens, it may drag the other along; Calkin et al., 2013). Insulin resistance may actually contribute to mood disorder treatment resistance (Calkin et al., 2015).

Thus we should ask: why use a medication that can induce this, when in mid-spectrum patients a direct antipsychotic effect is unnecessary? Alternative treatments would have to carry some very severe side effects or risks, or have very little evidence for efficacy, to fall lower on a list of options than antipsychotics.

Unfortunately, antipsychotics *will* be necessary for some patients with mid-spectrum mood disorders, when other treatments have not been sufficient. But before turning to them, several other options are worth considering. In each case I think the risk/benefit ratio is preferable. First, fish oil's risk is extremely low, even though potential for benefit may also be low. Carbamazepine and valproate are strong enough to serve as monotherapy, but carry greater risks, particularly for women. Even supraphysiologic thyroid, discussed in the next chapter, might be preferable to antipsychotics for some patients, or at least roughly comparable in risk/benefit balance. As before, readers are referred to prescribing guides for routine information. Here we will focus on details that directly affect choice among treatments, including where these medications fit for mid-spectrum patients.

Omega-3 Fatty Acids

"How much fish does one have to eat to get the same dose you used in your study?," I asked Andy Stoll, lead author of one of the first randomized trials of fish oil in patients with bipolar disorder, which was strikingly positive (Stoll et al., 1999). They used 9.6 grams of fish oil a day. He said their dose was roughly equivalent to "one large salmon steak per day, but it depends on what the fish were eating" (the fish's omega-3 composition depends on the omega-3s in their own diet).

Fish oil is the only source of omega-3 fatty acids yet studied for mood disorders in randomized trials. Flaxseed, though appealing in terms of cost and ease of use, has not been studied and does not provide the same eicosapentaenoic acid (EPA) and docosahexaenoic acid (DHA) that fish oil does (the pathway is different and outcomes depends partly on the diet of the user). Flaxseed oil might yet prove to be similarly beneficial, but at this point the only data we have suggesting a mood benefit come from fish oil trials.

Surprisingly, for an over-the-counter pill with no pharmaceutical company funding, fish oil has been studied as a treatment for mood in at least 19 randomized trials. Some were negative. But a meta-analysis showed a substantial difference between studies reaching a twin threshold: at least *1,000 mg of EPA*, using a fish oil that is at least *60 percent EPA* relative to DHA (Sublette et al., 2011). Nearly every study over this threshold was strongly positive, with a net effect size around 0.5. Every study below the threshold was negative. At minimum we may conclude that there is surely something psychoactive about this stuff at the right dose.

Unfortunately, in my practice at least, I've not had a single patient do well on monotherapy with fish oil (despite many motivated patients giving it a try). Lithium, yes; lamotrigine, yes; carbamazepine, yes; but monotherapy on fish oil, no. It just doesn't seem to have enough clout.

Why bother to discuss fish oil then? Because it is the perfect holding agent when you just need a little more time for a plan to evolve. One such situation is the subject of Chapter 12: As described there in detail, when a patient has continued mood cycling, rather than adding another mood stabilizer, sometimes you can just remove a destabilizing factor. If antidepressants are destabilizing in some patients, then removing them would theoretically lead to a smoother long-term course. For mid-spectrum patients, such a course means fewer episodes of depression—a net antidepressant effect, ironically, from tapering off an antidepressant.

But antidepressant tapers sometimes take months. During that time, depression can worsen, though usually only transiently, a few days to a week with each decrement. Through that phase, patients often need help, else they'll want to go back up on the antidepressant dose (and thus halt the effort to reach an antidepressant-free state, often for the first time in years). An interim step can be to add fish oil. It is clearly better than a placebo, and it adds minimal additional risk when all that may be needed is more time for the antidepressant taper.

However, helping patients accept the idea of fish oil as a mood treatment takes some time and effort, as you've probably discovered. And then you must help them pick the right version at the store! In addition to my webpage describing the meta-analysis of the putative threshold dose, I keep several bottles on the display shelf in my office. I ask patients to read the labels and tell me:

- how much EPA is in each pill (watching out for "serving size," often two capsules);
- how many pills it will take to deliver 1,000 mg EPA per day.

Thus armed I send them off to the closest grocery store with a map that describes which aisle and which shelf to hunt for; and which options on that shelf provide 1,000 mg EPA in adequate ratio with DHA, in just two pills per day.

(If nothing else, being able to knowledgeably describe an inexpensive, low-risk, nonpharmacologic treatment—and having examples right there on the shelf—is a great way to demonstrate that we psychiatric types are not here simply to write prescriptions for pharmaceuticals.)

What about risks? Does fish oil increase prostate cancer risk, for example, as was once broadcast widely (Fox, 2013)? That has not been borne out (Phelps, 2013). What about mercury and other heavy metals? No, such charged particles are extracted along with the protein. The hydrophobic oils are much lower in mercury than the whole fish, averaging 2.9 ppb (parts per billion; Labdoor, https://labdoor.com/rankings/fish-oil). The FDA recommended maximum is 1 part per million (FDA, http://www.fda.gov/OHRMS/DOCKETS/ac/02/briefing/3872_Advisory%207.pdf).

The main problem with fish oil is hassle. It's just too much for many patients, if only because of the sheer number of large pills. Being an oil from fish doesn't help matters. Liquids and even yogurts enriched with fish oil are available and more palatable that they sound, but still the barriers to initiation and adherence are higher than for pharmaceuticals for most patients. Even just having to pick a brand from the vast array of options in supermarket is a daunting challenge for many. There is a pharmaceutical brand, but its expense and being a prescription obviate some of the inherent appeal of fish oil.

N-Acetyl Cysteine (NAC)

In a similar niche—"natural," inexpensive, with tantalizing initial studies—is N-acetyl cysteine (NAC). This is actually just cysteine, an amino acid in our daily diet. An acetyl group in the N-position increases gastrointestinal absorbtion.

NAC has shown a remarkable range of psychotropic effects in small randomized trials, with at least one each in bipolar depression (Berk et al, 2008), pathologic gambling, trichotillomania, and autism; with efficacy as an adjunct therapy in obsessive-compulsive disorder, cocaine craving, and marijuana cessation (see reference links in Phelps, 2014a).

Tolerability is a bit of a problem: about one person in five gets nausea that does not seem to remit if NAC is continued. In my limited experience with NAC thus far, that nausea means "no way." Nevertheless, because it has no documented long-term risks, NAC is otherwise rather like lamotrigine: limited evidence for efficacy but very low potential for harm. Unfortunately, as of this writing, the first small study of NAC's potential for continued benefit in a maintenance role was negative (Berk et al., 2012). That accords with my patients' experience thus far: it might show some initial benefit, but that does not seem to stick. While awaiting further data, I've backed off regular use of this agent for now. I mention it here because, like fish oil, it is an appealing alternative to pharmaceuticals that some patients will have heard of and may ask about.

Finally, note that three of my patients who worsened on lamotrigine (per Chapter 7; in some patients it can act too much like an antidepressant) later worsened in a very similar way on NAC. One of several mood-related mechanisms of action of NAC is modulation of neuronal glutamate signaling, which is also thought to be a mechanism of action of lamotrigine. Perhaps there is a connection? To my knowledge there are no reports of NAC-induced worsening of mood, but if using it, keep an eye out for this, particularly if the patient already experienced worsening on lamotrigine.

Carbamazepine

Carbamazepine (CBZ) has not been associated with weight gain. If not for this attribute, CBZ would not have much risk/benefit advantage over atypicals such as quetiapine. But weight gain is such a significant problem in mood disorders, and such a psychological burden for many patients, a weight neutral option is attractive even if it has other problems. (In contrast, for residents in training in psychiatry, CBZ is not near the top of *their* list: 73 percent of them did not prescribe CBZ even once in an entire year; Rakofsky and Dunlop, 2013). The risks and complexity of prescribing CBZ appear to have strongly affected their view (and it has no pharmaceutical company marketing, having been generic for years).

To help patients maintain a balanced view as they hear the CBZ risk list, I precede it with a few more benefits in addition to weight-neutrality:

- Most patients experience no side effects at all, once the dose is stable.

- Some patients with chronic pain find analgesic benefit as well (particularly neuropathic pain, and sometimes fibromyalgia; but evidence here is weak; Wiffen et al., 2014)
- In my experience, when it works, CBZ very commonly helps people sleep, without making them sleepy during the day—even those who have tried "everything," from psychotherapies to melatonin to benzodiazepines and zolpidem.
- CBZ can have strong antianxiety effects in many patients.

But then comes the list of risks, which I remember by organ system: skin, blood, and liver.

1. Skin. Though less frequently than lamotrigine, CBZ can cause Stevens-Johnson syndrome and the related severe rashes. Like lamotrigine it frequently causes benign rashes that must be evaluated and managed. See Chapter 7 for an approach to this problem that can preserve patients' opportunity to try these medications even when a rash occurs.

Most prescribing resources would instruct you, but a reminder won't hurt: patients of Asian descent should have their human leukocyte antigen (HLA) types determined before being given CBZ. HLA-B*1502 is associated with a substantial increase in the severe rash risk, and is relatively common in Asians, particularly Han Chinese (Ferrell and McLeod, 2008).

2. Blood. White blood cell (WBC) count reductions are the most common blood dyscrasia, but red cells and platelets can be affected as well. Moderate reductions in WBCs are common, and alarming. Dangerous drops are less common, requiring weekly monitoring (and causing much anxiety) as the levels hover around minimum acceptable levels (WBCs less than 3,000 mm3, absolute neutrophil count less than 1,500 mm3, or platelet count less than 100,000 per mm3; Rahman et al., 2014).

One historic source (referenced in Daughton et al., 2006) gives the rate at 1 percent to 2 percent. I must say, I've been chasing blood counts in patients for years, and I've seen WBCs drop, then come back up again, many times. But in over 20 years of use I've seen only three patients become obviously and severely ill on CBZ. Their WBCs went down, but the patients were also very ill, with fever and malaise. We did not need a blood test to spot the problem. Perhaps I've been lucky. I cannot tell you to monitor less than the standard protocols, but I think that once again these may have suffered from the same kind of monitoring inflation described in the chapter on lithium.

Unfortunately, anxiety about risks and need for close monitoring is one of the main drivers of CBZ's dramatic underutilization by psychiatric residents. Thus, ironically the emphasis on monitoring may be driving patients away from CBZ to other treatments with far more common risks, such as diabetes—which occurred de novo in 8.5 percent of patients in a six-month quetiapine/divalproex trial (Weisler et al., 2011; I wish we had these data for each atypical as monotherapy). Even if that rate was 1 patient in 50, this is diabetes we're talking about: life-shortening, morbidity-generating, often irreversible. Granted, diabetes and agranulocytosis—or more problematic, the bone density problems discussed shortly—are like apples and oranges and pomegranates, hard to compare. But I'm sure I've caused more diabetes than I've caused life-threatening adverse reactions to CBZ, even with my hesitation to use atypical antipsychotics.

3. Liver. CBZ can cause enough hepatic irritation to raise trans-aminase levels, so while monitoring blood counts, one monitors liver function tests as well. Transient increases up to three times normal are generally acceptable, but continued elevations can be enough to force transition to another medication. How often does CBZ cause a dangerous hepatitis? This is a well-recognized phenomenon but still rare enough to warrant case reports (Haukeland et al., 2000). In most cases the transaminase elevations are part of a larger drug reaction/rash with eosinophilia and systemic symptoms (DRESS) syndrome, dangerous but also very uncommon: 1/1,000 to 1/10,000 (López-Rocha et al., 2014).

CBZ Interactions

Having toured through the dangerous but very infrequent problems, one can then turn to the frequent but manageable problem: enzyme induction. Most medications metabolized in the liver will be affected. Certainly any crucial medication must be evaluated, for example, antivirals in patients with HIV. Several specific interactions are worth noting.

1. Hormonal contraceptives. In the old days we would simply refer a woman to her gynecologist for an increase in the dose of her birth control pill to at least 50 mcg of ethinylestradiol (Crawford, 2002). But because that is not absolutely certain to be sufficient, some experts imply that women should not rely on such dose increases (e.g., see http://www .webmd.com/epilepsy/guide/birth-control-women-epilepsy?page=2).

What about intrauterine devices that emit small amounts of proges- terone (e.g., Mirena)? Here is the July 2015 summary linked by the Euro- pean National Institute for Health Care Excellence (the link is a separate website not directly associated with the NICE):

> 4.5 Interaction with other medicinal products and other forms of interaction. The metabolism of progestogens may be increased by concomitant use of substances known to induce drug-metabolising enzymes. . . . *The influence of these drugs on the contraceptive efficacy of Mirena has not been studied but is* <u>not believed</u> *to be of major impor- tance due to the local mechanism of action.* (http://www.medicines .org.uk/emc/medicine/1829; emphasis added)

By contrast, the Prescribing Information for the Mirena device (http: //labeling.bayerhealthcare.com/html/products/pi/Mirena_PI.pdf) lists CBZ among numerous enzyme inducers "that may decrease the serum concentration of LNG" (levonorgestrel). Look up this interaction when you are faced with it. Perhaps more information will be available by then, although the answer may depend more on liability concerns than science.

2. Quetiapine has two reported interactions with CBZ that could matter clinically. First, it can interfere with CBZ metabolism, leading to an increase in an epoxide metabolite that can cause significant side effects. Although I've never seen this, or at least not recognized it as such, a case report describes "ataxia and agitation" with this combina- tion that remitted when the patient was switched off carbamazepine

(Fitzgerald and Okos, 2002). Second, CBZ can lower quetiapine levels dramatically: a case report describes "undetectable" quetiapine levels in the presence of CBZ (Nickl-Jockschat et al., 2009). You would think these would be obvious interactions, but I have never recognized either of them despite using this combination occasionally over the past 15 years.

3. Thyroid hormone should not be affected by CBZ, since it is not metabolized by the liver. But reality is more complex, in part due to changes in binding globulins. One group found significant changes in thyroid indexes in patients taking CBZ but concluded that "patients receiving anticonvulsant drugs chronically are eumetabolic and do not need thyroxine supplementation" (Tiihonen et al., 1995). A more recent report in children concludes likewise (Kafadar et al., 2015). Yet other references on this subject are less certain. For example, in a recent case report, when two sisters were placed on CBZ, only the sister who was previously hypothyroid demonstrated hypothyroid changes (Krysiak and Stojko, 2014). As of this writing, I remain uncertain about all this and will continue to recheck thyroid status after adding CBZ, particularly since "euthyroid" is a slippery concept, as discussed in the next chapter.

4. Lamotrigine interaction was discussed in Chapter 7.

Carbamazepine or Oxcarbazepine?

What if one could have the key benefits of CBZ (e.g., weight-neutral; antianxiety and prosleep effects) without the blood or liver problems, and no need for blood testing? These potential attributes understandably tempt many into the use of oxcarbazepine (OXC), particularly for children where phlebotomy is a significant drawback.

Obviously OXC has some significant advantages over CBZ, but is it as effective? In the absence of head-to-head trials, one would need to switch patients from one to the other and compare symptom control and side effects. Having done this numerous times, my strong impression is that OXC lacks the "clout" of CBZ—it just doesn't work as well. I've had several patients who still had symptoms on OXC but after switching obtained completely adequate symptom control from CBZ alone.

Moreover, in my experience, when the dose is pushed to get more benefit, OXC has more side effects: daytime sedation, fuzzy thinking, and mild balance problems. These can happen with CBZ as well, of course. Some patients get these side effects early, during titration, and can never get past them. But for patients who tolerate CBZ enough to continue it, most have no side effects at all. That was not the case for my patients on OXC. I've stopped using it at all.

CBZ and Bone Density

How much certainty is required before a new risk is ascribed to an old medication? After using it routinely for 20 years, I've recently witnessed the growing concern that CBZ may reduce bone density with long-term use (Gold et al., 2015). Very unfortunate, if this is true. One particular reason: women with a concern about body weight are more likely to choose CBZ due to its weight-neutrality; yet thin women (particularly Caucasian women) are at the greatest risk of osteoporosis as they age. Of course bone mineral reduction is a concern for any patient, but it is ironic that bone loss might somehow be delivered preferentially to those who can least afford that risk.

As a further irony, CBZ seems to be particularly useful in mixed states where it can lower anxiety and improve sleep. But anxiety and sleep problems are also seen in PTSD. Women are at much greater risk for sexual abuse and thus civilian PTSD. Thus by their gender, trauma risk, resultant symptoms, and CBZ's potential for addressing those symptoms, women are being pointed toward a medication that carries greater risk for them, namely bone density reduction.

For all its other problems, CBZ is rarely a first choice. But once lamotrigine and lithium have been considered and perhaps tried, where does one turn? An antipsychotic, with metabolic and tardive dyskinetic risks? Or CBZ, with probable bone risk? This is a terrible choice. Many women have chosen CBZ as a short-run trial. If it works well, then the long-term risk can be weighed again. But it is often very difficult to give up a medication that is working, because of a probable but not certain long-term risk.

While presenting CBZ, given these concerns, it should probably be presented as "package deal" in which vitamin D and calcium are included. But that means three medications for one job, not a good ratio.

Finally, note: if oxcarbazepine did not affect bone density, while CBZ was shown more clearly to do so, this would radically tilt the balance between these two options. One study looked at bone density in 41 patients on OXC and found no consistent reductions in bone density, raising this possibility (Koo et al., 2014). But think mechanistically: most anticonvulsants that have been implicated in bone density reduction are enzyme inducers (valproate is the exception; Muzina et al., 2011). OXC is an enzyme inducer, just less so than CBZ. So if there is risk in CBZ, there is likely risk in OXC, just somewhat less perhaps. How much less bone risk would justify less efficacy? This is a complex calculus.

Valproate/Divalproex

Valproate (VPA) and its nausea-sparing version called divalproex can have the needed antidepressant effects in mid-spectrum mood disorders, primarily by preventing the next depressive episode, not having an antidepressant effect in the current one. Or so has been my impression. Small randomized trials have actually shown an antidepressant effect, particularly in rapid cycling Bipolar I (Ghaemi et al., 2007; Muzina et al., 2011), but I have not been impressed by this in my patients. Indeed, worsening of depression has been common: As these patients began working their way up toward 1,000 mg, each step seemed to take them deeper into depression, and stopping the VPA eased that problem rapidly. (But, remember the pitfalls of reasoning from limited experience. I am just raising a red flag.)

Nevertheless, if VPA does not have a strong antidepressant effect, it can still be useful to limit cycling. In bipolar disorder, most depressions are either cyclic or mixed, so a mood stabilizer that is primarily antimanic (as I think of VPA) can still contribute, usually as an add-on to something more directly antidepressant.

Unfortunately, VPA must be avoided in women of reproductive age because of the risk inducing of polycystic ovarian syndrome (Nonacs, 2007). But for mixed-state anxiety and insomnia, at least in men and postmenopausal women, VPA is a strong candidate. It even has a randomized trial showing benefit in Generalized Anxiety Disorder (Aliyev and Aliyev, 2008), so that if a patient's anxiety diagnosis is uncertain (mixed state versus GAD), VPA might help either way.

However, weight gain is a problem here, too, as anyone who has prescribed VPA more than a few times has witnessed. Weight gain on VPA can be as bad as the worst atypicals, such as olanzapine. However, in my experience there may be a dose threshold, in the case of VPA, below which appetite is not stimulated and dramatic weight gain is far less common. This seems to lie around 1000-1250 mg. Caution is warranted, but if aggressively managed with dose reduction for any appetite or weight increase, VPA may be a viable option for mid-spectrum patients with rapid cycling and/or mixed states when an additional (primarily anti-manic) mood stabilizer is needed.

Chapter 10

Managing Thyroid:
Not to Be Left to
Primary Care or
Endocrinology

Some things about thyroid and mood are not controversial. First, thyroid hormone affects mood; no one quibbles about this. Second, thyroid hormone can be used as an augmentation agent in Major Depression; no one quibbles about this either. So at minimum, use of thyroid hormone as a treatment is worth understanding and using regularly, at least for the unipolar end of the mood spectrum and perhaps across it.

But from there, discomfort, doubt, and mistrust spiral upward through the following controversies, addressed in turn through this chapter:

- What is a normal TSH level?
- High-normal TSH is associated with mood problems, that's clear; but can lowering a normal TSH with thyroid replacement improve mood?
- What benefit does thyroid hormone provide in bipolar depressions? Should one use T3 or T4?
- Supraphysiologic thyroid as a mood stabilizer: does it work?
- What are the risks of high-dose thyroid medications?
- Where in the spectrum of treatment options for mid-spectrum depression does thyroid treatment fall? Before antipsychotics, for example?

- Who should manage thyroid hormone in patients with mood disorders: primary care, endocrinology, or psychiatry?

What Is a Normal TSH Level?

The normal range for many laboratory tests is defined statistically, not clinically. In other words, "abnormal" is not defined by the point at which symptoms start to appear. It is defined as the range within which 95 percent of the population can be found, as shown in Figure 10.1.

When a test result follows a statistically normal distribution, the result is the classic "bell-shaped curve." The last 2.5 percent of the population on each end of the curve, as shown by the cutoff lines, is more than two standard deviations away from the average of the population by observation of clinical symptoms. They are "abnormal," according to the lab report, defined in this way.

Now consider thyroid-stimulating hormone (TSH). In most laboratories the upper limit of normal is around 4.25 (mIU/L). This is not the point at which people begin to develop symptoms of hypothyroidism. It is the point beyond which, on average, only 2.5 percent of asymptomatic people are found. Using these cutoffs allows a common language and set

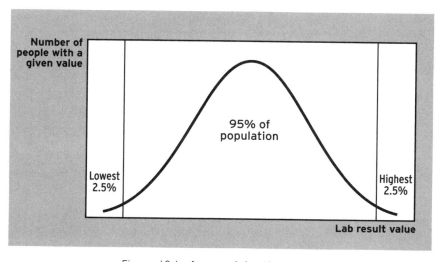

Figure 10.1. **A normal distribution**

of assumptions for how to interpret TSH values. But it does not mean that a patient with a TSH below 4.25 is normal, nor that a patient over 4.25 is abnormal (despite the readout from the lab indicating one or the other).

To make matters significantly more confusing, TSH values are not "normally distributed" (Hollowell et al., 2002). As shown in Figure 10.2 (reworked from Braverman and Cooper, 2012, fig. 11A.2, p. 185), the actual population curve has a significant skew, with the majority of the population far to the left and a long tail toward the right. The long tail drags the statistical "normal" cutoff much farther to the right than it would have fallen with a normal distribution.

The majority of the population live around 1.5–2.0 mIU/L. What do we make of someone whose TSH is in the normal range according to the lab result but out toward the tail, say, 3.0, where fewer people are found? Is that really "normal"?

A 2007 analysis suggested that the upper limit of TSH might be better considered anything over 2.5 (Davis and Tremont, 2007). The National Academy of Clinical Biochemists and the American Thyroid Association also suggested 2.5 as an upper limit of normal (Garber et al., 2012). Unfortunately this expert point of view is not widely known. Most clini-

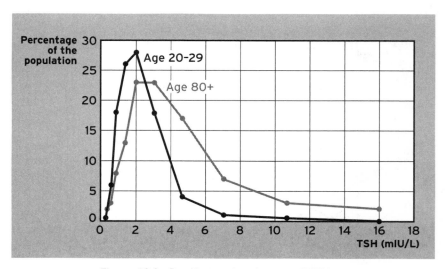

Figure 10.2. **Population distribution of TSH**

cians will use the laboratory's normal range and will have trouble conceptualizing 3.0 as "abnormal."

TSH in Mood Studies

In the realm of mood disorders, several studies have shown that a high "normal" TSH, say 3.0, is not the same as a TSH around 1.5. For example, in patients being treated for bipolar depression, at least two studies have looked specifically at the relationship between thyroid status and mood outcome. Replicating an earlier study (Frye et al., 1999), Cole and colleagues found that patients with a TSH values *below* 1.7, the median value in this study, improved far more quickly than those above 1.7, reaching remission four months faster (Cole et al., 2002).

The same inverse relationship between TSH and mood treatment response has been found in unipolar depression. For example, in one study from UCLA by Abulseoud and colleagues (2013), in which the mean TSH before treatment was 1.5, patients whose pretreatment TSH was above that mean were less likely to reach remission from their depression. This finding has not been consistent, however. Among other published investigations of this relationship detailed in the Abulseoud report, three found a correlation between TSH and treatment response, while six did not. A more recent study in unipolar depression found an inverse relationship looking at pretreatment TSH and serum brain-derived neurotrophic factor (BDNF) levels: the higher the TSH, the smaller the increase in BDNF during treatment (Baek et al., 2014). Interestingly, this relationship was not seen for T3 and T4 levels, only TSH.

Considering all these findings together, at a minimum we can say that a TSH of 3.0 mIU/L or higher is a significant finding, even though it is "normal" according to laboratory reference ranges. (This is why "her TSH was normal" is insufficient information!) A TSH of ≥3.0 does not establish the need for thyroid replacement even among depressed patients—unipolar, mid-spectrum, or bipolar. But when considering treatment options for a patient with a high normal TSH, thyroid replacement might precede use of antipsychotics as a treatment for depression: though the evidence base is very slim, so are the risks of giving a small amount of thyroid hormone.

T3 and T4 as Treatment

Thyroid hormone as an adjunctive treatment for depression has a very long history. Even the use of supraphysiologic thyroid, discussed later, dates back to the late 1930s (Gjessing, 1938). There are many studies using T3 in unipolar depression, but only a few using T4. By contrast, use of thyroid hormone as an augmentation in *bipolar* depression has been studied primarily with T4, though use of T3 was reported in one remarkable case series of 125 patients by independent investigator Tammas Kelly (Kelly and Lieberman, 2009).

The role of T3 as an adjunctive treatment for unipolar depression is well established. It even performed as well as lithium in the large STAR*D trial, with fewer side effects (perhaps accounted for by the dosing for lithium: 450 mg to start, increasing straight to 900 mg in the second week) (Nierenberg et al., 2006). In bipolar depression, limited data support T4 as an adjunct at low doses (Łojko and Ribakowski, 2007). More systematic study has been given to use of T4 at supraphysiologic doses, discussed shortly.

Which thyroid should one use in mid-spectrum patients? Following Dr. Kelly's data, should all augmentation be done with T3? This is an open question. In bipolar disorder, sheer weight of experience favors T4, with multiple reports from investigators at UCLA and in Berlin. But the converse is true in unipolar depression, where we have almost no data on use of T4 and many with T3. Here is my limited experience with these two forms of thyroid replacement in patients with bipolar disorder: in two cases of Bipolar II depression, I witnessed T3 produce a rapid positive response, followed within two months by a rapid cycling and mixed state experience which remitted when T3 was switched to T4. Kelly has far more experience with T3 and has not observed this (personal communication, 2010).

One setting in which T4 may have an edge over T3 is a mid-spectrum woman whose TSH is ≥3.0 who has not improved on lamotrigine. Low-dose lithium is a strong candidate for the next medication to try. But a woman with a TSH ≥3.0 is at high risk of becoming frankly hypothyroid when lithium is added. If that happens, conventionally she would be given T4 as replacement. So even though the data supporting T4 as an adjunct in depression are very limited, if she is very likely to end up on T4 anyway, why not try the T4 first, before lithium? (Joffe, 2012). The same logic was used in a study of lithium augmentation in unipolar depression long ago: patients who received T4 augmentation before lithium improved more than those who received lithium first (Spoov and Lahdelma, 1998).

This logic is even stronger if she has had rapid cycling mood shifts or mixed states, both of which have been associated with low thyroid levels (Carvalho et al., 2014; Chakrabarti, 2011; Chang et al., 1998). Levothyroxine has been invoked as an element in treatment for these harder-to-treat conditions (Kusumakar et al., 1997; Stancer and Persad, 1982) though not as prominently as I am placing it here. My logic for its use hinges on its extremely low risk relative to alternatives and the likelihood, presuming lamotrigine failed somehow, that lithium will be used.

What *doses* of T3 or T4 to use? The dose of T3 has been relatively consistent in augmentation studies, including the STAR*D: 25 mcg daily for a week and then, if tolerated but ineffective, 50 mcg daily. Dr. Kelly has used and advocates much higher doses for treatment-resistant cases, particularly bipolar depression (Kelly and Lieberman, 2009). But what dose for levothyroxine as an adjunctive treatment, for bipolar depression or mixed states? In a 2015 conference, Mark Frye suggested that the target is a "median TSH" (Frye, 2015). This is a crafty way of guiding clinicians to pursue a TSH around 1.5 in younger adults, or around 2.0 in older folks. Although the number sounds low and aggressive to some ears, because of the skew described above it is actually a *median* value, not aggressive at all. The dose of levothyroxine needed for this will vary substantially, depending primarily on the patient's starting TSH level.

When adding thyroid actually works, it is fast. I've seen this so many times I can predict (to myself at least) that if the patient responds, it will be about three to four days after the dose was increased (sometimes even after the first dose). How quickly can one advance the dose? Does one have to wait six weeks for steady state and check TSH at each step up? Many providers will do just that, starting with a relatively low dose out of caution. Of course this makes the titration quite slow.

Another approach is based on the relative short-term safety of supra-physiologic thyroid. In that regimen, dosing is based not on TSH but on the patient: any sign of hyperthyroidism is a signal to lower the dose. In published trials the dose has been 100 mcg to start, increasing weekly by that amount to 300 mcg or more (risks reviewed below). On this basis, if trying T4 first in a young patient without cardiovascular risk factors, I'll start with a 100 mcg pill: half daily for a week, then if no better and no problems, increase to one daily. For any signs of hyperthyroidism, lower the dose by half a pill or call if concerned. If the patient is hesitant, I might use a 50 mcg pill, started in similar fashion.

Using this approach will induce hyperthyroid symptoms in some patients, requiring dose reduction and reassurance that these will dissipate in a few days. But more often I've seen substantial improvements without any "side effects" at all. In general a dose of 100 mcg is on the high side, aggressive; 50 or 75 mcg is less likely to push TSH below normal levels. On the other hand, if the patient has no signs or symptoms of hyperthyroidism (no significant heat intolerance, tremor, gastrointestinal distress or diarrhea, or agitation), and she is better, does it matter what her TSH is? If she is better, and not clinically hyperthyroid, and has achieved her improvement without taking the risks of an atypical antipsychotic or even those of lithium, then we really need to know how much risk this approach poses, because it might be one of the most logical to try early on. Unfortunately, evaluating this risk turns out to be a complex question, best understood in the context of much higher doses of thyroid hormone, the so-called supraphysiologic approach.

Supraphysiologic Thyroid

Subho Chakrabarti's succinct history of this treatment, thoroughly referenced, is available online (2011). Briefly, from first reports in the 1980s to numerous additional case reports and open trials in the 1990s, the technique was shown to have surprisingly few adverse effects while benefiting highly treatment-resistant patients (primarily bipolar, but also in unipolar cases). Targets have included rapid cycling, looking for a mood stabilizer effect; and bipolar depression, looking for an antidepressant effect. One of the recent studies included pre- and posttreatment functional imaging, which showed significant decreases in limbic activity that correlated with reduction in depression scores, even with a small sample (Bauer et al., 2005).

A randomized trial of this approach was not available for many years, leaving supraphysiologic thyroid on the sidelines of most treatment guidelines, which tend to focus on efficacy data over tolerability. Finally a small double-blinded trial in bipolar depression was engineered by some of the pioneers of this method, notably Michael Bauer and Peter Whybrow. Following an approach they've studied over a decade, their six-week study increased levothyroxine to 300 mcg daily by 100 mcg per week (Stamm et al., 2014). The results were mixed. Overall, the results were significant only in women. A gender split has been seen before with this treatment, from the earliest studies (Stancer and Persad, 1982). In this study, the men experienced just as much reduction in depression scores as the women did. But their results were not statistically significant because the men were superb placebo responders; conversely, the women were not.

Even though in the levothyroxine group, men and women both improved nearly equally, the strong placebo response in men obliterated any statistical significance for that improvement and indeed for the study as a whole. Note that the entire group began the study in moderate depression, with an average HAM-D score of 21. This may partly explain the thyroid study's findings, as two recent meta-analyses of antidepressant trials found that active drug did not separate well from placebo unless pretreatment HAM-D was closer to 24 (Fournier et al., 2010; Kirsch et al., 2008).

Thus data in support of supraphysiologic thyroid as a mood treatment remain slim even after more than two decades of study. Here again, consideration of this treatment approach, relative to other options, will depend strongly on how one interprets evidence for *risk*. As per the logic for lamotrigine and low-dose lithium, if the risks of supraphysiologic thyroid are few, then even with only limited evidence of effectiveness, it may still be a strong candidate versus atypical antipsychotics in particular. What are the risks?

Risks of Supraphysiologic Thyroid

In this case, information on risk comes from two sources: experience with patients who are *endogenously* hyperthyroid, and patients who are taking high doses of thyroid hormone to suppress thyroid cancer. The latter is called "high-dose thyroid" (HDT) in that literature, but the process is the same as the supraphysiologic doses used as a mood treatment. Note that in all these instances, one expects TSH to be suppressed, less than the lower limit of normal, sometimes less than the lower limit of the assay.

Years of clinical experience with endogenous hyperthyroidism have highlighted two organ systems at risk: cardiac, principally atrial fibrillation but also cardiac dilatation and resultant congestive heart failure; and bone, namely decreased bone density.

1. Cardiac. Recognizing the key role of perceived cardiac risk in determining the use of supraphysiologic thyroid as a mood stabilizer, independent thinker Tam Kelly (2015) undertook an interesting literature review: what has been the cardiac experience of patients on HDT as part of treatment for well-differentiated thyroid cancer? Among several large population studies of HDT, little evidence for increased cardiovascular mortality was found: two large studies were negative, one positive, and the latter has some weaknesses according to Dr. Kelly. But that's mortality—what about simply the incidence of *arrhythmia* once HDT is undertaken? Here Kelly found one prospective study, in which 14 of 136 patients treated with HDT (10 percent) developed atrial fibrillation: 12 paroxysmal and 2 (1.5 percent) chronic. The latter carries a risk of arterial emboli from an atrial blood clot. Kelly notes several reasons why the cardiovascular risk of supraphysiologic thyroid for depression might differ from HDT for thyroid cancer, but does not completely remove this concern.

Dr. Kelly then goes on to present his experience using supraphysiologic thyroid for depression, though he used T3, not T4, so his patients are not directly comparable to the accumulated experience from Drs. Bauer and Whybrow and their colleagues and trainees (Bauer et al.,

2003; initially at UCLA, now international). He concludes that cardiac risk is minimal if present at all.

From the UCLA group and its colleagues, *no* reports of cardiac problems have emerged (to my knowledge at this writing). Those authors have noted, "Treating mood disorders with high dose levothyroxine does not result in excessive peripheral levels of T3 (the hormone with the highest biologic activity), in contrast with endogenous production of thyroid hormone secondary to hyperthyroidism" (Bauer et al., 2003). Together these authors have had several hundred patients on this regimen. The absence of published case reports of atrial fibrillation or other cardiac abnormalities associated with supraphysiologic T4, versus the 10 percent rate in the prospective HDT study, leaves the issue of cardiac risk uncertain. Given that it took two decades to mount a small trial of supraphysiologic thyroid for bipolar depressions, a trial large enough to reduce this uncertainty appears unlikely in the near future.

2. Bone. Some data suggest that patients with depression are already at risk for osteoporosis (Gebara et al., 2014). How much risk is added, with supraphysiologic thyroid? Again we have two sources of data: patients thus treated for mood, and patients treated with HDT for thyroid cancer.

Several studies have examined bone density in patients taking supraphysiologic thyroid for bipolar disorder (see Table 10.1 for a comparison).

Table 10.1. **Studies examining bone density**

Study	N, gender	Design	Time on treatment (avg.)	T4 dose (mean mcg)	Bone mineral density (BMD) findings
Gyulai et al., 1997	10 F	X-section	6 years	not shown	BMD loss same as 10 control women
Gyulai et al., 2001 premenopausal postmenopausal	13 F	X-section	3 years	281	Premenopausal same as population avg.; postmenopausal, 1 SD below
Bauer et al., 2004	21 F, M	Prospective	16–34 months	411	BMD declines no greater than age-matched reference population—except in one woman
Ricken et al., 2012 (extension of the Bauer 2004 study)	22 F, M	Prospective	5.75 years	380	Declines not statistically different from reference population—one male improved substantially

These data are moderately reassuring, but the trend in the largest, longest prospective study (Ricken et al., 2012) was toward BMD losses greater than population norms for gender and age. Although the net result was not statistically significant, the sample is small, perhaps underpowered to detect a slowly diverging BMD in the treatment group.

The separate literature on HDT's effects on bone is no more definitive (Kelly, 2014). Studies have both implicated and exonerated HDT in terms of bone density loss. Note that five years is a very long research time frame: keeping track of a study population becomes progressively more difficult. Yet patients who have responded to supraphysiologic thyroid could be taking it for several decades. By the time a decrease in BMD is detectable with repeat bone scans, a substantial loss of bone has already occurred, one that is very difficult to make up. So the lack of a definitive answer regarding BMD effects of long-term supraphysiologic thyroid is concerning. Note however that a short period of treatment is not subject to this concern. Thus a *trial* of supraphysiologic thyroid does not present a bone risk, nor does a brief overshoot of thyroid replacement.

Reconsidering a High-Normal TSH

After considering the foregoing issues, where does this leave a clinician whose patient is depressed and has a TSH ≥3.0 mIU/L but no signs of hypothyroidism? Is T4 a justified intervention?

In unipolar depression, determining treatment options for a patient with a high-normal TSH is relatively straightforward. For a patient already on a tolerable antidepressant who has not improved substantially, T3 is the standard, the one for which we have the most data and experience. There is no reason to consider T4.

But at the other end of the mood spectrum, T4 is the standard, largely defined by the research on supraphysiologic treatment. We have no randomized trial data on T3 augmentation in bipolar depression, analogous to T3 augmentation in unipolar depression. We have Dr. Kelly's large case series treated with T3, which included more than 100 patients with bipolar disorders, and my 2 patients with bipolar disorder treated with T3 whose experience suggested that it might exacerbate cycling and promote mixed states.

Thus several questions remain open:

1. Is thyroid augmentation as useful in bipolar depression as it is in unipolar depression?
2. If so, which is better, T3 or T4?
3. Does T3 act too much like an antidepressant in bipolar disorders, risking increased cycling and mixed states?

Extrapolating from all these sources, I think it reasonable to try T4 first, before lithium, in a woman with a family history of hypothyroidism whose TSH is ≥3.0 (presuming that lamotrigine was contraindicated or ineffective). With any fewer factors in favor of this approach, it probably falls behind lithium and even fish oil.

For a patient with a TSH ≥3.0 but *no* family history of thyroid problems (particularly if male), thyroid should be used as an adjunct (targeting a TSH around 1.0, not the supraphysiologic approach in which TSH is suppressed below 0.25), but not a primary intervention. A strong positive response to thyroid hormone could open the door to a discussion of supraphysiologic doses. Whether the high-dose treatment is effective for women only remains to be seen; the data seem to be pointing in that direction. For women, a detailed comparison of the risks of BMD loss versus the risks of weight gain and diabetes and tardive dyskinesia is warranted, where possible. This is a very difficult choice.

If considering T4 augmentation, familiarity with supraphysiologic thyroid and its risks makes possible a more aggressive approach to titration: increase as often as weekly until benefits are noted, or adverse effects (including any sign of hyperthyroidism), or at least 100 mcg, *before* the first follow-up TSH. After all, this is only the first step if one is taking the patient to 300 mcg, which has been done with no follow-up TSH in between. Monitor for hyperthyroid symptoms and get on with it. The risk here, compared with everything else except fish oil and nonpharmacologic approaches, is minimal in young healthy people. Ask yourself these questions, which at present have no clear answers: if the patient has no signs or symptoms of hyperthyroidism but the TSH is less than "normal," is she at risk at all? Which is the better indicator of hyperthyroidism, the patient or the lab?

Who Should Manage Thyroid?

This is another rhetorical question, because regardless of how you might answer it, you still have to work with the patient's primary care provider and perhaps an endocrinologist as well. I've found open communication and a respectful attempt to share the literature reviewed in this chapter is the best approach (surprise!). The patient must be kept out of the middle of ego and turf wars between providers.

I teach patients as much as possible and give them a copy of a review article to be carried with my greetings to their primary care provider. This has usually allowed continuation of treatment with the understanding that I am managing the doses and the monitoring—and the risk, whatever it is perceived to be. I educate patients about "irregularly irregular" tachycardia (if noted, go to the ER) and we discuss whether and when to do a bone density study. This is not a protection against risk, if there is one, but it may help in some cases to know we're watching.

Hopefully you've understood here that familiarity with supraphysiologic thyroid has value even if all it does is make you more willing to use thyroid replacement in patients with high-normal TSH. Atypical antipsychotics have far more evidence in their favor, as reflected in most treatment guidelines. We'll examine them in the next chapter.

Chapter 11

Antipsychotics:
Which and When from
a Mood Spectrum View

The medications generally referred to as antipsychotics all have anti-manic effects, some have very clear antidepressant effects, and most have antianxiety effects. Their class name reflects how they were developed, initially for the treatment of psychosis, usually first in schizophrenia. But that name is very narrow relative to their range of actions and contributes to stigma against them. "Antipsychotics" is an unfortunate term.

The old generation of these medications, so-called typical antipsychotics, had one function: treat psychosis. Calling these medications antipsychotics made sense. But the new generation, the "atypicals," have additional effects. Some are antidepressants, equal in efficacy to the medications usually referred to as such. Some have antianxiety effects. If they had not originally been used in schizophrenia, many might have been called antidepressants.

Because all these medications have anti-manic effects, even patients in the middle of the mood spectrum may sometimes have to consider their use when alternatives that target cycling are not viable or effective and some sort of mood stabilizing effect is needed. Antipsychotics that also have antidepressant effects in bipolar disorders (quetiapine, lurasidone, and olanzapine) are even more potentially relevant for mid-spectrum patients.

As in earlier chapters, routine details of use (precautions, titrations, etc.) are not reviewed here because they are available in many other resources. Some of the information here will become dated quickly, so I've tried to focus on things that won't change much over time.

Once again, begin with the principle that mid-spectrum patients do not need anti-manic prophylaxis. They need anticycling effects, which some but not all antipsychotics can provide. Some antipsychotics are actually pro-cycling, for at least a few patients. An *antidepressant* effect, in addition to suppression of cycling, would be particularly useful, especially for mid-spectrum patients. Any option that is truly weight-neutral has a tremendous advantage over the rest. With all those factors in mind, consider the following ranking of antipsychotics.

Procycling
    ziprasidone (albeit likely weight-neutral)
    risperidone
    paliperidone
Antidepressant
    quetiapine
    olanzapine/fluoxetine
    lurasidone (possibly weight neutral?)
Purely anti-manic
    perphenazine (less weight gain than most atypicals)
    other typicals

Procycling Effects

One of the primary goals in the treatment of all mood patients with *episodes* of depression is to stop the cycling in and out of those episodes. Unfortunately, some of our treatments can sometimes *induce* hypomanic or manic symptoms, including lamotrigine (as discussed in Chapter 7) and certainly antidepressants. But many clinicians are not aware that most atypical antipsychotics can also occasionally induce manic-side symptoms (Aubry et al., 2000; Benyamina and Samalin, 2012; Rachid et al., 2004). Because in many patients manic or hypomanic episodes appear to proceed into depressed episodes (the so-called manic-depressed-interval pattern, MDI), agents that induce manic episodes are also therefore presumably capable of inducing cycling.

Induction of a manic episode, as described in many case reports involving antipsychotics, is easier to detect than induction of hypomania. Of course, harkening back to Chapter 1 and the spectrum of hypomania, the more subtle the patient's symptoms, the less likely they are to be detected, and thus less likely to be ascribed to one of the patient's medications. Therefore recognizing that a medication that was supposed to suppress cycling is actually *causing* it requires close observation and a prepared mind. Otherwise the symptoms will simply be ascribed to the patient's own cycling, and the offending medication continued, creating a treatment-resistant case.

How common is this antipsychotic-induced cycling? Some medications are more frequently implicated than others. Typical antipsychotics are not among the case reports, only atypicals (Rachid et al., 2004). Among the latter, those with low-slow titrations appear to be more commonly recognized as inducing manic symptoms (Benyamina and Samalin, 2012). These findings suggest that the inherent antidepressant effects of the atypicals, perhaps through their serotonergic or noradrenergic effects, are responsible: these tend to kick in at low doses, whereas high doses are required for an anti-manic effect. On the other hand, even low doses of olanzapine are anti-manic, yet it is common among the case reports of mania induction. (Note that case reports are prompted by *new* findings. Olanzapine was one of the first atypicals and responsible for some of earliest cases of induced mania. Later cases on other medications are perhaps less likely to be reported, because the phenomenon already recognized, possibly creating an artificially high percentage of olanzapine cases).

The same difficulties that have plagued research efforts to determine the frequency of *antidepressant*-induced hypomania (detailed in the next chapter) are present with antipsychotics: what is the lowest threshold of hypomania that will be counted? How thorough was the search for those symptoms? How long after the medication was started will induction be attributed to the medication and not to the patient's own cycling? In the case of antipsychotics, the problem of attribution is even worse, because the frequency of the phenomenon is low and it is so counterintuitive—an anti-manic medication inducing *manic* symptoms? Only with close observation and a prepared mind are clinicians likely to recognize subtle cases.

A rank-ordering of culpability might help you know where to look, so I offer my working list (far too few data are available to rank on anything but clinical experience).

1. Ziprasidone. This one is clearly the worst. Indeed, not long after its introduction, low-dose ziprasidone was characterized as being more like a tricyclic antidepressant than an anti-manic or antipsychotic. Low doses have even been studied in the treatment of generalized anxiety disorder, as though efficacy comparable to an antidepressant might have been expected (results were negative and the dropout rate in the ziprasidone group far exceeded that in the placebo group; Lohoff et al., 2010).

Unfortunately ziprasidone absorption is highly affected by food intake, creating the ironic possibility that an anti-manic dose of 120 mg could drop down to a pro-manic dose of 80 mg simply by being taken at bedtime without food. Even though ziprasidone does appear to be weight-neutral, its side effects and erratic performance have kept this agent from wide use. That may have been fortunate, from the perspective of "do no harm" and the risk of inducing hypomania and cycling. Nevertheless, there are definitely a few patients with bipolar disorder out there who do well on it (Suppes et al., 2014). I wish I could tell in advance who they are. My tentative suspicion is that patients with intermittent manic symptoms and little else (few depressions, little comorbid anxiety or other problems) have the best chance at a good result on it.

2. Risperidone and its cousins. When risperidone was recognized as capable of inducing mania, case reports were still appearing for olanzapine, which had been introduced earlier (Henry and Demotes-Mainard, 2002). This is a weak suggestion that risperidone is more likely to cause this problem than olanzapine: it demonstrated this problem shortly after its appearance, in a more pronounced way, while olanzapine only slowly revealed its capacity to induce mania. For years I've worried that when risperidone is on board and the patient is still cycling, one has to consider risperidone as a possible culprit and ultimately take it out to be certain it is not the basis of the continued problem. I've never had to do that with olanzapine (when it had caused trouble, this was obvious early, and very rare in my experience).

Paliperidone has not been evaluated independently but has been around for years as an active first metabolite of risperidone. So far it does not appear to act significantly differently, except on the budget of agencies paying large sums for its injectable forms.

3. Aripiprazole. Low doses are antidepressant. When aripiprazole was studied as an adjunct to antidepressants in unipolar depression, the starting dose was 5 mg and clinicians were allowed to adjust from there. Many went down to *lower* doses (Berman et al., 2007; Marcus et al., 2008). Anti-manic doses are in the 15 mg range and up. Interestingly, a case report describes a pro-manic effect at 2 mg and successful anti-manic effect at 22 mg in the same patient (Park, 2014).

Even though aripiprazole has more recognized antidepressant effects than risperidone, I've not had the impression that induction of hypomania, or cycling, was worse than with risperidone. They might be about the same. I've not used it as much: it only recently came off patent and became more affordable. It may yet prove worse than risperidone, as its antidepressant effects appear to be more pronounced.

Aripiprazole is definitely not weight-neutral, even though the manufacturer's representatives did a very good job implying so early on. Case reports have demonstrated that although it is not as bad as olanzapine and perhaps not even as bad as quetiapine and risperidone, rapid substantial weight gain is possible on aripiprazole (Singh, 2005). One cannot wait for an appetite increase to signal impending metabolic problems: insulin shifts begin before appetite changes (Teff et al., 2015).

Finally, in my limited experience with it, aripiprazole seems to cause more trouble when stopping it than other atypicals. One of my patients had very clear exacerbation of mood symptoms when tapering slowly to 2 mg, and further worsening after she finally asked that we just stop rather than taper any further. After a period of increased mood lability, difficult but familiar for her, two months later she improved substantially compared to where she had been with aripiprazole on board, with no other medication changes in the interim. Note that her experience suggests more than withdrawal reaction, which has been reported for aripiprazole and most other atypicals (Sansone and Sawyer, 2013); it suggests that the aripiprazole was *causing* treatment resistance until discontinued.

4. Quetiapine. Though it has more case reports of inducing mania than other atypicals (Millard et al., 2015), in my experience quetiapine has not seemed to be as destabilizing as risperidone and perhaps also aripiprazole. Perhaps this is because sleep is relatively reliably preserved due to the antihistaminergic effects at low doses.

5. Olanzapine. Olanzapine's robust anti-manic effects, even at low doses, allow even a combination with an antidepressant (olanzapine/ fluoxetine) without significant induction of mania (Tohen et al., 2003). Yet in rare cases it can still induce hypomanic symptoms (Benyamina and Samalin, 2012).

Antidepressant Effects

Three atypicals have at least two large randomized trials showing efficacy in bipolar depression, and based on those data have received FDA indications for this purpose: quetiapine, olanzapine/fluoxetine combination, and lurasidone.

Olanzapine alone demonstrated significant antidepressant effects in bipolar depression, though this finding has been obscured in marketing of the trade-name combination with fluoxetine. In the same study that established the antidepressant efficacy of the combination, an olanzapine-only arm was included, as well as a placebo arm. Although olanzapine by itself was superior to placebo for bipolar depression (Tohen et al., 2003), Eli Lilly only sought FDA approval for and marketed the combination.

In *unipolar* depression, quetiapine and olanzapine both have trials showing benefit, but also some negative trials (similarly mixed results have also been found for most conventional antidepressants and even fish oil). So for these two antipsychotics, at least *some* antidepressant efficacy has been shown across the mood spectrum.

By contrast, aripiprazole did not show benefit in bipolar depression, only in unipolar as an add-on to antidepressants. The aripiprazole trials in bipolar depression were odd: apparent benefit initially, but somewhat variable, and then benefit lost by the last two weeks of an eight-week trial (Thase et al., 2008). So interpreting aripiprazole's value for mid-spectrum patients is difficult. Somewhere between unipolar and fully bipolar it loses benefit? Or in bipolar patients it can be too much like an antidepressant: work for a while, then stop working? More experience with it is needed to shed light on these questions.

Lurasidone has taken aripiprazole's place as a very expensive option that is readily available with samples. This availability has been enough to demonstrate that this medication does work, and so far appears to cause very few problems (only the cost, if the samples and the coupons run out). In bipolar depression trials for lurasidone, the results look very much like quetiapine: good separation from placebo throughout a six-week trial, though perhaps not quite as fast to show benefit as quetiapine (Loebel et al., 2014). No trials in unipolar depression have been posted on clinicaltrials.gov as of this writing (only in mixed states, and those trials have no publications 1.5 years after the extension's completion date). So lurasidone's role in mid-spectrum patients has yet to be defined.

Risperidone should not be considered for mid-spectrum depression for two reasons: first, it lacks placebo-controlled trial evidence as monotherapy in either unipolar or bipolar depression; and second, it may be likely to induce mixed states and exacerbate cycling, as already described. Risperidone did have a randomized trial in bipolar depression but only in comparison with paroxetine; the results were not strikingly positive for either alone, or in combination (Shelton and Stahl, 2004).

Purely Anti-manic Effects

Typical antipsychotics are not generally regarded as having any antidepressant effects at all, unlike the atypicals, each of which has been investigated for its antidepressant effects. Whereas each of the atypicals has been implicated in *inducing* manic symptoms, this has not been reported for the typical antipsychotics (Kavoor et al., 2014). Does this give the typical antipsychotics some role in the management of bipolar disorders? Here is an indirect answer.

Some patients with bipolar disorder only have manic symptoms: they never have a depressive phase at all (Pfohl et al., 1982). Might some patients only have *hypomania* and never depression? This, too, has been observed in epidemiologic research (Beesdo et al., 2009), but of course such patients are not likely to present for treatment, unless they were to have only dysphoric hypomanic episodes: irritable, agitated, insomniac, distractible, and impulsively imprudent phases. With these symptoms, but no phases of depression, such patients would not likely be diagnosed as bipolar, nor their symptoms recognized as hypomanic, but they might benefit from a purely anti-manic treatment.

Thus there are some patients, even mid-spectrum patients, who might occasionally need a *pure* anti-manic medication (a typical antipsychotic, as opposed to an atypical one). Another role for a pure anti-manic was common years ago. Patients with bipolar disorder who could not tolerate or did not respond to lithium were treated with a combination of an antipsychotic and an antidepressant: block the manic side with one and the depression with the other. A modern version of the approach is the olanzapine/fluoxetine combination. Tardive dyskinesia is an unfortunate risk of this long-term use of an antipsychotic.

By comparison, short-term use of an antipsychotic carries much less risk of tardive dyskinesia. Because the typical antipsychotics do not appear to carry a risk of inducing manic symptoms (or by extension, inducing rapid cycling and/or mixed states), sometimes they can be of value in treating acute manic-side symptoms. But in mid-spectrum patients this occasion will probably only arise when an astute clinician recognizes dysphoric hypomania in a patient who for some reason cannot use lamotrigine or lithium. In some cases a short course of a typical antipsychotic might carry less risk than turning to carbamazepine or divalproex with their attendant problems (as reviewed in Chapter 9). Which typical should we consider, then?

Before atypical antipsychotics appeared, there was a brief window in which *perphenazine* was regarded as the best of the available antipsychotics. It never quite received the attention of haloperidol and thorazine because at that time perphenazine was still protected by patent and thus a more expensive option (requiring prior authorization, for example, when nothing else did). Just before perphenazine became available as a generic, the atypicals started showing up: first clozapine, but then the more easily used olanzapine, which quickly amazed us with its rapid and broad efficacy and greater tolerability—and then with its weight gain.

The point of that historical tidbit is that perphenazine warrants consideration as possibly the best of the typicals. This was reflected in the large NIMH-sponsored comparison of antipsychotics, the so-called CATIE study (Lieberman et al., 2005). There, perphenazine was chosen as the sole typical to go head to head with the then exorbitantly expensive atypicals. It was found to be as effective as all but olanzapine and less likely to cause weight gain.

By contrast, haloperidol causes more extrapyramidal symptoms, which can occur with perphenazine but far less often. Thorazine causes much more sedation. Perphenazine can be tolerated without the blunting, thought-blocking effects that make patients hate antipsychotics, at least at the low doses which are commonly sufficient for mid-spectrum patients' symptoms (2–8 mg; rarely up to 12 mg, beyond which many of the side effects more common with other antipsychotics begin to emerge).

Managing Weight Gain

Weight gain is caused by mood disorders (Luppino et al., 2010). Of course, many other factors affect weight as well, but depression and bipolar disorders themselves are part of the driving force toward weight gain. Patients we treat for these conditions are already heading in that direction. So using a medication that pushes them further in that direction, in some cases very firmly, is ironic. Resistance to the very idea is completely understandable, and it is our responsibility as practitioners to minimize any addition to this problem.

The first step in that process is to avoid using medications that can cause weight gain. Would that it were that simple, right? Nearly every tool we have does so, with two notable exceptions: lamotrigine and carbamazepine. Ziprasidone is an exception, too, but it is almost unworkable in complexity and side effects and does not have reliable/sustainable antidepressant efficacy.

Perhaps lurasidone will be found to be weight-neutral? Not so far: in a pooled analysis of six 12-month studies (Meyer et al., 2015), 10 percent of patients went from normal or underweight to overweight or obese; not as bad as quetiapine or risperidone, at 15 percent and 27 percent, respectively, but far more than the one-pound average annual weight gain in the United States (Wetmore and Mokdad, 2012).

How about aripiprazole, often touted as less weight-gain-producing, an advantage over other medications? Unfortunately, in an antidepressant trial, aripiprazole was associated with an 8.5 kg gain at one year among patients who had gained significantly by week 6 of the trial. For those who did not gain significantly by week 6, their one-year gain was 4.5 kg. These far exceed population averages. Granted, depression itself is likely playing a role in these gains (there was no placebo continuation in this study for comparison); and the antidepressants to which aripiprazole was added as an adjunct may have also played a role. But these alone do not cause 10–20 pounds of weight gain in a year (Blumenthal et al., 2014).

Avoiding medications that cause weight gain is not easy. How can we help patients cope with this? Several weight gain "antidotes" have been studied, but when all risks and benefits are considered, non-medication approaches to weight control are at least as good. We start there and then consider the medication antidote options.

Non-Medication Approaches

Many studies of weight management in patients on psychotropics, particularly atypical antipsychotics, have included a group treated with lifestyle modification alone: dietary shifts, exercise programs, mindful eating practice, and so on. In many of those studies, substantial weight loss is seen in this control group.

Thus lifestyle modification alone was successful in controlling weight, sometimes lowering it, even while antipsychotics were continued. By comparison, the medication "antidotes" below are either minimally effective or rife with side effect problems. For most patients, the best approach to weight control is the one that nearly everyone in modern societies must use: avoidance of high-calorie/low-value foods, physical inactivity, and using food as a reward. Of course all of these strategies must be used carefully, mindfully, lest they become their own problems.

Unfortunately these behaviors are very difficult for most people to initiate and sustain, even without a mood disorder to contend with. Slips are almost unavoidable; wholesale abdication is common. On one hand, that leaves great room for improvement for many patients. But on the other hand, it means that lifestyle modification is challenging, even when mood is not impaired. For people who are depressed, where symptoms including lack of motivation and an inability to see the positives in things, managing diet and exercise for long-term health is far more difficult.

Research programs showing weight maintenance or loss through lifestyle modification almost always had a very detailed program providing guidance, support, motivation, and some form of short-term reward (monitoring and recognition of success, for example). They did not simply offer recommendations and then wait to see what happened: that is clearly insufficient for patients who are gaining weight on an atypical antipsychotic or any psychotropic (including antidepressants, nearly all of which have been associated with weight gain, though not of the proportions associated with the atypicals; Blumenthal et al., 2014).

Medication Approaches

For the foregoing reasons, and because many patients will have tried (sometimes very hard) to lose weight without success, "antidote" medications are important to understand and be able to explain: at this writing these include topiramate, metformin, zonisamide, and naltrexone.

1. Topiramate. Topiramate has been used for weight control for many years. Its efficacy in this role is accepted. For example, one study found substantial dose-related responses (Wilding et al., 2004); see Table 11.1.

Unfortunately, although topiramate's efficacy in weight loss is clear (not universal of course, but substantial), its cognitive side effects are similarly clear. Most of my patients, far more than 50 percent, describe cognitive impairment on it. This is much higher than reported in clinical trials. Formal assessments report deficits in working memory, process-

Table 11.1. **Dose-related responses of topiramate**

Dose of topiramate	% of Weight Lost (1 Year)	Lbs Lost (if 250 lbs or More to Start)	Lbs Lost (if 300 Pounds or More to Start)
Placebo	2	5	6
100 mg	7	15	20
200 mg	9	23	27
250 mg	10	25	30

ing speed, psychomotor speed, and verbal fluency in 20–25 percent of patients (Sommer et al., 2013). Either my patients are different, or the assay for cognitive impairment used in clinical trials is less sensitive than my interview. For example, I do not have a single patient in my practice who has stayed on topiramate who had a job, was going to school, or had children to take care of. They appreciate the weight control but cannot function. Evidently other practitioners have not encountered this problem as often. Suffice to say that before allowing patients' enthusiasm to ramp up, hearing that a medication might help them control weight even while taking one that is making their weight problem worse, I emphasize that there are significant problems with topiramate that occur at a high frequency (at least 25 percent, per the clinical trials).

Unlike other anticonvulsants reviewed in prior chapters (lamotrigine, divalproex, and carbamazepine), topiramate does *not* have mood-stabilizing properties: four randomized trials of topiramate in bipolar disorder were negative; none were positive (Kushner et al., 2006). On the other hand, multiple open trials have shown antidepressant effects and antianxiety effects. Some patients may respond, just not enough to rise above placebo rates. Some patients are highly predisposed to find it helpful based on optimism about its potential benefits for weight control, which could also contribute to placebo responses.

Of course, like all medications discussed in this book, there are other risks to factor into decisions about topiramate (e.g., renal stone formation at a rate of 1–2 percent). Clearly careful patient education is warranted when considering topiramate as an antidote to weight gain. To help patients understand the nature of the side effect, the slang names based on the trade name are informative: "Stupimax" or "Dopamax."

2. Metformin. Because it does not lower blood glucose in nondiabetics, metformin can be considered for its capacity to help preserve sensitivity to one's own insulin. The atypical antipsychotics and divalproex all decrease insulin sensitivity. On this basis, metformin has been tried both as preventive agent, before weight gain ensues on these medications, and as a treatment for weight gain after the fact. In both roles, metformin has demonstrated benefit—but the advantages it confers, relative to placebo, are not large (Correll et al., 2013).

On the other hand, metformin's risks are minimal in patients whose other organ systems are relatively healthy. Other than relatively frequent initial nausea (which remits with time, and is diminished if taken with meals), it is usually side effect–free. So the problem with metformin is the opposite of those with topiramate: tolerability is excellent, but efficacy is limited. Even when it works, it doesn't do anything particularly dramatic in the majority of patients. As such, it's hard to get excited about. Unless the significant problems with topiramate are underscored, it will be much more appealing to patients than metformin.

3. Zonisamide. Originally an anticonvulsant, zonisamide has been studied as a weight loss agent, following observations of weight loss when used in the treatment of epilepsy. One large trial demonstrated significant short-term benefit (Gadde et al., 2003) but in a longer trial, only the 400 mg dose was effective; a 200 mg dose was not better than placebo (Gadde et al., 2012). After the longer trial, weight *regain* in the 400 mg group was greater than in the placebo group (Shin et al., 2014).

But raising hope again, another trial in patients with schizophrenia showed substantial weight loss while on atypical antipsychotics, using a small 150 mg dose of zonisamide (Ghanizadeh et al., 2013). Like other anticonvulsants, zonisamide has been studied as a mood stabilizer. A small open trial found it beneficial for depressive as well as manic symptoms, and nine patients "improved markedly" (Ghaemi et al., 2008a). If it did have such mood benefits, zonisamide would be a strong candidate for weight control. Unfortunately, that has not been seen in other trials. A randomized study in bipolar mania or mixed states was negative (Dauphinais et al., 2011). Almost half of the patients in another small study discontinued zonisamide because of *worsening* mood symptoms after having begun the trial in euthymia (Wang et al., 2008).

Moreover, whether it works for mood or for weight, zonisamide has had the same kind of cognitive effects as topiramate in all the patients for whom I've tried it (at least 15 or so). Only one patient stayed on it, and she had a complex eating disorder playing into that choice. All the rest eventually stopped it because of cognitive impairment: they just felt dull and slowed on it. Several had not noticed the extent of this effect until stopping zonisamide. One said that tapering off it was like "slowly waking up." However, in clinical trials the reported rates of somnolence and memory impairment are far less that what I have observed. Again, like topiramate, either my patients are just different or the assay for cognitive impairment in those studies is less sensitive than my interview. Given the stakes, it would be wonderful if one of these medications was actually tolerable, so neither patients nor I have a reason to bias these observations.

4. Naltrexone/bupropion combination. While patients struggled with whether to use metformin (is it worth it?) or topiramate (will this be the lucky patient who doesn't get cognitive impairment?) new data arrived suggesting naltrexone might be another option (Caixàs et al., 2014). Generally known as an opiate antagonist and commonly used to help maintain sobriety in chronic alcohol use, it has been investigated for weight loss for many years. Early studies of naltrexone alone did not suggest great efficacy: weight loss was minimal or absent (Lee and Fujioka, 2009).

More recently naltrexone has been combined with bupropion, which itself has some evidence for mild weight loss. The combination is a new trade-name medication, complete with very odd dosages (360 mg bupropion/32 mg naltrexone), to force practitioners into using the new product instead of just writing prescriptions for the closest available doses of the generics separately.

But of course bupropion is an antidepressant, and antidepressants can exacerbate bipolarity, as reviewed in the next chapter—potentially worsening the very condition that a weight-promoting antipsychotic is treating. Thus for mid-spectrum patients who are seeking weight control, a bupropion/naltrexone approach is almost contraindicated.

Almost but not quite: at least one atypical has so much anti-manic effect, it has been used successfully in combination with fluoxetine for bipolar depression and was not associated with worsening of cycling or inductions of manic or mixed states: olanzapine (Tohen et al., 2003). Of course the stability of response to olanzapine/fluoxetine combination has not been followed for more than a year in research studies, as they do not generally continue beyond that. But if one has to use an atypical, olanzapine is probably the most reliable.

Thus with trepidation I sometimes consider continuing olanzapine if weight can be controlled. I might consider the naltrexone/bupropion combination in this context. Using generics, one could start with naltrexone alone, establish its tolerability, and assess for efficacy before adding bupropion. Indeed, in one recent study of patients taking atypical antipsychotics, naltrexone alone was strikingly effective (not consistent with prior studies of naltrexone by itself for weight loss): patients on placebo gained 1.4 kg in 8 weeks, while those receiving 25 mg of naltrexone lost 3.4 kg (Tek et al., 2014). Got that? *Lost* weight, *on* atypicals. A larger study by the same team is recruiting at this writing, per ClinicalTrials. gov. Unfortunately even at low doses naltrexone causes quite a bit of nausea, so careful instruction (e.g., take with dinner, not too late) and encouragement is often necessary for a successful trial.

Newer Medications

As this book ages, newer medications will appear. As of this writing several are emerging: asenapine and iloperidone among the misnamed antipsychotic class, vortioxetine as a nominal antidepressant, and more. The problem with new medications is that they are new. Establishing benefit enough to obtain regulatory approval for use requires several randomized trials, but discovering the full range of adverse effects requires many years of widespread use. Consider the bone density concerns now arising for carbamazepine, which has been around for decades, or the slow process of determining that valproate/divalproex is indeed causing (not just associated with) polycystic ovarian syndrome, which also finally came to light after several decades of use.

When a new medication appears, for the first several years of its use, patients are essentially invited to participate in a grand experiment: what are the real risks? At first, there is no way to know the answer. The older I get, the slower I am to begin using new medications. I wait until patients are starting to come in to my practice on one of the new medications—started by another practitioner—and describe very significant benefit. Then I start paying attention.

In the case of olanzapine, this happened very early, within a year of the drug's release. It is strikingly effective, which became apparent very quickly. Lurasidone is now crossing this threshold for me because it appears closer to weight-neutral, with few side effects, and significant antidepressant effects. I was slower to begin using it because other atypicals are now generic and far more reasonable in price, and because we know now that weight effects can only really be known through many months of use. In my first 20 patients or so, I've seen spectacular responses in patients who had been through many other treatments with only slight improvement, raising my hopes that we have another truly valuable tool here. On the other hand, consider the old adage: "when a new medication comes out, use it quickly before it stops working" (i.e., initial enthusiasm can be infectious but later succumbs to reality). Time will tell.

In general, when a new medication is available, a very slow, repeated balancing is required: does early clinical experience suggest that we have a highly effective new tool? On that basis, is it worth exposing patients to the risks of using a medication that has not been around for long, and whose long-term risks are thus unknown, when it is expensive and others are not? In the case of aripiprazole, my foot-dragging lasted nearly the entire duration of the drug's patent, because for mid-spectrum patients, clinical experience did not suggest enough benefit to leap past the invisible risk of the long-term unknowns, plus the high costs.

One more complex risk-benefit balancing process is the subject of the final chapter, on controversies regarding the role of antidepressants in the treatment of bipolar disorders.

Chapter 12

Antidepressants:
Four Controversies and Nine Solutions

Few topics in psychiatry generate as much controversy as the role of antidepressants in the treatment of bipolar disorders. Four different questions provoke differences of opinion:

1. Do antidepressants work better than a placebo in bipolar depression?
2. How often do they induce hypomanic or manic symptoms?
3. Are antidepressants mood "destabilizers," inducing rapid cycling, mixed states, treatment resistance, or suicidality?
4. If a patient is on an antidepressant and a mood stabilizer and doing well, should she stay on the antidepressant, or taper off and stay on the mood stabilizer alone?

(And for each question: are there subgroups of patients for whom the answers are clearer?)

Fortunately, at least nine alternative treatments have as much evidence for efficacy in bipolar depression as do antidepressants, or carry fewer risks—and most of those alternatives have *both* of these advantages. After considering all factors from efficacy to short-term and long-term risk, the alternatives usually seem a better place to start than antidepressants for bipolar depression.

However, the further down the mood spectrum one goes, the less clear this conclusion becomes. As reviewed shortly, antidepressant efficacy in Bipolar II appears to be higher than in Bipolar I. The International Society for Bipolar Disorders recommends against antidepressants in Bipolar I in almost all circumstances, but exempts Bipolar II from this caution (Pacchiarotti et al., 2013a). For a patient in the middle of the mood spectrum who has never had a medication approach, whether to start an antidepressant or lamotrigine is a very open question. Some specialists regard it as an open question even in patients with Bipolar II.

In the face of all this, a thorough understanding of the pro and con views on each of the four controversies is useful. But the bottom line—in my view—is that *at least five of the nine alternatives to antidepressants are preferable as a starting point for treatment of depression in most mid-spectrum patients*. An even greater reliance on the alternatives is warranted as bipolarity increases from that midpoint. A convenient way of remembering and presenting these alternatives to patients concludes this chapter, along with my personal strategies.

Controversy 1: Do They Work?

No. Yes. Maybe. (What evidence will you accept?) In the STEP-BD study of this question, the answer was clear: no (Sachs et al., 2007). But that study has been repeatedly criticized (e.g., Henry et al., 2007). Meanwhile, diligent work over decades from Jay Amsterdam and his colleagues has repeatedly shown that antidepressants, even without a mood stabilizer, work better than placebo in Bipolar II depression, better even than lithium (e.g., Amsterdam et al., 2013, 2015). Yet those studies have also been criticized for design features that weaken the findings (Thase, 2013; Xenitidis et al., 2013).

Perhaps more telling: no one really seems to believe the STEP-BD results. Even the lead investigator on that study said that when a patient with bipolar disorder calls to report dramatic, rapid improvement one should say, "Well, that's great. Let's celebrate. Let's lower the dose of your antidepressant." Anyone with much experience with antidepressants, including in patients with bipolar disorders, knows these pills are not duds. They may be volatile, they may cause unwanted consequences, but they are not inactive, as the STEP-BD results appear to suggest.

Indeed, in the recent randomized trial by Dr. Amsterdam and colleagues, venlafaxine worked better than lithium in preventing subsyndromal depressive symptoms in patients with Bipolar II. On the other hand, as its critics point out, these patients were selected for randomization after having done well on venlafaxine for *six months*.

So it goes, you see: point and counterpoint. The unfortunate bottom line for Controversy 1 is that providers can easily find studies to support their position: yes, antidepressants work in bipolar disorder, no they don't, maybe they work in some groups (e.g., Bipolar II patients, but not those with rapid cycling or any degree of mixed state).

Conclusion: antidepressants do not appear to work the same in Bipolar I as they do in unipolar depression. Some patients with Bipolar II do well on them for quite a while, even as monotherapy. How long that lasts has not been reported beyond one year of follow-up.

Controversy 2: How Often Do They Induce Hypomania/Mania?

Depending on the study one chooses, the answer to this question ranges from a 4 percent to 30 percent "switch" rate. How can that range be so large? Often it seems that the results on this subject reflect the views of the authors before they undertook the study, despite very careful methodology. Here are two examples.

First, consider the view from across the Atlantic, where antidepressants are not regarded as problematic when combined with a mood stabilizer. For example, in the NICE guidelines (National Institute for Health and Care Excellence, for Britain's National Health System) the number one recommendation for treatment of bipolar depression is fluoxetine combined with olanzapine (NICE, 2014c). When a team from Oxford conducted a meta-analysis of bipolar disorder switch rates on antidepressants, they found a rate of 4 percent, no greater than placebo (75 percent of the patients were also on a mood stabilizer; Gijsman et al., 2004).

Conversely, a U.S. team led by Bob Post, who from his experience with life charting at the NIMH has long had a deep concern about anti-depressant-induced worsening of bipolar disorders, looked specifically at switching into hypomania or mania on antidepressants. All patients were on mood stabilizers. They found a 30 percent switch rate in Bipolar I, 19 percent in Bipolar II. Switch rates also varied with the antidepressant used, venlafaxine > sertraline > bupropion (Leverich et al., 2006).

The subtlety of hypomania is one factor accounting for the large range in switch rate findings. Imagine the difficulty determining when an antidepressant has induced a switch. First, a cutoff below which hypomania is "subthreshold" and not to be counted is necessary. This must include both symptom intensity and duration. In addition, to define causality firmly, a cutoff in time-after-antidepressant-initiation is also required. But all of these variables are recognized as falling on a spectrum: the symptoms for making the diagnosis of bipolar disorder and the timing of switching as well. Most switches happen within the first several weeks, certainly the first two months, and yet there is at least one case of a well-documented switch seven years after antidepressant initiation (Phelps, 2005).

Nevertheless, from the last decade of work in this controversial area, a few conclusions seem relatively firm:

1. Antidepressants can definitely induce switches into hypomania and mania, even when a patient is already on a mood stabilizer; how often this switching happens is not clear, but it certainly isn't rare.
2. Concurrent treatment with a mood stabilizer lowers switching.
3. Switches are more common in Bipolar I than Bipolar II.
4. Switch rates further down the mood spectrum are not known; but remember that switching in apparently unipolar patients is well recognized. Presumably this reflects unrecognized bipolarity.

Switching into a full manic episode is not the biggest problem with antidepressants. For example, even though primary care providers prescribe very large volumes of antidepressants, most of them have had few patients, if any, who switched into a full mania—based on my queries of primary care colleagues over the years. Far more common, though less easily studied, is switching into rapid cycling, mixed states, or a treatment-resistant bipolar variation, which brings us to the third controversy.

Controversy 3: How Destabilizing Are They?

"Destabilizing" includes induction of rapid cycling, mixed states, treatment resistance, suicidality—and even, through increased cycling, depression itself. The bottom line: each of these suspected inductions has some evidence suggesting it does indeed occur, and very little evidence to the contrary, but research trials firmly establishing a causal connection are few. Enough evidence exists to leave worriers feeling supported but little enough to leave the skeptics feeling justified in their doubts. In my opinion, given the magnitude of these concerns, including induction of suicidal ideation, the burden of proof has shifted to the doubters: we should assume that antidepressants do commonly cause each of these negative outcomes.

Indeed, this set of potential negatives is my main reason for working so hard to avoid antidepressants: not because they cause manic symptoms, which they can, though with uncertain frequency. Rather I avoid antidepressants because:

- they can cause mixed states, which are associated with an increased risk of suicidal ideation;
- they can cause rapid cycling, ironically inducing depressive episodes, the very symptoms they were added to treat;
- they can make otherwise effective mood stabilizers appear to be ineffective, creating an unjustified hopelessness that itself is dangerous.

Unlike mania, which is relatively easy to detect, each of these types of worsening can be subtle. Many patients have these problems even without antidepressants, so causality when they appear can easily be dismissed as a product of the illness, when it may be iatrogenic.

This is a major clinical problem. The only way to know if the antidepressant might be responsible for rapid cycling, mixed states, and treatment nonresponse is to taper it off and observe the results. As noted earlier, the answer is not immediately forthcoming once one has done this: antidepressant discontinuation–associated neural changes may take several months to resolve (Phelps, 2011). Tapering off requires a committed patient who thoroughly understands and accepts the rationale and is willing to endure some transient worsenings to determine whether the antidepressant may have been part of the reason for their continued symptoms.

Look at that last paragraph again. The potential for arriving in this position, wondering whether a poor outcome might have an iatrogenic component, *is itself a good reason not to start antidepressants when alternatives are available.* Don't dig yourself or your successors a clinical hole that is very difficult to work out of. Granted, that was emphatic. This issue warrants a thorough examination of the available evidence. Unfortunately, in my experience, those who already think like I do will find these data at least supportive if not convincing, whereas skeptics will be unmoved.

This persistent disagreement is worth wondering about. Appendix A examines why providing data on these controversial points will often not change opinions. It examines why these issues seem more like politics and religion than science, and how research on moral decision making may shed light here: for example, why "do no harm" drives my thinking while many colleagues, though still respecting that dictum, are more concerned with respecting the integrity of the DSM and following known clinical paths. With Appendix A as a caveat (I commend it to you), here are further data on antidepressant destabilization.

1. Rapid cycling. Do antidepressants cause rapid cycling? The short answer is yes: when all available evidence is assembled, there remains little doubt.

Fred Goodwin and Tom Wehr at the NIMH started documenting this phenomenon in 1979 in a series of case reports (Wehr and Goodwin, 1979). Their investigations culminated in a 1988 study of 51 patients with bipolar disorder who underwent an on/off/on/off trial of antidepressants (Wehr et al., 1988a). A subset of these patients showed a very striking pattern of increased cycling while on antidepressants and decreased cycling when off them (each subject serving as his or her own control). Another line of evidence comes from Joe Goldberg and colleagues, who found evidence that rapid mood switching has become more prevalent since antidepressants came into widespread use (Wolpert et al., 1990).

A contrary finding comes from the University of Iowa team that for years has managed to come up with evidence that diminishes concerns about antidepressants worsening bipolar disorders (they're rather like the Oxfordians in this respect, only more so). Their report (Coryell et al., 2003) is a retrospective analysis of a study from several decades prior; that is, the original study was not designed to examine the relationship between rapid cycling and antidepressants. In patients with Bipolar I and Bipolar II, they did not find evidence of any such connection.

A more definitive finding comes from the large STEP-BD study. One team of their investigators looked specifically for an effect of antidepressants on the frequency of cycling, in the context of an examination of rapid cycling overall (Schneck et al., 2008). Even though antidepressant use diminished over the course of the study, remaining on one was clearly associated with rapid cycling. A more recent prospective study led the authors to conclude "the development of rapid cycling is associated with a higher use of antidepressants" (Valentí et al., 2015).

Rapid cycling itself is not particularly dangerous, but it means far more time symptomatic, and in mid-spectrum patients, that means more time *depressed*. Thus antidepressants are here implicated in precipitating the very symptoms they are supposed to be alleviating. The good news is the corollary: sometimes when an antidepressant effect is desperately needed, one way to get there is to taper the antidepressant. Sounds backward, doesn't it? It certainly does to patients if you don't provide an elaborate explanation. But it is my ace-up-my-sleeve strategy, discussed further shortly.

If it were clearer that antidepressants can *induce* depression, then it would be more clear that stopping them, although counterintuitive, is a potential treatment for long-standing depression. To my knowledge this has never been directly tested. But the director of the University of Kentucky's Mood Disorders program has been nurturing this hypothesis for over a decade, writing in the *Journal of Clinical Psychiatry*, "Can long-term antidepressant use be depressogenic?" (El-Mallakh et al., 1999).

After using a previous term for this possible phenomenon, ACID syndrome (antidepressant-induced chronic irritable dysphoria; El-Mallakh et al., 2008), Dr. El-Mallakh has more recently referred to this putative problem as "tardive dysphoria" (El-Mallakh et al., 2011), an obvious reference to a problem well known to be associated with antipsychotics. Suffice to say that I am following a respected source in worrying that antidepressants can induce the very problem they are supposed to solve, and in believing that one way to treat chronic depression is, ironically, to taper the antidepressant.

2. Mixed states. Do antidepressants induce mixed states? In one of his books on Bipolar II, one of Australia's senior bipolar specialists, Gordon Parker, noted that "mixed states have been associated with antidepressant use, though these data are more observational" (Parker, 2012). Here some of those data, including some that postdate his conclusion.

In the Barcelona Bipolar Disorder Program, 40 percent of patients treated with antidepressants experienced a mixed episode, although interestingly a statistically significant association was found only for serotonin/norepinephrine reuptake inhibitors (SNRIs; Valentí et al., 2011). One suggestive study found that antidepressants induced mixed symptoms in patients with depression who went on to exhibit bipolar symptoms versus those who did not so progress. The authors noted that induction of "serious symptoms" by the antidepressant (agitation, rage, or suicidality, that is, mixed state symptoms) occurred more commonly in the group that later developed bipolar disorder (O'Donovan et al., 2008). Finally, the Barcelona group analyzed data on patients hospitalized with bipolar disorder and found that mixed states were associated with anxious temperament, higher rates of suicidal ideation—and higher frequencies of antidepressant use (Pacchiarotti et al., 2013b).

"Activation syndrome" (AS) is a transient worsening in anxiety, agitation, and irritability shortly after antidepressants are started. This is common, though published incidence rates vary from 4 percent to 65 percent of patients (Sinclair et al., 2009). Is AS related to bipolar mixed states? There is significant overlap, certainly. The FDA description of AS includes symptoms show in Table 12.1 (Culpepper et al., 2004).

Table 12.1. **Symptoms of activation syndrome**

Anxiety	Hostility
Agitation	Impulsivity
Insomnia	Hypomania
Irritability	Mania

Obviously this is almost identical to the list of symptoms that make a depression "mixed", as reviewed in Chapter 3. Yet many who experience such symptoms just after starting an antidepressant go on to do well, with a decrease in these symptoms, and often subsequently a decrease in depression symptoms. Others will become progressively more mixed. Is there any way to tell which patients will go which way? One would think that bipolarity—not just a history of hypomania, but all the other non-manic markers—would be a strong variable determining which course patients will follow. Yet a post hoc analysis of the STAR*D database did not find that patients with such histories did worse on antidepressants than those without (Perlis et al., 2011). On the other hand, Takeshima and Oka (2013) found that in 157 consecutive patients, those with Bipolar II and Bipolar NOS experienced AS 52 percent of the time, versus only 13 percent of those with unipolar disorders.

For now one might conclude, as Gordon Parker does in his text (2012; parentheses his): "though the data are limited, many (most?) clinicians believe that, as in rapid cycling, one of the best ways to address mixed states is to begin by gradually withdrawing the antidepressant."

3. Suicidal ideation.   Can antidepressants induce suicidal thinking or action? Mixed states clearly can do so (Swann et al., 2013). Antidepressants appear to induce mixed states, as just reviewed. This syllogism obviously implicates antidepressants in suicidality. Evidence supporting this concern predate the FDA's controversial 2004 labeling change, beginning at least as far back as Teicher's report of six cases (Teicher et al., 1990; the story of that report and the related FDA hearing—described by one attorney in attendance as a "kangaroo court" [Zuckoff, 2000]—is fascinating though difficult to discern through competing interests).

Fourteen years later the FDA warned that antidepressants were associated with suicidal ideation in children and adolescents (later expanded to include young adults to age 24), albeit at a very low rate, about 2 percent of cases (Culpepper et al., 2004). Why this association with young age? Is it possible that what the FDA was detecting was an association not between antidepressants and suicidal ideation directly but between antidepressant-induced mixed states and bipolar disorder, which because of their age had not been detected when these young people presented with depression?

Several well-known mood specialists have suggested this might be the simplest explanation (Berk and Dodd, 2005; Rihmer and Akiskal, 2006). Others have trotted out the old concept of "rollback," in which antidepressants are said to sometimes improve the low-energy state of depression before they improve mood (Culpepper et al., 2004). Though frequently invoked, I've not seen any study of this rollback explanation. The more parsimonious "occult bipolarity" hypothesis may not be the only mechanism, but is likely at least a partial explanation. If so, screening for bipolarity before antidepressants and avoiding them in a patient who screens positive lowers their propensity to induce suicidal ideation. Such screens do not make diagnoses, of course; further evaluation is warranted. Statistics and issues around screening for bipolar disorder are presented in the latter part of Appendix B.

Controversy 4: Stay On, or Taper Off?

In part of the STEP-BD study, willing euthymic patients who were on a mood stabilizer and an antidepressant were randomly assigned to stay on their antidepressant or taper it off. No placebos were used; patients were aware of their assignment. The result: in patients with a history of rapid cycling, those who stayed on their antidepressant had three times more depressive episodes in the following three years than those who tapered off (Ghaemi et al., 2010). As the authors point out, this was despite their preselection for good antidepressant response! Patients who had earlier had adverse reactions to antidepressants and were no longer taking them were not part of the pool of patients being randomized (El-Mallakh et al., 2015).

Patients who did not have a history of rapid cycling were also in the randomization pool. What became of them, when half were assigned to antidepressant taper? There was a transient but substantial worsening, which when factored into the overall scores for the trial left the discontinuation group with more depression than experienced by those who stayed on their antidepressant. But wait a minute: discontinuation rates were rapid, over one to four weeks, with an average of two weeks!

In contrast, I once heard Dr. Sachs (the principal investigator of the STEP-BD, but not directly part of this component of that research program) suggest at a conference that antidepressant tapers should take four months, 25 percent per month. When I started to follow his recommendation I had dramatically more patients actually make it to zero antidepressant. In light of this experience, I would never taper an antidepressant over two weeks, unless the patient was manic.

Antidepressant discontinuation is highly destabilizing in many patients. Indeed, it can induce mania, per numerous case reports (e.g., see Andrade, 2004). Indirect physiologic evidence also supports Sachs's four-month approach (Phelps, 2011). If the taper in the STEP-BD study had been much slower, I suspect that even more patients would have done well, relative to those who stayed on their antidepressant. If so, then even those without a history of rapid cycling might have done better when tapered. In that case, the entire sample in this component of the STEP-BD study would have come out better off with antidepressant tapering rather than continuation. Remember, this is the only randomized trial we have to go on, so such speculation is warranted.

At minimum we can conclude that in the absence of any other randomized trial data, patients with rapid cycling bipolar disorder—even those for whom an antidepressant has shown clear benefit—should try to taper off antidepressants within months of any improvement. But what about a mid-spectrum patient? Perhaps cyclicity, not polarity, is the relevant factor: those with the most volatile mood course are those who should be tapered, regardless of bipolarity? Once again, we have no direct data with which to address this question. As discussed shortly, tapering is at least an ace-up-the-sleeve strategy.

Nine Alternatives to Antidepressants

Fortunately, given all the controversies, there are numerous alternatives to antidepressants for treating bipolar depression. To make the following informal list, a treatment must meet two criteria:

a. It must have at least as much evidence for efficacy as do antidepressants in Bipolar I (this is a very low bar: one solid randomized trial would do).
b. It must not, unlike antidepressants, have evidence for routinely making bipolar disorders worse.

To make it easier to remember nine options, they can be divided into three columns of three, where "natural" means "not originally synthesized by a pharmaceutical company" (see Table 12.2).

Table 12.2. **Nine alternative options**

Not pills	Natural	Pharmaceutical
Exercise	Lithium	Lamotrigine
Psychotherapy	Fish oil	Quetiapine
Dawn simulators	Thyroid hormone	Lurasidone

The items in the first two columns have not been shown to make bipolar disorder worse, or have only very rare exceptions; for example, there has been one case report of hypomania on fish oil (Kinrys, 2000).

These lists are not inclusive. Some would include electroconvulsive therapy (ECT) in the first column. N-acetylcysteine could certainly be included in the second column. Olanzapine warrants inclusion in the third column. But three columns of three is easier to remember and in most cases these other options rank below the rest: ECT because of its reputation, not its realities; olanzapine because of its weight gain risk; and NAC because in my practice it has yet to demonstrate the value of the others. Nine alternatives to antidepressants for bipolar depression is enough to make the point.

Exercise as an Antidepressant

All of these tools have been discussed in prior chapters, except exercise. Although exercise is almost universally regarded as an effective antidepressant, a recent Cochrane review found surprisingly few high-quality data supporting this belief (Cooney et al., 2013). But a new trial is one of the best demonstrations of antidepressant efficacy to date. The same Duke team that earlier conducted a randomized trial of exercise versus sertraline (Blumenthal et al., 1999; equal improvement in both groups but no control group, so some doubt remained) has now completed another trial in depressed patients with coronary disease. It was firmly positive: equal improvement in both the sertraline and exercise groups, both greater than placebo (Blumenthal et al., 2012).

Exercise offers numerous other health benefits (though perhaps not as many as often touted; Phelps, 1987). But developing and maintaining a pattern of regular physical activity is difficult even for people who are not depressed: most readers will not have to look further than their own experience to understand this. Now add the lack of energy, lack of motivation, and hopelessness that characterize depression, and the recommendation to adopt a regular exercise program is even further out of reach. Indeed, simply offering it up as a treatment option is potentially counterproductive: one could increase the patient's despair. Do not proffer exercise without understanding how possible—or seemingly impossible—it seems to your patient; and begin with small steps carefully selected to be within reach. Of course, modeling your belief in the value of exercise by maintaining your own fitness will help.

An Ace Up Your Sleeve: Taper the Antidepressant

Illustrating how powerful a tool I believe antidepressant tapers to be: a patient comes for a consultation saying he has "tried everything" for his recurrent depressions, and I find myself *hoping* that he is on an antidepressant.

As a mood specialist, it is nice to have an alternative that is very unlikely to have been tried—an "ace up your sleeve" in poker parlance. For many patients, "tried everything" means they have tried five or more antidepressants. Often significant bipolarity has been missed, which means that ironically, even though they think they are at the end of the string of possible treatments, they are actually at the beginning. It is simple to start anew.

Some patients will have tried lamotrigine and lithium. They may have had divalproex. They will often have had several antipsychotics. They may not yet have had carbamazepine. They probably have not yet had supraphysiologic thyroid. They often will not have had fish oil of proper type and dose. But a few will have tried all these things.

For such patients, the one thing they may *not* have tried is to get rid of their antidepressant. After all, they are still having episodes of severe depression. That is why they are seeing me. Why, in the face of that, would I think about tapering off their antidepressant? Indeed, if I suggest this without proper preparation, they will think that I have completely failed to understand them and move on if they can.

To quickly review the logic which patients will need to comprehend and accept before proceeding:

1. Antidepressants can induce manic symptoms, that's clear.
2. Manic symptoms can lead to depressive symptoms (so well recognized it has an acronym, the MDI pattern: manic, depressed, well interval).
3. Therefore antidepressants can in some people induce cycling, which means inducing episodes of depression, including potentially the one the patient is in now, which their antidepressant clearly did not prevent.
4. Thus one way out of the repeated depressions is to taper off the antidepressant and replace it with antidepressant modalities that do not induce cycling.

Some crucial elements in this strategy are discussed next. But first: are there any data in support of this approach? Perhaps. The STEP-BD antidepressant discontinuation trial applies here: at least for patients with a history of rapid cycling, tapering an antidepressant left them better off (Ghaemi et al., 2010). As for the other end of the mood spectrum, my chief resident colleague and I published 12 cases of Major Depression whose anxiety dramatically diminished when their antidepressant was tapered. Many also had suicidal ideation, which also remitted (Phelps and Manipod, 2012). Finally, I would add that many clinicians I have met at the International Society for Bipolar Disorders meetings have arrived at the same strategy independently.

Not much to go on? Remember, the patient at this stage is on an antidepressant that is manifestly not working. Little evidence is required to justify taking it out.

Tips for Tapering Antidepressants Successfully

Most patients start this process with trepidation. Here are five ingredients of a successful taper, from my and ISBD colleagues' experience. Some patients will not require all five steps.

1. Do something else first. Mid-spectrum patients for whom this strategy is considered will be either depressed or mixed, as opposed to Bipolar I patients who might be in a manic phase. So their depression or depression/agitation is going to need some direct treatment. A slow antidepressant taper may ultimately help (that is the reason for this strategy, of course) but not quickly.

Moreover, if the patient is new to you, he may need to develop confidence in your skill and trust that you will be able to help him. Start out with something that eases symptoms a little and you'll be in a better position to sell a counterintuitive, potentially difficult procedure.

What if all the usual options one might consider (low-dose lithium augmentation; optimizing thyroid; initiating some rapidly acting psychotherapy such as behavioral activation) have all been tried, along with many other agents? At this point I go back through the patient's prior treatments with a fine-tooth comb, looking for anything that might have been just a little helpful—not helpful enough, not even remembered as clearly helpful, but perhaps a hint of some response. I make a list of all such agents and any adverse effects experienced. I remind the patient that in theory, the antidepressant might have interfered with a more substantial response. Then I propose that we add a low dose of anything that once helped a little, turning it up slowly until something good happens or something bad happens or a routine dose or blood level is reached. If still no improvement, we might add another agent that is slightly positively remembered and hope for some synergy between the two. We keep doing this until some slight improvement is seen, and then begin the antidepressant taper.

2. Make sure the patient has bought in. If the patient is hesitant, and fearful that lowering the antidepressant dose is going to make things worse, then of course he is more likely to have just the response he fears. Or if the patient really thinks that another antidepressant is the right thing to try, then going in the opposite direction will meet resistance. Sometimes I've deliberately gone along with a patient's preference to try another antidepressant even when I thought it was the wrong thing to do, so as to put myself in a stronger position when her strategy doesn't work out (and of course, sometimes it does help after all, in which case, fine, however we get there is good, if the risks and costs are not too great, and the result sticks).

3. Go slowly. This is perhaps the most important ingredient. As mentioned, Dr. Sachs recommended four months, 25 percent a month as a general timeframe. But the key is the size of the steps down: *the more hesitant the patient, the smaller the decrement.* Think about it: if the very first step goes badly, he is going to want to go right back up to the full dose and will be more resistant to the idea of ever trying this strategy again. If getting off the antidepressant might eventually be a key ingredient in this patient's improvement, then taking too big a first step could lock him in to treatment resistance.

So the first step is crucial. It really is worth the hassle of prescribing a new, smaller size of the antidepressant—and then instructing your patient to cut it in half, and if feasible, to quarters. If the quarters are inaccurate, that's fine: have your patient cut up several pills, and start with the largest quarters, to create the smallest decrement. It really is worth all these gyrations, because if that first step goes all right—nothing is worse, nothing has changed at all—then confidence builds to continue with another step down.

Explain that even with small decrements, a transient increase in depressed or mixed symptoms may occur, but this worsening should diminish rapidly (a few days, not more than a week) back to where symptoms were before the last step down. Don't take another step until things are settled again: the whole idea here is to be able to taper with no worsening. Many patients will start to see a gradual improvement as their antidepressant dose goes down: less severe depression, particularly less severe depressive shifts; and fewer mixed state symptoms such as anxiety, agitation, irritability, insomnia, and distractibility.

If they do not see such improvement, but do not worsen, all the way to zero, then at minimum one will have tapered off one medication and perhaps thereby made room for another. (The patient's sexual function might have improved as well).

4. Look for other destabilizers. Sometimes other factors are contributing to continued cycling or mixed features, such that there will be no improvement as the antidepressant is tapered. This is demoralizing and can interfere with successfully tapering to zero then staying there long enough to see if mood and energy settle into a reasonable balance. Common destabilizers to watch for include:

- significant alcohol use (and certainly any street drugs, except possibly marijuana)
- continued life trauma, or grossly unaddressed past trauma
- undetected or untreated sleep apnea (so he has a CPAP machine; is he using it?)
- over-the-counter antidepressants: St. John's wort, SAM-e

Why except marijuana? As discussed in Appendix C, in Bipolar I it can cause psychosis, particularly in young people; but in Bipolar II and mid-spectrum presentations, patients often report that "just a little puff before bed helps shut my mind off so that I can go to sleep," and this is not always a cover story for heavy recreational use. I've had numerous patients who tried my medications, trying to replace their marijuana use, and after trials of several agents we both concluded that the marijuana was working better, including overall level of function. So the drug could be neutral and even helpful.

5. Carefully balance hope and realism. Hope is one of the most important ingredients in treatment. Without it, getting good outcomes is harder, and risk increases. But hope is also dangerous, as raised hopes can lead to dashed hopes, and dashed hopes can lead patients to give up on treatment or even contemplate suicide.

Thus as all providers learn, one of the most important things we provide is a careful balance between hope and realism. We can maintain hope and project it when patients do not feel it. We can caution against too much hope after many previous failed trials, yet not abandon hope entirely. This balancing act becomes particularly important during antidepressant tapers, because the process is so long and the gains—if there will be any—are so slow to appear.

Anxiety: Same Logic, Same Procedures

For patients with continued severe anxiety, agitation, intractable insomnia, and distractibility, the same logic applies:

1. Antidepressants can induce mixed states.
2. Mixed states can present with these anxiety symptoms (as discussed in Chapter 4).
3. If a patient is having such symptoms, despite her antidepressant (whether added to treat depression or a comorbid anxiety disorder), and if she is already on a raft of mood stabilizers for bipolarity, one must consider the possibility that she is having anxious symptoms because of her antidepressant.
4. Perhaps if the antidepressant was tapered off, her mood stabilizers might be sufficient treatment after all.

At least this is an option to consider, one that becomes more plausible when many other treatment approaches have been tried without much success. As noted, I hope to find an antidepressant on the patient's medication list when she arrives with long-standing, treatment-resistant anxiety: if some degree of bipolarity is found, this opens up the slow-taper option, should other options have been exhausted (e.g., she's already had four or more antidepressant trials), impractical (e.g., benzodiazepines in a patient with history of alcohol problems), or judged by the patient as too dangerous (e.g., atypical antipsychotics at sustained full doses).

Appendix A

Bipolar Disorders, Politics, and Religion

In some psychiatric circles, utter the word "bipolar" and energy shields go up, armor goes on, sometimes even metaphoric swords are drawn. This is not the realm of scientific method. It much more resembles the realm of politics and religion. Opinions are strong and often apparently immutable.

Recent research on moral reasoning, which examines the origins of strongly held beliefs, may shed light on why discussions of bipolar disorder are frequently divisive and unproductive. The bottom line: just like liberals and conservatives, different camps within psychiatry begin these discussions with radically different perceptions of what is good for patients and good for the field.

This appendix presents an overview of some recent investigations in moral decision making, then examines how findings from that research may explain the difficulties we in psychiatry have talking with one another about bipolar disorders, and sometimes likewise with our mental health colleagues.

Research on Moral Reasoning

Taking just a slice from this field, consider the work of Jonathan Haidt. His team has invited self-identified liberals, conservatives, and those in between to answer questions about moral dilemmas. These questions are designed around issues like:

- Whether someone acted unfairly.
- Whether some people were treated differently than others.
- Whether someone cared for someone weak or vulnerable.
- Whether someone's action showed love for his or her country.
- Whether someone showed a lack of loyalty.

Multiple investigations in social psychology have been launched from this foundation (see http://YourMorals.org). For our purposes here, consider Haidt's early results (Haidt, 2012). He and his colleagues found that five principles seem to guide moral decision making, such as whether to approve of a person's actions in a moral dilemma. Those principles are (my translation):

1. Do no harm.
2. Be fair.
3. Stick with your group.
4. Respect authority.
5. Some things are sacred, don't violate them.

Self-identified highly liberal people regard two of the above principles as far more important than the other three. Can you tell which those are? (You might first want to take the questionnaire online at yourmorals.org)

Here is a peek at Haidt's results. Self-identified liberals make moral decisions based primarily on two principles: do no harm, and be fair. Self-identified conservatives value these principles, but also the three others, such that all five are considered important. Among conservatives, none of these principles are ranked as strongly as the liberals rank their top two. Conservatives' emphasis is roughly uniform across all principles. These differences in moral reasoning are most pronounced among people who self-identify as strongly liberal or strongly conservative; less strong political stances in the middle are associated with intermediate mixing of principles, forming a relatively smooth line from extreme to extreme—a spectrum.

What does this have to do with bipolar disorders? As Dr. Haidt has elegantly demonstrated (2012), certain topics "automatically activate moral concerns and emotions." These topics include politics, religion, and his current area of exploration, economic models such as capitalism. In our field, I think bipolar disorder may be another such topic.

Of such activation, he says (Haidt, 2014; transcribed from the video, emphases mine) "I'm a social psychologist, I've studied morality for 27 years, and one thing I've learned that I'm pretty confident about is that you can't really convince people on moral and political issues by giving them facts." He continues: "And the reason is because human reasoning does not take place in a logical world based on fact; it takes place in an emotional world, based on stories. And we don't even write these stories: we imbibe them, we drink them in as we grow up. When we hear something, when we see something that fits with our favorite stories, we get a feeling of *familiarity*—and that tags it as *true*." His book presents an extremely useful way to understand the very odd behaviors of politicians, and very unfortunate arguments about religion. These are not realms of logic; nor is bipolar diagnosis, I fear.

Applied to Bipolar Disorders

Somehow invoking a bipolar diagnosis seems to activate moral concerns and entry into a world of emotional reasoning. That might seem a truism: just look at the faces and listen to the voices of two people having an animated conversation about whether a patient has bipolar disorder or not. In many instances, they are in an emotional world. But the key insight here is that these emotions about bipolar disorder are arising—or so I theorize—from moral concerns. Haidt shows us that in the realm of moral concerns, people's values can differ so profoundly that understanding one another is almost impossible. Liberals and conservatives approach the world very differently. So too may some psychiatrists, psychologists, and other mental health colleagues, around the issues of bipolar diagnosis and treatment.

For example, consider a liberal approaching bipolar diagnosis. According to Haidt's data, his moral reasoning will be driven primarily by two principles: do no harm and be fair. What does this do to his diagnostic reasoning? He will be calculating, perhaps intuitively, the likelihood of harm to the patient based on diagnosis. He knows that if the patient "actually" (according to some gold standard we don't have) has bipolar disorder, and that diagnosis is missed, she will most likely end up with a diagnosis of Major Depression. If she is then treated with a medication, it is likely to be an antidepressant. Antidepressants can make bipolar disorder worse—that is, doing harm. Thus for a liberal, the downside of doing harm by missing a diagnosis of bipolar disorder will loom very large.

By contrast, compare a conservative's approach to bipolar diagnosis. According to Haidt's data, conservatives, much more than liberals, value conforming with group norms, respecting authority, and protecting the sacred. For the conservative then, the DSM system of diagnosis is important: it is the rulebook our group has agreed to use, created by experts, so not using it is a violation of group norms and disrespect for authority. Indeed, there is something almost sacred about having a system of diagnosis that has been crafted with great effort to reflect psychiatry's best understanding of how to view an illness like bipolar disorder. Don't violate the sacred.

When seeing a patient with depression, the diligent conservative diagnostician will begin by asking for the DSM-5 A criteria: "have you ever had phases of feeling really elated, really positive about the world, or really irritable, while full of energy?" If none of these symptoms are endorsed, then by the DSM the patient cannot have bipolar disorder. There is no point in asking any more questions. Bipolar disorder has been ruled out, following the accepted diagnostic system for psychiatry. What could be wrong about that? Indeed, anyone who suggests that there is something wrong about this approach is not respecting the authority of the DSM (relative to any other diagnostic approach) and is endangering the integrity (Baldessarini, 2000) of the bipolar diagnosis.

Another intense concern about bipolar "overdiagnosis" is that applying this label allows and often quickly leads to use of antipsychotic medications, which are perceived to carry far more risk than antidepressants (or, better yet, family or cognitive-behavioral therapy). This is a do-no-harm concern: laudable, understandable, and also, according to Haidt's data, a prompt for emotional reasoning.

Haidt's data and conclusions, applied to the differential diagnosis of depression, predict that two psychiatrists could see the same patient and arrive at different diagnoses based on their moral reasoning. One's diagnosis might arise from a determination to minimize potential harm to the patient, while the other's diagnosis would be driven by a belief in the importance of standards and rigor and preserving the integrity of the diagnostic system. Neither is wrong. These are all important principles. But when these two practitioners talk to one another and find their diagnoses opposed, their reactions can be fueled by a righteous indignation that attends moral reasoning:

A: *Bipolar* disorder? She has nothing even close to DSM criteria for that diagnosis.

B: But look at her family history, it's chock-full of people with bipolar disorder, and she's got racing thoughts and insomnia.

A: Insomnia is not a DSM criteria. She doesn't have *decreased need* for sleep—look, she's been asking for lorazepam.

B: But she's using lorazepam during the day as well. Maybe she's treating a mixed state that the antidepressant is inducing. We should begin a taper.

A: She's *depressed*. We should be turning *up* her antidepressant, not turning it down.

Moral reasoning leads to emotional arousal that promotes and seemingly justifies defense of one's position. Important principles are at stake. But it does not lead to good patient care. Often patients end up in the middle of these arguments: two different diagnoses, two differing treatment recommendations. We clinicians are responsible for this. Yet as you may have experienced, trying to work out a middle ground or an agreed-on plan can be very difficult when two practitioners flatly disagree about a patient's diagnosis. Commonly we agree to disagree because we've learned from experience that we can do no better. But that leaves the patient in the middle. Perhaps Haidt's data might help open channels for more constructive discussion.

Potential Solutions

Suppose this hypothesis about bipolar diagnosis and moral reasoning is the basis for the divisiveness of diagnosis-related discussions, at least to some degree. What can be done?

In politics, divisiveness is tolerated and almost expected (despite being so often utterly counterproductive). But in mental health, we have long recognized the risks of emotionally driven reasoning and behavior, at least in one realm: handling countertransference. We understand the importance of a third eye, observing our own feelings and thoughts as provoked by a clinical encounter. We take responsibility for managing our behavior so that countertransference is not running the show. We invite feedback from peers if we are failing to do so successfully, and seek supervision when we are at risk of failing. (Imagine if this were the norm in the culture of politics!)

So we actually need no new tools for management of morally driven reasoning. Resonating around the perceived importance of doing no harm is not very different from resonating around the perception that one truly understands a patient's needs where others have failed (having been drawn into a splitting dynamic). Finding oneself angry with a colleague about the importance of using a uniform, DSM-based approach is not very different from being angry toward a patient who repeatedly transgresses boundaries (e.g., coming up with creative excuses for yet again having run out of benzodiazepines too early).

We can use our training in identifying and managing countertransference to handle our own emotional reasoning arising from moral principles (not from the patient's actual problem or needs). For example, consider the management of splitting as recommended by a recognized authority on borderline personality disorder, Marsha Linehan. "Splitting is an iatrogenic phenomenon," says Dr. Linehan, in her game-changing monograph (Linehan, 1993). Identifying with a patient's projections instead of recognizing them as such can lead to thinking that another team member has failed to understand the patient. That other team member may be identifying with an all-bad projection and respond with anger when her colleague talks about what needs to be done. Now the team is split. Yet this split arose not solely because of the patient's dynamics, but more proximally because of team members' failure to recognize their own countertransference and behaving instead on the received projections.

Likewise when one fails to recognize one's own moral reasoning, and instead acts to defend a principle such as doing no harm or respecting

authority, thereby creating a rift in the team, this is an iatrogenic phenomenon as well. The solution is the same, whether managing borderlinity or bipolarity: monitor your moral reasoning. Recognize the principles
you are feeling called to defend. Let go of that defense and listen for your
colleague's *moral* reasoning. Disarm his defensiveness by naming the
principles that he feels called to defend. If you can do so in the context
of the patient you have both seen, all the better. For example, the earlier
conversation might go something more like:

A: You're thinking that her depression might have a significant
bipolar component, based on her family history and her severe
insomnia.

B: True, but I know that she doesn't meet formal criteria for a
bipolar diagnosis. She doesn't have decreased *need* for sleep.

A: Well, if she did have a bipolar component then the antidepressant could be inducing a mixed state; maybe that would
account for all the lorazepam she seems to need.

B: Perhaps, but if we turn it down we'd need to come up with
some other means of addressing her depression; that's still her
main problem.

In other words, the views of our colleagues that do not match our own
are predictable. One can learn this from repeated disagreements, but
using Haidt's data, one can also predict them from the different moral
stances that may underlie their different diagnosis in the first place. If I
know that my spectrum way of thinking is going to offend my partner's
dedicated belief in the importance of a uniform approach to diagnosis,
then I can predict what she will think when I invoke bipolar disorder. I
can put her predicted view forth with respect. Perhaps this will disarm
her otherwise predictable defensiveness and allow her to stay mindful
enough to do the same for me, putting my very predictable view forth
with respect as well.

These stances are easier if one follows another dictum from Dr. Linehan, also designed to avoid iatrogenic splitting: "assume competence."
In other words, begin with a respect for your colleague's views. That

should make it easier to predict them and offer them at least neutrally, if not supportively.

Notice that this proposed approach does not rely on invoking research data or clinical logic. Those are like Haidt's "facts": when the shields are up, facts simply don't work. Either one must avoid provoking a defensive position in the first place, by knowing what words and concepts will provoke it; or have a means to disarm defensiveness—perhaps via Rogerian empathy with moral sentiments behind it. Meanwhile, ideally everyone would use their skills in monitoring for transference, in this case monitoring for their own emotional reasoning.

None of this is easy. Failures to monitor and manage emotional reasoning will occur. I have certainly been guilty of this many times. Haidt's findings may have helped me a little bit; I hope for further improvement yet. Nevertheless, throughout this book readers will find me on a moral high horse. I would not be able to explain my views clearly without that tone coming through: concerns about doing no harm have driven my thinking for years, enough to power books and websites and trying to keep up with relevant literature. (Moral values do have some advantages, e.g., energizing effort.)

Appendix B

Overdiagnosis, Predictive Value, and Screening Tests

If the overdiagnosis of bipolar disorder is of concern to you, a study led by Mark Zimmerman is worth a detailed look. There are actually only a few other studies of this issue, and none so directly assess the over-/underdiagnosis question with so large a sample (Ghouse et al., 2013).

When a clinician offers a patient a diagnosis, how accurate is she? In other words: what is the predictive value of her diagnosis? That is what Dr. Zimmerman's team studied. Yet predictive value is determined not just by the sensitivity and specificity of the test or examiner, but by another key factor that is often overlooked—and holds the key to more accurate diagnosis. Following a review of Dr. Zimmerman's study, we turn to a review of predictive value and this key factor.

The Brown University Study

Zimmerman and colleagues used data from patients referred to the outpatient program at Brown University to examine their prior diagnoses from a categorical view: how many of these referred patients had been told that they have bipolar disorder, and how did that community diagnosis line up with the team's research/consultation diagnosis? (Zimmerman et al., 2008).

In Table B.1, the Brown University area clinicians' diagnoses are shown in the left column: yes, the patient had been told she/he has bipolar disorder or no, she/he had not been told that.

The middle columns show the results of a Structured Clinical Interview for Diagnosis (SCID), which follows DSM criteria and asks closed questions in strict order. In this study, the SCID serves as the gold standard against which the diagnoses of the Brown University area clinicians are compared.

Table B.1. **The Brown University bipolar diagnosis study.**

BP DX	Structured Clinical Interview (SCID)		Total
	BP	Not BP	
Yes	63	82	145
No	27	528	555
Total	90	610	700

As you can see, only 63 of the 145 patients (44 percent) who had been told they have bipolar disorder were found to have it using the SCID. This is obviously a serious problem.

But remember the epigraph at the beginning of this book: "Dichotomies are useful for education, communication, and simplification. Unfortunately, simplicity is useful, but untrue; whereas complexity is true, but useless" (Vieta and Suppes, 2008). Perhaps it is an oversimplification to say that all those "misdiagnosed" patients don't have bipolar disorder. Zimmerman and colleagues went on to show that by the SCID, many of those previously told they had bipolar disorder actually warranted a diagnosis of borderline personality disorder. By the structured interview, using DSM criteria, this may be true. But consider the overlap in symptoms between these two conditions (presented in Chapter 4). Suffice to say that Zimmerman's study was well structured and conducted, and that within a categorical framework it does indeed demonstrate overdiagnosis of bipolar disorder.

It also demonstrated underdiagnosis of bipolar disorder. As you can see in the table, the authors also found 90 patients who according to the

SCID did indeed have bipolar disorder, of whom 27 were *not* told they had it—a 30 percent underdiagnosis rate. Unfortunately, despite mixed findings, three papers from this research group have "overdiagnosis" in their titles, contributing to polarization of this issue.

By contrast, a team led by Nassir Ghaemi, while at Emory University, conducted a similar investigation among children referred to their mood disorder clinic. Their categorical results were roughly the opposite of what the Brown University team found: 62 percent underdiagnosis of bipolar disorder, 5 percent overdiagnosis (Chilakamarri et al., 2011).

Watch your reaction here: if you found yourself insisting "that can't be right," or found yourself irritated by my language describing Dr. Zimmerman's work, then you and I may be in the realm of moral reasoning, which is not mutable with data, according to Jonathan Haidt. (See Appendix A.)

In the end we all have the same problem: our clinical diagnoses are not perfectly accurate relative to a gold standard. Our predictive value can be quite low. Yet the analysis that follows suggests it can be improved relatively simply.

Predictive Value: For Clinicians

Remember that positive predictive value (PPV) means: "when a clinician offers a diagnosis, or a screening test comes up positive, how often is that truly positive—as opposed to false positive?" The following analysis describes how clinicians' and screening tests' PPVs can be increased. Categorical yes/no rules are used here by necessity, but consider a spectrum view as well as you go; I'll offer such an interpretation in closing this appendix.

The clinicians' diagnoses studied by Zimmerman and colleagues had low PPV relative to a structured clinical interview: only 44 percent of patients given the diagnosis where found to have it using the SCID (63/145). Screening tests for bipolar disorder, applied to a primary care population with depression for example, also have a very low PPV, so low that it has been recommended they not be used at all (NICE, 2014a; Zimmerman and Galione, 2011).

In case you find these terms confusing or ancient history, here is a quick review, and then we'll focus on the clinical impact of all this. Fear not the two-by-two table: this is the same thing you saw above, I simply add a few labels (Figure B.1).

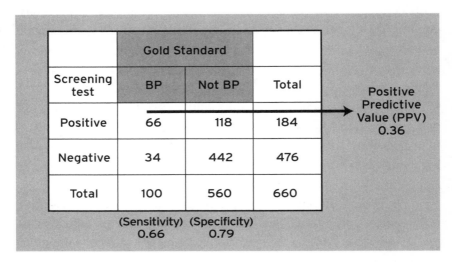

Figure B.1 **Predictive value of a common bipolar screening tool**

This example uses an average sensitivity and specificity of the MDQ bipolar screening test (Carvalho et al., 2014) in a hypothetical sample. As you can see the PPV is very low at 36 percent. Yet the test's average sensitivity and specificity are not extremely low, nor were those of the Brown University area clinicians (see Table B.2).

Table B.2. **Average sensitivity and specificity of common bipolar screening tools (Carvalho et al., 2014), and the Brown University area clinicians**

	Sensitivity	Specificity
MDQ	0.66	0.79
BSDS	0.69	0.86
HCL-32	0.81	0.67
Area clinicians	0.70	0.87

Why then is PPV so low, when sensitivity and specificity are not?

The Key Factor in PPV

PPV is very powerfully affected by prevalence. Think about it: if a good-but-not-perfect test is given to a population with low prevalence of the illness in question, many positives will be false positives. And in most populations, the prevalence of bipolar disorder is low.

The key to obtaining higher PPVs—that is, the key to making practitioners' diagnosis and the positive screening test more often correct—is to increase the prevalence. (It doesn't really work to try to increase specificity, e.g. by applying criteria more rigorously: sensitivity goes down and PPV doesn't go up very much at all; Phelps and Ghaemi, 2012.) But how does one increase prevalence?

Prevalence is simply the frequency of bipolar disorder in the population at hand; it cannot be increased. However, prevalence is just one form of "prior probability": the likelihood of the illness before the diagnosis was made or the test given. Prior probability *can* be increased, by using family history and all the other non-manic markers to estimate how likely bipolar disorder is before applying DSM criteria or before interpreting a screening test result.

For example: suppose Ms. Brown seeks psychiatric help for depression. Assume that the prevalence of bipolar disorder is 16 percent in the clinic Ms. Brown is attending (as reported in Angst et al., 2011). Suppose Ms. Brown has a first-degree relative with a reliable diagnosis of bipolar disorder. Now her probability of bipolar disorder is much higher than 16 percent. And suppose she had her first depression in her late teens, multiple discrete episodes since, and postpartum depression as well. At this point the probability that she has bipolar disorder might be well over 50 percent (to my knowledge, no study has been done that allows a quantitative assessment based on these non-manic markers).

Assume that given this history, Ms. Brown's prior probability of bipolar disorder is now 66 percent, a two-to-one chance. (Remember that the authors of the Bipolarity Index gave the markers for which Ms. Brown is positive more than 50 percent of the 100 points possible; so 66 percent, a two thirds chance, is not a wild guess.) *Now* have her take the MDQ. With the same sensitivity and specificity as before, the predictive value of a positive MDQ in this context is 80 percent. (Where do these numbers come from? One simply constructs two-by-two tables and varies the prevalence, holding sensitivity and specificity constant; Phelps and Ghaemi, 2012.)

A clinician who knows Ms. Brown's non-manic markers and considers her DSM criteria in that light—that is, knowing that the prior probability of bipolar disorder is high—is theoretically operating just as the screening test does: with a higher PPV, if his diagnosis is bipolar disorder. Obviously this is a testable hypothesis. But of course this is just an elaborate way of saying that a better history leads to a better diagnosis.

To summarize: having data on the non-manic markers, which carry much of the weight of the Bipolarity Index, can change the context for interpretation of answers to questions about DSM criteria—however those answers are obtained, whether via a screening questionnaire, or an interview. The result is a higher PPV of bipolar disorder when the test is positive or the clinician makes that diagnosis.

Now consider all this from a spectrum view. By necessity all the language of sensitivity, prior probability and prevalence is categorical: a gold standard (a structured interview, in the Zimmerman studies, for example) was used to say whether bipolar disorder was present, or absent—yes or no. But as discussed in Chapter 1, mood disorders form a continuum from purely unipolar to clearly bipolar. Here we see the value of the Bipolarity Index (Chapter 2). It frames and answers the question: "how bipolar is Ms. Brown?" If she presents with few markers and few positives on her DSM criteria, her bipolarity is low. The more positive markers, and the more DSM criteria met, the higher her bipolarity.

Remember, this is still just a way of thinking, a heuristic. The Bipolarity Index has been validated in categorical terms (Aiken et al., 2015) but not in dimensional terms. Nevertheless, the preceding analysis suggests that assessing non-manic markers as a means of improving PPV is clearly warranted. Importantly, for those of us concerned about identification of bipolarity in primary care, it also suggests that the MoodCheck questionnaire (Chapter 2) allows for PPVs high enough to justify screening in that busy setting.

Appendix C

Non-Medication Approaches to Treatment

Changing Mood-Destabilizing Behaviors

First among the non-medication approaches is behavior change. Before adding a mood stabilizer, look at the known mood-*destabilizers* and reduce them where possible. Often the most obvious targets, though not necessarily the easiest, are behaviors.

What specific behaviors should be encouraged? Clinicians will not be surprised at anything on the list below, which reads like a "usual suspects" for health-related behavior change. But note the exception or emphasis for each in regard to mid-spectrum mood disorders:

1. Abstinence from street drugs—except perhaps marijuana
2. Regular, sufficient sleep—in a darkened environment
3. Healthy diet—low in refined carbohydrates, but perhaps also low in gluten
4. Regular physical activity—though in hypomanic phases, perhaps less exercise
5. Smoking cessation—except when emphasis on this erodes therapeutic alliance
6. Stress reduction—many approaches, including community connection

Absence of these behaviors may contribute directly to inflammatory factors now increasingly thought to play a major role in most forms of depression and bipolar disorder (Kiecolt-Glaser et al, 2015). For example, Michael Berk in Melbourne and his collaborators around the world have investigated multiple risk factors for mood disorders, and the biological underpinnings of those factors. Berk and colleagues' oxidative and nitrosative stress model (Morris et al., 2015) emphasizes the central role of basic behavioral choices (1–6 above) in the development and perpetuation of mood problems (Moylan et al., 2014). Thus we're not just looking at good health here, we're looking at core ingredients in mood stability. Changing adverse habits as much as possible is more than a good place to start. It is a core ingredient in treatment. Let's look at each item in terms of its importance for mid-spectrum patients.

1. Abstinence from street drugs and alcohol. Stimulants like cocaine and methamphetamine are obviously capable of causing mood "cycling": first due to the drug, then due to withdrawal, then through craving leading to further use (not to mention the stress of life chaos that generally attends their use and the legal problems that can follow). Although one might think these would be most used during depressions, they are statistically more closely tied with hypomania and mania, likely because of lower thresholds for impulsive risk-taking during those bipolar phases. But they clearly exacerbate manic shifts. Mood stability is very difficult to achieve when these street drugs remain in use, whether in Bipolar I or any other mood disorder on the spectrum.

LSD and other hallucinogens are also problematic in patients with Bipolar I, contributing to psychosis. Exactly how much direct risk to mood stability they pose in mid-spectrum patients is moot, given their potential for disrupting constructive lifestyles. Ecstasy's capacity to destroy neurons is similarly sufficient to warrant complete abstinence.

Marijuana is a more complex issue. In some parts of the United States, it is not an illicit drug anymore. The resulting increase in access is amplifying concern about its negative effects. Marijuana clearly increases risk of psychosis in susceptible young people, and appears to contribute directly to the development of bipolar disorder (Tyler et al., 2015). It may have mood-destabilizing effects in some users (stopping it when manic is associated with better response to treatment than continuing it; Zorilla et al., 2015).

But low-THC/high-cannabidiol strains may be different. Cannabidiol appears to have anxiolytic properties, particularly in social anxiety disorder (Schier et al., 2012), a very high-prevalence problem in mid-spectrum mood disorder patients. Cannabidiol has even been studied as an antipsychotic, and although data are limited, that possibility remains (Roser et al., 2010; Leweke et al, 2012). Thus a blanket antimarijuana stance reflects an ignorance of its psychopharmacology. This ignorance is not lost on patients, who recognize that often they know more than we do about this stuff. Many of my patients have figured out, through on/off/on trials, that "a little puff before bedtime helps turn my mind off so I can sleep." These patients regard an antimarijuana edict from their providers as a failure to understand their experience—not good for the therapeutic alliance.

While awaiting further research on cannabidiol and perhaps other cannabinoids, at minimum we can adopt more nuanced stances toward use of marijuana by patients with mood disorders. For some, it is extremely risky and obviously should be avoided; for others, it may be a useful adjunct. Simply requiring abstinence from marijuana, as many practitioners do, is narrow-minded and potentially counterproductive.

By contrast, alcohol has very few recognized benefits beyond some reduction in social anxiety with carefully controlled use. Given the very high prevalence of social anxiety in patients with mood disorders, a blanket requirement for complete abstinence from alcohol may—like abstinence from marijuana—be unrealistic and for some patients a detriment. But for the large majority of patients with mood disorders, regular consumption of more than a few drinks per week can be mood-destabilizing (Rakofsky and Dunlop, 2013).

All this taken into account, for most patients with active mood symptoms, abstinence from street drugs and alcohol is a reasonable starting point while other treatments are being initiated. Zero is easier to rigorously quantify than one or two drinks or puffs or pills. Just as discussed in Chapter 5 regarding treatment duration and relapse prevention, one should plan on patients going off one's recommended routes. I encourage them to be scientists about it, if they are not going to commit to sustained abstinence.

First, they should wait to resume their substance use until they have actually achieved mood stability, so they have a baseline against which to compare should they later resume some degree of drug or alcohol use. Of course this is an exercise in motivational interviewing. In that spirit, the following discussion has worked well for me when achieving sustained abstinence looks dubious: "So, you could go a week with no marijuana?" I ask, eliciting an assured nod. "Really? Okay, great. Think you could make it two weeks?" Then I keep upping the ante until that assurance begins to flicker. At that point I back up a step to what looked more likely to be achievable, based on their confidence and determination. I invite an agreement to maintain zero use for that long, as a baseline. This may not be as long as I'd have wished, to really assess a new treatment. But per the motivational interviewing literature, this approach increases the likelihood of reduction or cessation of substance use, at least for a while.

Then as a second step, if the patient is determined to return to use of a potentially destabilizing drug, encourage that he or she proceed as a scientist. Begin with small amounts and intermittent use and look for any weakening of that mood stability. Use the prodrome detection method (Chapter 5) to detect early changes (decreased sleep, accelerated or intensifying thought, irritability, impulsive actions, for example). Walk through how worsening will be identified, who will help if insight is low, and what steps should be taken right away to abort a possible recurrence of hypomania or depression. Of course all these are part of any good relapse prevention plan, drug-induced or otherwise.

2. Regular, sufficient, uninterrupted (non-apneic) sleep—in the dark. Sleep regularity is a central ingredient in social rhythm therapy, detailed in Chapter 6. Regular, sufficient sleep is almost certainly a mood stabilizer unto itself (but not studied alone, thus the uncertainty). Sleep also modulates the inflammatory response: too little is associated with the increased production of inflammatory factors (Prather et al., 2009). Apneic sleep further promotes mood disorder risk; sleep apnea is very common in patients with Major Depression and bipolar disorders (Crawford-Achour et al., 2014; Gupta and Simpson, 2015).

How best to screen for sleep apnea, short of an overnight sleep study, is still under research. The STOP-BANG questionnaire performs reasonably well for severe apnea, but less well in mild to moderate cases (Silva et al., 2011). Some experts recommend screening all patients with bipolar disorder for sleep apnea, finding a point prevalence of at least 20 percent (Kelly et al., 2013). At a minimum, a high clinical suspicion is warranted, and treatment-resistant patients in particular often warrant the full sleep study approach to apnea diagnosis (polysomnography).

The relevance of a dark environment for sleep, and indeed for the several hours preceding sleep, is discussed in Chapter 6. Even though data supporting dark therapy are scant, the intervention is inexpensive and almost entirely without risk.

3. Healthy diet. This is much more than a platitude. Inflammation is strongly associated with diet, and as noted already, inflammation is now thought to play a significant role in mood disorders (Kiecolt-Glaser et al, 2015). Imagine if making dietary changes to lower inflammatory factors could lower risk of mood disorder recurrence or even treat a current episode. Neither has yet been clearly demonstrated as of this writing. All we have are a few preliminary efforts to use anti-inflammatories as adjunct treatments for depression. The results so far are mixed, though there's a suggestion that for patients who have high levels of inflammatory factors, such as the easily measured C-reactive protein (CRP), a strong anti-inflammatory like infliximab can indeed have antidepressant effects (Raison et al., 2013). Even sleep improved in response to infliximab in this high-CRP subgroup (Weinberger et al., 2015). These findings come from the remarkable work of Andrew Miller and Charles Raison, including Dr. Raison's innovative nonpharmacologic anti-inflammatory interventions.

What about celiac and nonceliac gluten sensitivity, inflammatory markers, and mood? This is a small mixed literature as of this writing, but expanding (Porcelli et al., 2014). One study in patients with bipolar disorders found that compared with controls, patients with bipolar disorder had elevated IgA for gliadin, a dietary gluten protein (Dickerson et al., 2012). That Johns Hopkins team has embarked on a randomized trial of probiotics as a treatment in bipolar disorder, and results are pending at this point. Obviously this is a literature worth following!

Why are we looking at interventions with almost no evidence for efficacy? Remember: the difference between treating mid-spectrum mood disorders, relative to Bipolar I, is the absence of the need to prevent manic relapses. This takes the pressure off, allowing trials of approaches with less evidence for efficacy, if they are simple and inexpensive and very low risk. Of course some patients will want to move quickly to interventions with a high likelihood of rapid improvement. But others—those with less severe symptoms, for example—may want to focus on interventions that have the lowest risk. If dietary changes to lower inflammatory factors could actually treat or prevent mood disorders, this would be very appealing to many patients.

Many people are reporting mood improvement with gluten-free diets, for example. At this writing, a brief literature review revealed only one randomized trial of a gluten-free diet with mood as an outcome measure (a small trial, with an interesting result: mood was better with placebo supplementation than with an identical gluten-containing capsule; Di Sabatino et al., 2015). Dietary changes to lower inflammatory factors have already been studied and found effective, even with relatively minor substitutions. For example, replacing two red meat meals with legume protein three days a week lowered multiple inflammatory markers in patients with type 2 diabetes (Hosseinpour-Niazi et al., 2015).

These are dietary changes many people need to make anyway. So we need not wait for randomized trials; we can just fall in behind our primary care colleagues who are already advocating these changes. For example, soft drinks containing sugars are an obvious target; following that, anything else made with added sugar or white flour ("if it's white, don't bite").

By comparison, a ketogenic diet is not easy, cheap, or safe. This diet is based on an almost zero-carbohydrate approach to eating. It has a long history in medicine as a treatment for seizures, mostly for children with severe epilepsy not responding to medications. Since some (but not all) anticonvulsants are mood stabilizers, might a ketogenic diet also help in bipolar disorders? In some respect this question is moot, because these diets are extremely difficult to maintain and not without risk. But two people with Bipolar II maintained a ketotic state for months (affirmed by urine ketostick) and observed an apparent mood stabilizer effect (Phelps et al., 2013).

4. Regular physical activity. This is so important that it is included as a specific alternative to antidepressants in Chapter 12.

5. Smoking cessation. Cigarette smoking is so deleterious, cessation is warranted for any diagnostic group at any point on the mood spectrum. Quitting may be more difficult for patients with severe mood symptoms, however: when life seems pointless and the potential for change nil, why bother with smoking cessation? Perhaps this is a target for later, after some mood improvement, but it must not be forgotten. Motivational interviewing skills are essential, but so may be timing. I have a few patients where we've worked for years on mood and never been able to shift into targeting cigarettes (in case you've seen a few of these kinds of patients as well). Several have said that quitting cigarettes was much harder than quitting heroin.

6. Stress reduction. Because stress is so prevalent in our society (nearly ubiquitous?), addressing obvious sources of it is almost as important as smoking cessation. Many tools are available. A mid-spectrum patient may be more able than a patient with Bipolar I to incorporate things like yoga, walking meditation, and other mindfulness practices, because their value in depression may be more obvious than for the prevention of mania. See the free downloadable audio and scripts from the UCLA Mindfulness Institute (at http://marc.ucla.edu/body.cfm?id=22). For irritable mixed states, additional tools include positive psychology exercises such as practicing forgiveness, gratitude, and optimism and Zen-based anger management techniques (Chodron, 2001; Hanh, 2002).

Though these behavior changes are a logical starting place, they are also difficult to implement—even for people who are not depressed! For many patients, help with their depression by some other means will be necessary before they can take on these challenges. But that does not mean turning directly to formal psychotherapy or prescription medications. Many patients will be interested in over-the-counter approaches and online information; for them these options are likely on the table whether or not you put them there. Bring them into the discussion of options in terms of evidence for efficacy versus evidence for risk.

Over-the-Counter Pills

Over-the-counter options for mid-spectrum mood problems include at least fish oil and N- acetyl cysteine. Both have multiple randomized trials supporting their use (discussed in Chapter 9). After that, however, patients are vulnerable to the vast array of "cure what ails you" remedies available in health food stores and online. Nevertheless, remember the efficacy of placebo in treatment of depression and anxiety. If a patient has a strongly positive feeling about a particular treatment, this raises the likelihood of benefiting from it. Do not puncture belief simply because of a lack of randomized trial evidence. For example, omega-3 fatty acids from flaxseed have not been tested as have those from fish oil, but if your patient has strong positive associations between flax and mood benefit, leave that be—unless she is really suffering and reliance on flaxseed is interfering with acceptance of other treatments with greater likelihood of benefit.

In general, if a treatment is extremely inexpensive, unlikely to cause harm, and the patient has a strong belief in its efficacy, I try to leave those alone. Vitamin D, for example, is another treatment commonly believed to help mood. The evidence for this (at this writing) is extremely slim, based almost entirely on association studies, with several failed randomized trials (Gowda et al., 2015). Some studies showed benefit when limited only to those whose vitamin D was deficient to begin with and changed with treatment (Spedding, 2014). But vitamin D is relatively inexpensive, has other potential health benefits, and if not used in excess, appears to be very safe.

On the other hand, most patients dislike juggling handfuls of pills every day. It reminds them that they have an illness they would rather not have. One of the goals of treatment is to so thoroughly control symptoms that effectively they don't *have* the illness anymore—they just have a condition that requires continued management. Even with that good symptom control, the pill ritual is a daily reminder of an unfortunate circumstance. For many, taking the pills is dysphoric. Often that dysphoria is proportional to the number of pills they are taking!

So every pill in the regimen must be truly essential. This is a problem with the low-benefit (albeit low-risk and hopefully low-cost) over-the-counter pills. They're adding to the burden which may one day cause the patient to wonder: "Why am I taking all this stuff?" (and "I'm tired of all this" or "I feel fine anyway; maybe I don't need them."). Thus they do add risk, in a way, for some patients.

Somatic Therapies, Including Light Therapies

ECT and TMS. At the top of this list should be electroconvulsive therapy (ECT), based on its efficacy and (more recently, with new techniques) relatively low risk. But it also has an unfortunate reputation and is rarely considered by patients who are not having severe symptoms. Access can be limited as well, especially on the West Coast of the United States (Oregon, for example, has only three hospitals in the state offering ECT).

What about transcranial magnetic stimulation (TMS)? It clearly has an antidepressant effect, including in bipolar depression (Dell'osso et al., 2011). But it has also induced hypomania (Xia et al., 2008). Until these modalities are shown to have mood-stabilizing effects, they should be regarded as antidepressants and handled accordingly in mid-spectrum patients.

Direct current and magnetic seizure therapies, like ketamine, are not yet well defined for unipolar depression, nor in routine use—and so are not in consideration at this point for use in mid-spectrum patients. In general, these techniques, like TMS, are antidepressant interventions, subject to many of the same concerns as antidepressants themselves (Chapter 12). Magnetic seizure therapy, for example, has at least once case report of inducing hypomania (Arul-Anandam et al., 2010).

Light therapy. Triple chronotherapy is the definitive version of this approach, but most patients will know only of light boxes.

Light boxes have substantial evidence for efficacy and years of use in mid-spectrum patients. Indeed seasonality is one of the non-manic mood markers, albeit a relatively weak one—that is, it does not strongly distinguish unipolar from bipolar patients. For many reasons, patients can find their way to this treatment on their own. The Center for Environmental Therapeutics has made guidance and tools available online (cet.org) for years, such as their Morningness-Eveningness Questionnaire (AutoMEQ). Many patients simply buy some kind of light box—unfortunately not the research-grade device, which now costs little more than its knock-offs—and turn it on, without education about risks, dose, or timing. Practitioners should be familiar with what's available and have a routine for instructing patients in a systematic one- to two-week assessment of efficacy (for an example, see the Light Therapy page at Psycheducation.org).

There have been remarkably few studies of light therapy in bipolar disorder, but one small trial in nine women found that over half of them went from depressed to a mixed state with standard dose and timing (30 minutes each a.m.; Sit et al., 2007). However, four out of the five went on to a good outcome when the dose was reduced and delayed (15 minutes, midday). So the little evidence we have suggests that in bipolar disorder, light must be used differently than in unipolar depressions, and carefully.

Based on that one small study, can we guess at where along the mood spectrum should one shift the dose of light and the timing? If patients with unipolar depression (e.g., seasonal affective disorder with no other indications of bipolarity) do best with 30 minutes in the morning, timed relative to their MEQ results; and patients with Bipolar I or II do better with smaller doses at midday; then might mid-spectrum patients need some intermediate dose and timing? At this writing, we have no more data to guide the choice—except for the intriguing work on chronotherapy.

Triple chronotherapy combines light therapy with overnight wake therapy and a circadian phase delay. The latter is a deliberate shifting of the timing of light and sleep to move the biological clock toward an earlier bedtime and earlier rise time. This form of chronotherapy is an underused treatment, especially given several very positive results in randomized trials, and its low risk (Benedetti, 2012). Adoption has been limited by the need for overnight supervision of wake therapy—at one time known by the less appealing name of "sleep deprivation," though in most recent protocols this is only a single night's regimen, relying on the other two chronotherapeutic modalities (light and phase delay) to maintain the overnight improvement in mood routinely seen with this treatment. Innovative psychiatrist John Gottlieb has pioneered several different means of delivering this treatment in his clinic in Chicago (Gottlieb and Terman, 2012; see also http://www.chicagochronotherapy.com).

These forms of light therapy minimize the risk of regular exposure to short-wavelength (high energy) light, but that risk still must be taken into account for some patient populations. So overall, light therapy is a treatment modality best handled by well-informed physicians and psychologists and therapists, not patients and families—unless they cannot access professionals with appropriate knowledge and skill. In that case, many have successfully educated themselves about the risks as well as the protocols and devices.

Patients undertaking their own treatment in this fashion, after thorough self-education and with appropriate monitoring of risk, is increasingly common in management of mood disorders generally and perhaps most common in mid-spectrum mood disorders. So familiarity with these modalities, and ability to help patients understand and properly use them, is helpful.

References

Abulseoud OA, Gitlin M, Altshuler L, Frye MA. Baseline thyroid indices and the subsequent response to citalopram treatment, a pilot study. Brain Behav. 2013 Mar;3(2):89–94.

Adam D. Mental health: on the spectrum. Nature. 2013 April 25; 496:416–18. http://www.nature.com/news/mental-health-on-the-spec trum-1.12842; accessed 8/17/15.

Aiff H, Attman PO, Aurell M, et al. Effects of 10 to 30 years of lithium treatment on kidney function. J Psychopharmacol. 2015 May; 29(5):608–14.

Aiken CB, Orr C. Rechallenge with lamotrigine after a rash: a prospective case series and review of the literature. Psychiatry (Edgmont). 2010 May;7(5):27–32.

Aiken CB, Weisler RH, Sachs GS. The Bipolarity Index: a clinician-rated measure of diagnostic confidence. J Affect Disord. 2015 May 15;177:59–64.

Akiskal HS, Akiskal KK, Perugi G, et al. Bipolar II and anxious reactive "comorbidity": toward better phenotypic characterization suitable for genotyping. J Affect Disord. 2006 Dec;96(3):239–47.

Algorta GP, Youngstrom EA, Phelps, J et al. An inexpensive family index of risk for mood issues improves identification of pediatric bipolar disorder. Psychol Assess. 2013 Mar;25(1):12–22.

Aliyev NA, Aliyev ZN. Valproate in the acute treatment of outpatients with generalized anxiety disorder without psychiatric comorbidity: randomized, double-blind placebo-controlled study. Eur Psychiatry. 2008 Mar;23(2):109–14.

Alvarez PA, Pahissa J. QT alterations in psychopharmacology: proven candidates and suspects. Curr Drug Saf. 2010 Jan;5(1):97–104.

Amsterdam JD, Lorenzo-Luaces L, Soeller I, et al. Safety and effectiveness of continuation antidepressant versus mood stabilizer monotherapy for relapse-prevention of Bipolar II depression: a randomized, double-blind, parallel-group, prospective study. J Affect Disord. 2015 Oct 1;185:31–7.

Amsterdam JD, Luo L, Shults J. Efficacy and mood conversion rate during long-term fluoxetine v. lithium monotherapy in rapid- and non-rapid-cycling Bipolar II disorder. Br J Psychiatry 2013;202:301–6.

Andrade C. Antidepressant-withdrawal mania: a critical review and synthesis of the literature. J Clin Psychiatry. 2004 Jul;65(7):987–93.

Angst J, Azorin JM, Bowden CL, et al. Prevalence and characteristics of undiagnosed bipolar disorders in patients with a major depressive episode: the BRIDGE study. Arch Gen Psychiatry. 2011 Aug;68(8):791–8.

Arnedo J, Svrakic DM, Del Val C, et al. Uncovering the hidden risk architecture of the schizophrenias: confirmation in three independent genome-wide association studies. Am J Psychiatry. 2015 Feb 1;172(2):139–53.

Arul-Anandam AP, Loo C, Mitchell P. Induction of hypomanic episode with transcranial direct current stimulation. J ECT. 2010 Mar; 26(1):68–9.

Aubry JM, Simon AE, Bertschy G.Possible induction of mania and hypomania by olanzapine or risperidone: a critical review of reported cases. J Clin Psychiatry. 2000 Sep;61(9):649–55.

Baek JH, Kang ES, Fava M, et al. Thyroid stimulating hormone and serum, plasma, and platelet brain-derived neurotrophic factor during a 3-month follow-up in patients with major depressive disorder. J Affect Disord. 2014 Dec;169:112–7.

Baldessarini RJ. A plea for integrity of the bipolar disorder concept. Bipolar Disord. 2000 Mar;2(1):3–7.

Bandelow B, Reitt M, Röver C, et al. Efficacy of treatments for anxiety disorders: a meta-analysis. Int Clin Psychopharmacol. 2015 Jul;30(4):183–92.

Barbini B, Benedetti F, Colombo C, et al. Dark therapy for mania: a pilot study. Bipolar Disord. 2005 Feb;7(1):98–101.

Basco M, Rush AJ. Cognitive-Behavioral Therapy for Bipolar Disorder. Guilford Press, 2005.

Bateman A, Fonagy P. Randomized controlled trial of outpatient mentalization-based treatment versus structured clinical management for borderline personality disorder. Am J Psychiatry. 2009 Dec;166(12):1355–64.

Bauer M, Adli M, Bschor T, et al. Clinical applications of levothyroxine in refractory mood disorders. Clin Approach Bipolar Disord. 2003;2:49–56.

Bauer M, Fairbanks L, Berghöfer A, et al. Bone mineral density during maintenance treatment with supraphysiological doses of levothyroxine in affective disorders: a longitudinal study. J Affect Disord. 2004 Dec;83(2–3):183–90.

Bauer M, London ED, Rasgon N, et al. Supraphysiological doses of levothyroxine alter regional cerebral metabolism and improve mood in bipolar depression. Mol Psychiatry. 2005 May;10(5):456–69.

Bauer M, Ludman E, Greenwald D, Kilbourne A. Overcoming Bipolar Disorder: A Comprehensive Workbook for Managing Your Symptoms and Achieving Your Life Goals. New Harbinger, 2009.

Beesdo K, Höfler M, Leibenluft E, et al. Mood episodes and mood disorders: patterns of incidence and conversion in the first three decades of life. Bipolar Disord. 2009 Sep;11(6):637–49.

Benedetti F. Antidepressant chronotherapeutics for bipolar depression. Dialogues Clin Neurosci. 2012 Dec;14(4):401–11.

Benyamina A, Samalin L. Atypical antipsychotic-induced mania/hypomania: a review of recent case reports and clinical studies. Int J Psychiatry Clin Pract. 2012 Mar;16(1):2–7.

Berger M, Vollmann J, Hohagen F, et al. Sleep deprivation combined with consecutive sleep phase advance as a fast-acting therapy in depression: an open pilot trial in medicated and unmedicated patients. Am J Psychiatry, 1997;154(6):870–2.

Berk M, Copolov DL, Dean O, et al. N-acetyl cysteine for depressive symptoms in bipolar disorder—a double-blind randomizeed placebo-controlled trial. Biol Psychiatry. 2008 Sep 15;64(6):468-75.

Berk M, Dean OM, Cotton SM, et al. Maintenance N-acetyl cysteine treatment for bipolar disorder: a double-blind randomized placebo controlled trial. BMC Med. 2012 Aug 14;10:91.

Berk M, Dodd S. Are treatment emergent suicidality and decreased response to antidepressants in younger patients due to bipolar disorder being misdiagnosed as unipolar depression? Med Hypotheses. 2005;65(1):39-43.

Berman RM, Marcus RN, Swanink R, et al. The efficacy and safety of aripiprazole as adjunctive therapy in major depressive disorder: a multicenter, randomized, double-blind, placebo-controlled study. J Clin Psychiatry. 2007;68:843–53.

Blanc X, Collet TH, Auer R, et al. Publication trends of shared decision making in 15 high impact medical journals: a full-text review with bibliometric analysis. BMC Med Inform Decis Mak. 2014 Aug 9;14:71.

Blum N, St John D, Pfohl B, et al. Systems training for emotional predictability and problem solving (STEPPS) for outpatients with borderline personality disorder: a randomized controlled trial and 1-year follow-up. Am J Psychiatry. 2008 Apr;165(4):468–78.

Blumenthal JA, Babyak MA, Moore KA, et al. Effects of exercise training on older patients with major depression. Arch Intern Med. 1999 Oct 25;159(19):2349–56.

Blumenthal JA, Sherwood A, Babyak MA, et al. Exercise and pharmacological treatment of depressive symptoms in patients with coronary heart disease: results from the UPBEAT (Understanding the Prognostic Benefits of Exercise and Antidepressant Therapy) study. J Am Coll Cardiol. 2012 Sep 18;60(12):1053–63.

Blumenthal SR, Castro VM, Clements CC, et al. An electronic health records study of long-term weight gain following antidepressant use. JAMA Psychiatry. 2014 Aug;71(8):889–96.

Bocchetta A, Loviselli A. Lithium treatment and thyroid abnormalities. Clin Pract Epidemiol Mental Health. 2006;2:article 23.

Bowden CL, Singh V. Lamotrigine (Lamictal IR) for the treatment of bipolar disorder. Expert Opin Pharmacother. 2012;13:2565-71.

Brainard GC, Hanifin JP, Greeson JM, et al. Action spectrum for melatonin regulation in humans: evidence for a novel circadian photoreceptor. J Neurosci. 2001 Aug 15;21(16):6405–12.

Braverman LE, Cooper DS. *Werner & Ingbar's The Thyroid: A Fundamental and Clinical Text*, 10th ed. Wolters Kluwer Health, 2012.

Brodie MJ, Mintzer S, Pack AM, et al. Enzyme induction with antiepileptic drugs: cause for concern? Epilepsia. 2013 Jan;54(1):11–27.

Bromley R, Weston J, Adab N, et al. Treatment for epilepsy in pregnancy: neurodevelopmental outcomes in the child. Cochrane Database Syst Rev. 2014 Oct 30;10:CD010236.

Brooks M. Chronotherapy for depression: rapid, large, stable effect. Medscape Med News. 2015 Feb 23. http://www.medscape.com/viewarticle/840191; accessed 7/24/15.

Brown EB, McElroy SL, Keck PE Jr, et al. A 7-week, randomized, double-blind trial of olanzapine/fluoxetine combination versus lamotrigine in the treatment of Bipolar I depression. J Clin Psychiatry. 2006 Jul; 67(7):1025–33.

Bschor T, Lewitzka U, Sasse J, et al. Lithium augmentation in treatment-resistant depression: clinical evidence, serotonergic and endocrine mechanisms. Pharmacopsychiatry. 2003 Nov;36 Suppl 3:S230–4.

Bucht G, Smigan L, Wahlin A, Eriksson P. ECG changes during lithium therapy. A prospective study. Acta Med Scand. 1984;216(1):101–4.

Burkhart K, Phelps JR. Amber lenses to block blue light and improve sleep: a randomized trial. Chronobiol Int. 2009 Dec;26(8):1602–12.

Caixàs A, Albert L, Capel I, Rigla M. Naltrexone sustained-release/bupropion sustained-release for the management of obesity: review of the data to date. Drug Des Devel Ther. 2014 Sep 18;8:1419–27.

Calabrese JR, Huffman RF, White RL, et al. Lamotrigine in the acute treatment of bipolar depression: results of five double-blind, placebo-controlled clinical trials. Bipolar Disord. 2008 Mar;10(2):323–33.

Calkin CV, Gardner DM, Ransom T, Alda M. The relationship between bipolar disorder and type 2 diabetes: more than just co-morbid disorders. Ann Med. 2013 Mar;45(2):171–81.

Calkin CV, Ruzickova M, Uher R, et al. Insulin resistance and outcome in bipolar disorder. Br J Psychiatry. 2015 Jan;206(1):52–7.

Carvalho AF, Dimellis D, Gonda X, et al. Rapid cycling in bipolar disorder: a systematic review. J Clin Psychiatry. 2014 Jun;75(6):e578–86.

Cassano GB, Rucci P, Frank E, et al. The mood spectrum in unipolar and bipolar disorder: arguments for a unitary approach. Am J Psychiatry. 2004 Jul;161(7):1264–9.

Chakrabarti S. Thyroid functions and bipolar affective disorder. J Thyroid Res. 2011;2011:306367.

Chang KD, Keck PE, Stanton SP, McElroy SL, Strakowski SM, Geracioti TD. Differences in thyroid function between bipolar manic and mixed states. Biol Psychiatry. 1998;43:730–733.

Chilakamarri JK, Filkowski MM, Ghaemi SN. Misdiagnosis of bipolar disorder in children and adolescents: a comparison with ADHD and major depressive disorder. Ann Clin Psychiatry. 2011; 23:25-9.

Chodron T. Working with Anger. Snow Lion, 2001.

Christensen J, Petrenaite V, Atterman J, et al. Oral contraceptives induce lamotrigine metabolism: evidence from a double-blind, placebo-controlled trial. Epilepsia. 2007 Mar;48(3):484–9.

Cohen L. Psychiatric medications and lactation: Informing clinical decisions. 2013; MGH Center for Women's Health. http://womens mentalhealth.org/mcm_obgyn/4012-2/; accessed 10/7/15.

Cohen LS, Friedman JM, Jefferson JW, et al. A reevaluation of risk of in utero exposure to lithium. JAMA 1994;271:146–50.

Cole DP, Thase ME, Mallinger AG, et al. Slower treatment response in bipolar depression predicted by lower pretreatment thyroid function. Am J Psychiatry. 2002 Jan;159(1):116–21.

Colom F, Vieta E, Martinez-Aran A, et al. A randomized trial on the efficacy of group psychoeducation in the prophylaxis of recurrences in bipolar patients whose disease is in remission. Arch Gen Psychiatry. 2003 Apr;60(4):402–7.

Colom F, Vieta E, Sánchez-Moreno J, et al. Group psychoeducation for stabilised bipolar disorders: 5-year outcome of a randomised clinical trial. Br J Psychiatry. 2009 Mar;194(3):260–5.

Colom F, Vieta E, Scott J. *Psychoeducation Manual for Bipolar Disorders.* Cambridge University Press, 2006.

Colombo C, Lucca A, Benedetti F, et al. Total sleep deprivation combined with lithium and light therapy in the treatment of bipolar depression: replication of main effects and interaction. Psychiatry Res. 2000;95(1):43–53.

Cooney GM, Dwan K, Greig CA, et al. Exercise for depression. Cochrane Database Syst Rev. 2013 Sep 12;9:CD004366.

Correll CU, Sikich L, Reeves G, Riddle M. Metformin for antipsychotic-related weight gain and metabolic abnormalities: when, for whom, and for how long? Am J Psychiatry. 2013 Sep;170(9):947–52.

Coryell W, Solomon D, Turvey C, et al. The long-term course of rapid-cycling bipolar disorder. Arch Gen Psychiatry. 2003 Sep; 60(9):914–20.

Coulston CM, Tanious M, Mulder RT, Porter RJ, Malhi GS. Bordering on bipolar: the overlap between borderline personality and bipolarity. Aust N Z J Psychiatry. 2012 Jun;46(6):506–21.

Crawford P. Interactions between antiepileptic drugs and hormonal contraception. CNS Drugs. 2002;16(4):263–72.

Crawford-Achour E, Saint Martin M, Roche F. Stress hormones in obstructive sleep apnea complications: the role of cortisol. Sleep Med. 2014 Jan;15(1):3–4.

Culpepper L, Davidson JR, Dietrich AJ, et al. Suicidality as a possible side effect of antidepressant treatment. Prim Care Companion J Clin Psychiatry. 2004;6(2):79–86.

Daughton JM, Padala PR, Gabel TL. Careful monitoring for agranulocytosis during carbamazepine treatment. Prim Care Companion J Clin Psychiatry. 2006;8(5):310–1.

Dauphinais D, Knable M, Rosenthal J, Polanski M, Rosenthal N. Zonisamide for bipolar disorder, mania or mixed states: a randomized, double blind, placebo-controlled adjunctive trial. Psychopharmacol Bull. 2011;44(1):5–17.

Davis JD, Tremont G. Neuropsychiatric aspects of hypothyroidism and treatment reversibility. Minerva Endocrinol. 2007 March;32(1):49–65.

Dell'osso B, D'Urso N, Castellano F, Ciabatti M, Altamura AC. Long-term efficacy after acute augmentative repetitive transcranial magnetic stimulation in bipolar depression: a 1-year follow-up study. J ECT. 2011;27(2):141–4.

Di Sabatino A, Volta U, Salvatore C et al. Small amounts of gluten in subjects with suspected nonceliac gluten sensitivity: a randomized, double-blind, placebo-controlled, cross-over trial. Clin Gastroenterol Hepatol. 2015 Feb 19;S1542-3565(15)00153-6.

Dickerson F, Stallings C, Origoni A, Vaughan C, Khushalani S, Yolken R. Markers of gluten sensitivity in acute mania: a longitudinal study. Psychiatry Res. 2012;196:68–71.

El-Mallakh RS, Gao Y, Briscoe BT, Roberts RJ. Antidepressant-induced tardive dysphoria. Psychother Psychosom. 2011;80(1):57–9.

El-Mallakh RS, Ghaemi SN, Sagduyu K, et al. Antidepressant-associated chronic irritable dysphoria (ACID) in STEP-BD patients. J Affect Disord. 2008 Dec;111(2–3):372–7.

El-Mallakh RS, Vöhringer PA, Ostacher MM, et al. Antidepressants worsen rapid-cycling course in bipolar depression: a STEP-BD randomized clinical trial. J Affect Disord. 2015 Sep 15;184:318–21.

El-Mallakh RS, Waltrip C, Peters C. Can long-term antidepressant use be depressogenic? . Clin Psychiatry. 1999;60:263.

Etain B, Jamain S, Milhiet V, et al. Association between circadian genes, bipolar disorders and chronotypes. Chronobiol Int. 2014 Aug; 31(7):807–14.

Faedda GL, Marangoni C, Reginaldi D. Depressive mixed states: a reappraisal of Koukopoulos' criteria. J Affect Disord. 2015 May 1; 176:18–23.

Fagiolini A, Kupfer DJ, Scott J, et al. Hypothyroidism in patients with Bipolar I disorder treated primarily with lithium. Epidemiol Psichiatr Soc. 2006 Apr–Jun;15(2):123–7.

Fels, A. Should we all take a little bit of lithium? New York Times, 2014 Sept 13. http://www.nytimes.com/2014/09/14/opinion/sunday/should-we-all-take-a-bit-of-lithium.html; accessed 8/8/2015.

Ferrell PB Jr, McLeod HL. Carbamazepine, HLA-B*1502 and risk of Stevens-Johnson syndrome and toxic epidermal necrolysis: US FDA recommendations. Pharmacogenomics. 2008 Oct;9(10):1543–6.

Fiala SJ. A piece of my mind. Normal is a place I visit. JAMA. 2004 Jun 23;291(24):2924–6.

Finer LB, Zolna MR. Shifts in intended and unintended pregnancies in the United States, 2001–2008. Am J Public Health. 2014;04(S1):S44–8.

First, M. Dimensional aspects of psychiatric diagnosis. In DSM-5 Research Planning Conference Summaries and Monographs. 2006 July 26–28. http://www.dsm5.org/Research/Pages/DimensionalAspects ofPsychiatricDiagnosis ().aspx; accessed 5/9/15.

Fitzgerald BJ, Okos AJ. Elevation of carbamazepine-10,11-epoxide by quetiapine. Pharmacotherapy. 2002 Nov;22(11):1500–3.

Foer J, Siffre M. Caveman: an interview with Michel Siffre. Cabinet. 2008:30. http://www.cabinetmagazine.org/issues/30/foer.php; accessed 9/30/15.

Forlenza OV, De-Paula VJ, Diniz BS. Neuroprotective effects of lithium: implications for the treatment of Alzheimer's disease and related neurodegenerative disorders. ACS Chem Neurosci. 2014 Jun 18;5(6):443–50.

Forlenza OV, Diniz BS, Radanovic M, et al. Disease-modifying properties of long-term lithium treatment for amnestic mild cognitive impairment: randomised controlled trial. Br J Psychiatry. 2011 May;198(5):351–6.

Fournier JC, DeRubeis RJ, Hollon SD, et al. Antidepressant drug effects and depression severity: a patient-level meta-analysis. JAMA. 2010 Jan 6;303(1):47–53.

Fox M. Fish oils may raise prostate cancer risks, study confirms. NBC News. 2013 July 10. http://www.nbcnews.com/health/fish-oils-may-raise-prostate-cancer-risks-study-confirms-6C10597283; accessed 8/12/15.

Frank E. Treating Bipolar Disorder: A Clinician's Guide to IPTSRT. Guilford Press, 2007.

Frye M. Case presentations. In Diagnosing and Managing Depressive Episodes in the DSM-5 Era. Presented at the International Society for Bipolar Disorders, Toronto, 2015.

Frye MA, Denicoff KD, Bryan AL, et al. Association between lower serum free T4 and greater mood instability and depression in lithium-maintained bipolar patients. Am J Psychiatry. 1999 Dec; 156(12):1909–14.

Frye MA, Helleman G, McElroy SL, et al. Correlates of treatment-emergent mania associated with antidepressant treatment in bipolar depression. Am J Psychiatry. 2009;166:164–72.

Gadde KM, Franciscy DM, Wagner HR II, Krishnan KR. Zonisamide for weight loss in obese adults: a randomized controlled trial. JAMA. 2003;289:1820–25.

Gadde KM, Kopping MF, Wagner HR II, Yonish GM, Allison DB, Bray GA. Zonisamide for weight reduction in obese adults: a 1-year randomized controlled trial. Arch Intern Med. 2012;172:1557–64.

Gamez J, Salvado M, Martínez de la Ossa A, Badia M. Lithium for treatment of amyotrophic lateral sclerosis: much ado about nothing. Neurologia. 2013 Apr 10.

Garber JR, Cobin RH, Gharib H, et al. Clinical practice guidelines for hypothyroidism in adults: cosponsored by the American Association of Clinical Endocrinologists and the American Thyroid Association. 2012. https://www.aace.com/files/final-file-hypo-guidelines.pdf; accessed 8/13/15.

Gebara MA, Shea ML, Lipsey KL, et al. Depression, antidepressants, and bone health in older adults: a systematic review. J Am Geriatr Soc. 2014 Aug;62(8):1434–41.

Geddes JR, Calabrese JR, Goodwin GM. Lamotrigine for treatment of bipolar depression: independent meta-analysis and meta-regression of individual patient data from five randomised trials. Br J Psychiatry. 2009 Jan;194(1):4–9.

Gelenberg AJ, Kane JM, Keller MB, et al. Comparison of standard and low serum levels of lithium for maintenance treatment of bipolar disorder. N Engl J Med. 1989; 321:1489–93.

Gerhard T, Devanand DP, Huang C, Crystal S, Olfson M. Lithium treatment and risk for dementia in adults with bipolar disorder: population-based cohort study. Br J Psychiatry. 2015 Jul; 207(1):46–51.

Gever J. APA: add-on lithium no help in bipolar disorder. Medpage Today. 2011. http://www.medpagetoday.com/MeetingCoverage/APA/26544; accessed 6/16/15.

Ghaemi SN. The failure to know what isn't known: negative publication bias with lamotrigine and a glimpse inside peer review. Evid Based Mental Health 2009;12:65–68.

Ghaemi SN, Dalley S, Catania C, Barroilhet S. Bipolar or borderline: a clinical overview. Acta Psychiatr Scand. 2014 Aug;130(2):99–108.

Ghaemi SN, Gilmer WS, Goldberg JF et al. Divalproex in the treatment of acute bipolar depression: a preliminary double-blind, randomized, placebo-controlled pilot study. J Clin Psychiatry. 2007 Dec;68(12):1840–4.

Ghaemi SN, Ko JY, Goodwin FK. "Cade's disease" and beyond: misdiagnosis, antidepressant use, and a proposed definition for bipolar spectrum disorder. Can J Psychiatry. 2002 Mar;47(2):125–34.

Ghaemi NS, Miller CJ, Berv DA et al. Sensitivity and specificity of a new bipolar spectrum diagnostic scale. J Affect Disord. 2005 Feb;84(2–3):273–7.

Ghaemi SN, Ostacher MM, El-Mallakh RS et al. Antidepressant discontinuation in bipolar depression: a Systematic Treatment Enhancement Program for Bipolar Disorder (STEP-BD) randomized clinical trial of long-term effectiveness and safety. J Clin Psychiatry. 2010 Apr;71(4):372–80.

Ghaemi SN, Shirzadi AA, Klugman J, Berv DA, Pardo TB, Filkowski MM. Is adjunctive open-label zonisamide effective for bipolar disorder? J Affect Disord. 2008a Jan;105(1–3):311–4.

Ghaemi SN, Shirzadi AA, Filkowski M. Publication bias and the pharmaceutical industry: the case of lamotrigine in bipolar disorder. Medscape J Med. 2008b;10(9):211. http://www.medscape.com/view article/579046_1; accessed 7/28/15.

Ghanizadeh A, Nikseresht MS, Sahraian A. The effect of zonisamide on antipsychotic-associated weight gain in patients with schizophrenia: a randomized, double-blind, placebo-controlled clinical trial. Schizophr Res. 2013 Jun;147(1):110–5.

Ghouse AA, Sanches M, Zunta-Soares G, Swann AC, Soares JC. Overdiagnosis of bipolar disorder: a critical analysis of the literature. ScientificWorldJournal. 2013 Nov 20;2013:297087.

Gjessing R. Disturbances of somatic function in catatonia with a periodic course and their compensation. J Ment Sci. 1938;84:608–21

Gijsman HJ, Geddes JR, Rendell JM, Nolen WA, Goodwin GM. Antidepressants for bipolar depression: a systematic review of randomized, controlled trials. Am J Psychiatry. 2004 Sep;161(9):1537–47.

Gold PW, Pavlatou MG, Michelson D, et al. Chronic administration of anticonvulsants but not antidepressants impairs bone strength: clinical implications. Transl Psychiatry. 2015 Jun 2;5:e576.

Goldberg JF. Mixed depression: a farewell to differential diagnosis? J Clin Psychiatry. 2015 Mar;76(3):e378–80.

Goldberg JF, Perlis RH, Bowden CL, et al. Manic symptoms during depressive episodes in 1,380 patients with bipolar disorder: findings from the STEP-BD. Am J Psychiatry. 2009 Feb;166(2):173–81.

Gottlieb JF, Terman M. Outpatient triple chronotherapy for bipolar depression: case report. J Psychiatr Pract. 2012 Sep;18(5):373–80.

Gowda U, Mutowo MP, Smith BJ, Wluka AE, Renzaho AM. Vitamin D supplementation to reduce depression in adults: meta-analysis of randomized controlled trials. Nutrition. 2015 Mar;31(3):421–9.

Grandjean EM, Aubry JM. Lithium: updated human knowledge using an evidence-based approach: part III: clinical safety. CNS Drugs. 2009;23(5):397–418.

Grover S, Avasthi A. Mood stabilizers in pregnancy and lactation. Indian J Psychiatry. 2015 Jul;57(Suppl 2):S308–23.

Gupta MA, Simpson FC. Obstructive sleep apnea and psychiatric disorders: a systematic review. J Clin Sleep Med. 2015 Jan 15;11(2):165–75.

Gyulai L, Bauer M, Garcia-Espana F, et al. Bone mineral density in pre- and post-menopausal women with affective disorder treated with long-term L-thyroxine augmentation. J Affect Disord. 2001 Oct; 66(2–3):185–91.

Gyulai L, Jaggi J, Bauer MS, et al. Bone mineral density and L-thyroxine treatment in rapidly cycling bipolar disorder. Biological Psychiatry. 1997;41(4):503–6.

Haidt J. The Righteous Mind: Why Good People Are Divided by Politics and Religion. Pantheon, 2012.

Haidt J. Three stories about capitalism. Righteous Mind. July 2014. http://righteousmind.com/three-stories-about-capitalism/; accessed 9/9/2015.

Hampel H, Ewers M, Bürger K, et al. Lithium trial in Alzheimer's disease: a randomized, single-blind, placebo-controlled, multicenter 10-week study. J Clin Psychiatry. 2009 Jun;70(6):922–31.

Hanh TN. Anger: Wisdom for Cooling the Flames. Riverhead Books, 2002.

Haukeland JW, Jahnsen J, Raknerud N. Carbamazepine-induced hepatitis. Tidsskr Nor Laegeforen. 2000 Oct 10;120(24):2875–7.

Heath C, Heath D. *Made to Stick*. Random House, 2007.

Henriksen TE, Skrede S, Fasmer OB, et al. Blocking blue light during mania—markedly increased regularity of sleep and rapid improvement of symptoms: a case report. Bipolar Disord. 2014 Dec;16(8):894–8.

Henry C, Demotes-Mainard J. Olanzapine-induced mania in bipolar disorders. J Psychiatry Neurosci. 2002 May;27(3):200–1.

Henry C, Demotes-Mainard J, Leboyer M. Adjunctive antidepressant treatment for bipolar depression. N Engl J Med. 2007 Aug 9; 357(6):614–5.

Hollowell JG, Staehling NW, Flanders WD, et al. Serum TSH, T(4), and thyroid antibodies in the United States population (1988 to 1994): National Health and Nutrition Examination Survey (NHANES III). J Clin Endocrinol Metab. 2002 Feb;87(2):489–99.

Hosseinpour-Niazi S, Mirmiran P, Fallah-Ghohroudi A, Azizi F. Non-soya legume-based therapeutic lifestyle change diet reduces inflammatory status in diabetic patients: a randomised cross-over clinical trial. Br J Nutr. 2015 Jun 16;1–7.

Huthwaite MA, Stanley J. Lithium in drinking water. Br J Psychiatry. 2010 Feb;196(2):159.

Ives-Deliperi VL, Howells F, Stein DJ, Meintjes EM, Horn N. The effects of mindfulness-based cognitive therapy in patients with bipolar disorder: a controlled functional MRI investigation. J Affect Disord. 2013 Sep 25;150(3):1152–7.

Jamison K. *An Unquiet Mind*. Alfred A. Knopf, 1995.

Jentink J, Loane MA, Dolk H, et al. N Valproic acid monotherapy in pregnancy and major congenital malformations. N Engl J Med. 2010 Jun 10;362(23):2185–93.

Jeong Jeong H, Moon E, Min Park J, et al. The relationship between chronotype and mood fluctuation in the general population. Psychiatry Res. 2015 Oct 30;229(3):867–71.

Joffe RT. How should lithium-induced thyroid dysfunction be managed in patients with bipolar disorder? J Psychiatry Neurosci. 2002 Sep;27(5):392.

Kabacs N, Memon A, Obinwa T, Stochl J, Perez J. Lithium in drinking water and suicide rates across the east of England. Br J Psychiatry. 2011 May;198(5):406–7.

Kafadar İ, Kılıç BA, Arapoglu M, Yalçın K, Dalgıç N. Evaluation of thyroid hormones in children receiving carbamazepine or valproate: a prospective study. J Child Neurol. 2015 Jan;30(1):63–8.

Kanner AM. When thinking of lamotrigine and valproic acid, think "pharmacokinetically"! Epilepsy Curr. 2004 Sep–Oct;4(5):206–7.

Kavoor AR, Mitra S, Mondal SK, Das B. Risperidone-induced mania: an emergent complication of treatment. J Pharmacol Pharmacother. 2014 Oct;5(4):258–60.

Kayumov L, Casper RF, Hawa RJ, et al. Blocking low-wavelength light prevents nocturnal melatonin suppression with no adverse effect on performance during simulated shift work. J Clin Endocrinol Metab. 2005 May;90(5):2755–61.

Kelly T. A favorable risk-benefit analysis of high dose thyroid for treatment of bipolar disorders with regard to osteoporosis. J Affect Disord. 2014 Sep;166:353–8.

Kelly T. An examination of myth: a favorable cardiovascular risk-benefit analysis of high-dose thyroid for affective disorders. J Affect Disord. 2015 May 15;177:49–58.

Kelly T, Douglas L, Denmark L, Brasuell G, Lieberman DZ. The high prevalence of obstructive sleep apnea among patients with bipolar disorders. J Affect Disord. 2013 Oct;151(1):54–8.

Kelly T, Lieberman DZ. The use of triiodothyronine as an augmentation agent in treatment-resistant Bipolar II and bipolar disorder NOS. J Affect Disord. 2009 Aug;116(3):222–6.

Kessing LV, Søndergård L, Forman JL, Andersen PK. Lithium treatment and risk of dementia. Arch Gen Psychiatry. 2008 Nov;65(11):1331–5.

Ketter TA, Miller S, Dell'Osso B et al. Balancing benefits and harms of treatments for acute bipolar depression. J Affect Disord. 2014 Dec;169 Suppl 1:S24–33.

Kibirige D, Luzinda K, Ssekitoleko R. Spectrum of lithium induced thyroid abnormalities: a current perspective. Thyroid Res. 2013 Feb 7;6(1):3.

Kiecolt-Glaser JK, Derry HM, Fagundes CP. Inflammation: Depression Fans the Flames and Feasts on the Heat. Am J Psychiatry. 2015;172(11):1075-91.

Kinrys G. Hypomania associated with omega3 fatty acids. Arch Gen Psychiatry. 2000 Jul;57(7):715–6.

Kirsch I, Deacon BJ, Huedo-Medina TB et al. Initial severity and antidepressant benefits: a meta-analysis of data submitted to the Food and Drug Administration. PLoS Med. 2008 Feb;5(2):e45.

Kirova G, Tredget J, John R, Owen M, Lazarus J. A cross-sectional and a prospective study of thyroid disorders in lithium-treated patients. J Affect Disord. 2005;87:313–7.

Koo DL, Hwang KJ, Han SW, et al. Effect of oxcarbazepine on bone mineral density and biochemical markers of bone metabolism in patients with epilepsy. Epilepsy Res. 2014 Mar;108(3):442–7.

Koukopoulos A, Sani G, Ghaemi SN. (2013). Mixed features of depression: why DSM-5 is wrong (and so was DSM-IV). Br J Psychiatry 203:3-5.

Kraai EP, Seifert SA. Citalopram overdose: a fatal case. J Med Toxicol. 2015 Jun;11(2):232–6.

Krysiak R, Stojko R. Transient hypothyroidism induced by anticonvulsant agents. Neuro Endocrinol Lett. 2014;35(3):183–5.

Kushner SF, Khan A, Lane R, Olson WH. Topiramate monotherapy in the management of acute mania: results of four double-blind placebo-controlled trials. Bipolar Disord. 2006 Feb;8(1):15–27.

Kusumakar V, Yatha LN, Haslam D. Treatment of mania, mixed state, and rapid cycling. Can J Psychiatry 1997;42 Suppl 2:79S–86S.

Lam RW. Psychopharmacology for the clinician. J Psychiatry Neurosci. 2013 Mar;38(2):E5–6.

Lee MW, Fujioka K. Naltrexone for the treatment of obesity: review and update. Expert Opin Pharmacother. 2009 Aug;10(11):1841–5.

Leverich GS, Altshuler LL, Frye MA, et al. Risk of switch in mood polarity to hypomania or mania in patients with bipolar depression during acute and continuation trials of venlafaxine, sertraline, and bupropion as adjuncts to mood stabilizers. Am J Psychiatry. 2006 Feb;163(2):232–9.

Leweke FM, Piomelli D, Pahlisch F et al. Cannabidiol enhances anandamide signaling and alleviates psychotic symptoms of schizophrenia. Transl Psychiatry. 2012;2:e94

Lieberman JA, Stroup TS, McEvoy JP, et al. Effectiveness of antipsychotic drugs in patients with chronic schizophrenia. N Engl J Med. 2005 Sep 22;353(12):1209–23.

Linehan M. *Cognitive Behavioral Therapy for Borderline Personality Disorder.* Guilford Publications, 1993.

Loebel A, Cucchiaro J, Silva R et al. Lurasidone monotherapy in the treatment of Bipolar I depression: a randomized, double-blind, placebo-controlled study. Am J Psychiatry. 2014 Feb;171(2):160–8.

Lohoff FW, Etemad B, Mandos LA, Gallop R, Rickels K. Ziprasidone treatment of refractory generalized anxiety disorder: a placebo-controlled, double-blind study. J Clin Psychopharmacol. 2010 Apr;30(2):185–9.

Łojko D, Rybakowski JK. L-thyroxine augmentation of serotonergic antidepressants in female patients with refractory depression. J Affect Disord. 2007 Nov;103(1–3):253–6.

López-Rocha E, Blancas L, Rodríguez-Mireles K, et al. Prevalence of DRESS syndrome. Alerg Mex. 2014 Jan–Mar;61(1):14–23.

Luppino FS, de Wit LM, Bouvy PF et al. Overweight, obesity, and depression: a systematic review and meta-analysis of longitudinal studies. Arch Gen Psychiatry. 2010 Mar;67(3):220–9.

MacKinnon DF, Pies R. Affective instability as rapid cycling: theoretical and clinical implications for borderline personality and bipolar spectrum disorders. Bipolar Disord. 2006 Feb;8(1):1–14.

Marcus R, McQuade R, Carson W, et al. The efficacy and safety of aripiprazole as adjunctive therapy in major depressive disorder: a second multicenter, randomized, double-blind placebo-controlled study. J Clin Psychopharmacol. 2008;28:156–65.

Malhi GS, Adams D, Berk M. Medicating mood with maintenance in mind: bipolar depression pharmacotherapy. Bipolar Disord. 2009 Jun;11 Suppl 2:55–76.

Malhi GS, Tanious M, Das P, Berk M. The science and practice of lithium therapy. Aust N Z J Psychiatry. 2012 Mar;46(3):192–211.

Mansur RB, Brietzke E, McIntyre RS. Is there a "metabolic-mood syndrome"? A review of the relationship between obesity and mood disorders. Neurosci Biobehav Rev. 2015 May;52:89–104.

Margolese HC, Beauclair L, Szkrumelak N, Chouinard G. Hypomania induced by adjunctive lamotrigine. Am J Psychiatry. 2003 Jan;160(1):183–4.

Markowitz JC, Weissman MM. Interpersonal psychotherapy: principles and applications. World Psychiatry. 2004 Oct;3(3):136–9.

Martín-Merino E, de Abajo FJ, Gil M. Risk of toxic epidermal necrolysis and Stevens-Johnson syndrome associated with benzodiazepines: a population-based cohort study. Eur J Clin Pharmacol. 2015 Jun;71(6):759–66.

McElroy SL, Strakowski SM, Keck PE Jr, et al. Differences and similarities in mixed and pure mania. Compr Psychiatry. 1995 May–Jun;36(3):187–94.

McIntyre R, Frye M, Nierenberg A. Diagnosing and managing depressive episodes in the DSM-5 era. International Society for Bipolar Disorders Meeting, Toronto, 2015.

McKnight RF, Adida M, Budge K, et al. Lithium toxicity profile: a systematic review and meta-analysis. Lancet. 2012 Feb 25;379(9817):721–8.

Merikangas KR, Akiskal HS, Angst J, et al. Lifetime and 12-month prevalence of bipolar spectrum disorder in the National Comorbidity Survey replication. Arch Gen Psychiatry. 2007 May;64(5):543–52.

Meyer JM, Mao Y, Pikalov A, Cucchiaro J, Loebel A.Weight change during long-term treatment with lurasidone: pooled analysis of studies in patients with schizophrenia. Int Clin Psychopharmacol. 2015 Nov;30(6):342–50.

Miklowitz D. *Bipolar Disorder: A Family-Focused Treatment Approach*, 2nd ed. Guilford Press, 2007.

Miklowitz DJ, Otto MW, Frank E, et al. Psychosocial treatments for bipolar depression: a 1-year randomized trial from the Systematic Treatment Enhancement Program. Arch Gen Psychiatry. 2007 Apr;64(4):419–26.

Miklowitz DJ, Schneck CD, George EL, et al. Pharmacotherapy and family-focused treatment for adolescents with Bipolar I and II disorders: a 2-year randomized trial. Am J Psychiatry. 2014 Jun;171(6):658–67.

Millard HY, Wilson BA, Noordsy DL. Low-dose quetiapine induced or worsened mania in the context of possible undertreatment. J Am Board Fam Med. 2015 Jan–Feb;28(1):154–8.

Mitchell JE, Mackenzie TB. Cardiac effects of lithium therapy in man: a review. J Clin Psychiatry. 1982 Feb;43(2):47–51.

Mitchell PB. Bipolar disorder: the shift to overdiagnosis. Can J Psychiatry. 2012 Nov;57(11):659–65.

Mitchell PB, Goodwin GM, Johnson GF, Hirschfeld RM. Diagnostic guidelines for bipolar depression: a probabilistic approach. Bipolar Disord. 2008 Feb;10(1 Pt 2):144–52.

Mockenhaupt M, Messenheimer J, Tennis P, Schlingmann J. Risk of Stevens-Johnson syndrome and toxic epidermal necrolysis in new users of antiepileptics. Neurology. 2005 Apr 12;64(7):1134–8.

Monk T. Enhancing circadian zeitgebers. Sleep. 2010 Apr 1;33(4):421–22.

Montalescot G, Levy Y, Farge D, Brochard L, Fantin B, Arnoux C, Hatt PY. Lithium causing a serious sinus-node dysfunction at therapeutic doses. Clin Cardiol. 1984 Nov;7(11):617-20.

Morris G, Walder K, Puri BK, Berk M, Maes M. The deleterious effects of oxidative and nitrosative stress on palmitoylation, membrane lipid rafts and lipid-based cellular signalling: new drug targets in neuroimmune disorders. Mol Neurobiol. 2015 Aug 27. [Epub ahead of print].

Movig KL, Baumgarten R, Leufkens HG, et al. Risk factors for the development of lithium-induced polyuria. Br J Psychiatry. 2003;182:319–23.

Moylan S, Berk M, Dean OM, et al. Oxidative & nitrosative stress in depression: why so much stress? Neurosci Biobehav Rev. 2014 Sep;45:46–62.

Murray G, Leitan ND, Berk M, et al. Online mindfulness-based intervention for late-stage bipolar disorder: pilot evidence for feasibility and effectiveness. J Affect Disord. 2015 Jun 1;178:46–51.

Muzina DJ, Gao K, Kemp DE, et al. Acute efficacy of divalproex sodium versus placebo in mood stabilizer-naive Bipolar I or II depression: a double-blind, randomized, placebo-controlled trial. J Clin Psychiatry. 2011 Jun;72(6):813–9.

NICE (National Institute for Health and Care Excellence). Guideline 1.2.3 in Bipolar disorder: the assessment and management of bipolar disorder in adults, children and young people in primary and secondary care. NICE. 2014a. http://www.nice.org.uk/guidance/cg185/chapter/1-recommendations#recognising-and-managing-bipolar-disorder-in-adults-in-primary-care-2; accessed 9/11/15.

NICE. Recommendation 1.6.3. NICE. 2014b. http://www.nice.org.uk/ guidance/cg185/chapter/1-recommendations#managing-bipolar-depression-in-adults-in-secondary-care-2; accessed 8/8/2015.

NICE. Pharmacological interventions for moderate or severe bipolar depression. NICE Pathways: Bipolar Disorder. 2014c. http:// pathways.nice.org.uk/pathways/bipolar-disorder#path=view%3A/ pathways/bipolar-disorder/managing-bipolar-depression-in-adults. xml&content=view-node%3Anodes-pharmacological-interventions-for-moderate-or-severe-bipolar-depression; accessed 9/5/15.

Nickl-Jockschat T, Paulzen M, Schneider F, Grözinger M. Drug interaction can lead to undetectable serum concentrations of quetiapine in the presence of carbamazepine. Clin Neuropharmacol. 2009 Jan–Feb;32(1):55.

Nierenberg AA, Fava M, Trivedi MH, et al. A comparison of lithium and T(3) augmentation following two failed medication treatments for depression: a STAR*D report. Am J Psychiatry. 2006 Sep; 163(9):1519–30.

Nierenberg AA, Friedman ES, Bowden CL, et al. Lithium treatment moderate-dose use study (LiTMUS) for bipolar disorder: a randomized comparative effectiveness trial of optimized personalized treatment with and without lithium. Am J Psychiatry. 2013 Jan;170(1):102–10.

Nierenberg AA, McIntyre RS, Sachs GS. Improving outcomes in patients with bipolar depression: a comprehensive review. J Clin Psychiatry. 2015 Mar;76(3):e10.

Nonacs, R. Polycystic ovarian syndrome in women taking valproate. MGH Center For Women's Mental Health. 2007. http://womensmental health.org/posts/polycystic-ovarian-syndrome-in-women-taking-valproate/; accessed 8/10/15.

Nonacs R. Lamotrigine and breastfeeding: an update. MGH Center For Women's Mental Health. 2010. http://womensmentalhealth.org/posts/ lamotrigine-and-breastfeeding-an-update/; accessed 10/7/15.

Nonacs R. You asked: should lamotrigine (lamictal) dose be adjusted during pregnancy? MGH Center For Women's Mental Health. 2015. http://womensmentalhealth.org/posts/you-asked-should-lamotri gine-lamictal-dose-be-adjusted-during-pregnancy/; accessed 10/7/15.

Novick DM, Swartz HA, Frank E. Suicide attempts in Bipolar I and Bipolar II disorder: a review and meta-analysis of the evidence. Bipolar Disord. 2010 Feb;12(1):1–9.

Nunes MA, Viel TA, Buck HS. Microdose lithium treatment stabilized cognitive impairment in patients with Alzheimer's disease. Curr Alzheimer Res. 2013 Jan;10(1):104–7.

Nurnberger JI Jr, Koller DL, Jung J, et al. Identification of pathways for bipolar disorder: a meta-analysis. JAMA Psychiatry. 2014 Jun;71(6):657–64.

O'Donovan C, Garnham JS, Hajek T, Alda M. Antidepressant monotherapy in pre-bipolar depression; predictive value and inherent risk. J Affect Disord. 2008 Apr;107(1–3):293–8

Ohgami H, Terao T, Shiotsuki I, Ishii N, Iwata N. Lithium levels in drinking water and risk of suicide. Br J Psychiatry. 2009 May;194(5):464-5

Otto M, Reilly-Harrington N, Kogan J, et al. *Managing Bipolar Disorder: A Cognitive-Behavioral Approach.* Oxford University Press, 2008.

Pacchiarotti I, Bond DJ, Baldessarini RJ, et al. The International Society for Bipolar Disorders (ISBD) task force report on antidepressant use in bipolar disorders. Am J Psychiatry. 2013a Nov;170(11):1249–62.

Pacchiarotti I, Nivoli AM, Mazzarini L, et al. The symptom structure of bipolar acute episodes: in search for the mixing link. J Affect Disord. 2013b Jul;149(1–3):56–66.

Paris J. Borderline personality and bipolar disorder: the limits of phenomenology. Acta Psychiatr Scand. 2013 Nov;128(5):384.

Paris J, Black DW. Borderline personality disorder and bipolar disorder: what is the difference and why does it matter? J Nerv Ment Dis. 2015 Jan;203(1):3–7.

Park YM. Low-dose manic switch and high-dose antimanic effect and extrapyramidal symptoms by aripiprazole in a single bipolar patient. Am J Ther. 2014 Nov–Dec;21(6):e218–20.

Parker G. How should mood disorders be modelled? Aust N Z J Psychiatry. 2008 Oct;42(10):841–50.

Parker G. *Bipolar II: Modelling, Measuring and Managing.* Cambridge University Press, 2012.

Parker G, Graham R, Synnott H, Anderson J. Is the DSM-5 duration criterion valid for the definition of hypomania? J Affect Disord. 2014;156:87–91.

Parker G, McCraw S. The "disconnect" between initial judgments of lamotrigine vs. its real-world effectiveness in managing bipolar disorder. A tale with wider ramifications. Acta Psychiatr Scand. 2015 Apr 27.

Pennell PB, Newport DJ, Stowe ZN, et al. The impact of pregnancy and childbirth on the metabolism of lamotrigine. Neurology. 2004 Jan 27;62(2):292–5.

Perlis RH, Sachs GS, Lafer B, et al. Effect of abrupt change from standard to low serum levels of lithium: a reanalysis of double-blind lithium maintenance data. Am J Psychiatry. 2002; 159:1155–9.

Perlis RH, Uher R, Ostacher M, et al. Association between bipolar spectrum features and treatment outcomes in outpatients with major depressive disorder. Arch Gen Psychiatry. 2011 Apr;68(4):351–60.

Perry A, Tarrier N, Morriss R, McCarthy E, Limb K. Randomised controlled trial of efficacy of teaching patients with bipolar disorder to identify early symptoms of relapse and obtain treatment. BMJ. 1999 Jan 16;318(7177):149–53.

Perucca E. Clinically relevant drug interactions with antiepileptic drugs. Br J Clin Pharmacol. 2006 Mar;61(3):246–55.

Perugi G, Angst J, Azorin JM, Bowden C, Vieta E, Young AH; BRIDGE Study Group. The bipolar-borderline personality disorders connection in major depressive patients. Acta Psychiatr Scand. 2013 Nov; 128(5):376-83.

Peruzzolo TL, Tramontina S, Rohde LA, Zeni CP. Pharmacotherapy of bipolar disorder in children and adolescents: an update. Rev Bras Psiquiatr. 2013 Oct–Dec;35(4):393–405.

Pfohl B, Vasquez N, Nasrallah H. Unipolar vs. bipolar mania: a review of 247 patients. Br J Psychiatry. 1982;141:453–8.

Phelps J. Physical activity and health maintenance—exactly what is known? West J Med. 1987 Feb;146(2):200–6.

Phelps JR. Agitated dysphoria after late-onset loss of response to antidepressants: a case report. J Affect Disord. 2005 Jun;86(2–3):277–80.

Phelps J. Dark therapy for bipolar disorder using amber lenses for blue light blockade. Med Hypotheses. 2008;70(2):224–9.

Phelps J. Tapering antidepressants: is 3 months slow enough? Med Hypotheses. 2011 Dec;77(6):1006–8.

Phelps J. Omega-3s and prostate cancer. PsychEducation.org. 2013. http://psycheducation.org/treatment/mood-stabilizers/omega-3-fatty-acids/824-2/; accessed 8/12/15.

Phelps J. N-Acetyl cysteine. PsychEducation.org. 2014a. http://psych education.org/treatment/mood-stabilizers/n-acetyl-cysteine-nac/; accessed 10/7/15.

Phelps J. No need for blood: nine alternatives to the antidepressant debate. *Psychiatric Times*. 2014b Jan 23. http://www.psychiatrictimes.com/ bipolar-disorder/no-need-blood-nine-alternatives-antidepressant-debate; accessed 6/15/2015.

Phelps J, Angst J, Katzow J, Sadler J. Validity and utility of bipolar spectrum models. Bipolar Disord. 2008 Feb;10(1 Pt 2):179–93.

Phelps J, Ghaemi SN. The mistaken claim of bipolar 'overdiagnosis': solving the false positives problem for DSM-5/ICD-11. Acta Psychiatr Scand. 2012 Dec;126(6):395–401.

Phelps J, Manipod V. Treating anxiety by discontinuing antidepressants: a case series. Med Hypotheses. 2012 Sep;79(3):338–41.

Phelps JR, Siemers SV, El-Mallakh RS. The ketogenic diet for type II bipolar disorder. Neurocase. 2013;19(5):423–6.

Phillips ML, Kupfer DJ. Bipolar disorder diagnosis: challenges and future directions. Lancet. 2013 May 11;381(9878):1663–71.

Pies R. WHIPLASHED: a mnemonic for recognizing bipolar depression. Psychiatric Times. 2007. http://www.psychiatrictimes.com/bipolar-disorder/whiplashed-mnemonic-recognizing-bipolar-depression; accessed 5/24/15.

Porcelli B, Verdino V, Bossini L, Terzuoli L, Fagiolini A. Celiac and non-celiac gluten sensitivity: a review on the association with schizo-phrenia and mood disorders. Auto Immun Highlights. 2014 Oct 16; 5(2):55–61.

Prather AA, Marsland AL, Hall M, et al. Normative variation in self-reported sleep quality and sleep debt is associated with stimu-lated pro-inflammatory cytokine production. Biol Psychol. 2009 Sep;82(1):12–7.

Printz D, Clark J, Stricks L, Malaspina D. Weight gain in bipolar disor-der: causes and treatments. Primary Psychiatry. 2003;10(11):29–33.

Rachid F, Bertschy G, Bondolfi G, Aubry JM. Possible induction of mania or hypomania by atypical antipsychotics: an updated review of reported cases. J Clin Psychiatry. 2004 Nov;65(11):1537–45.

Rakofsky JJ, Dunlop BW. Do alcohol use disorders destabilize the course of bipolar disorder. J Affect Disord. 2013;145:1–10.

Rao AV, Hariharasubramanian N. Electrocardiographic changes during lithium treatment. Indian J Psychiatry. 1980 Apr;22(2):135–41.

Rahman T, Campbell A, O'Connell CR, Nallapula K. Carbamazepine in bipolar disorder with pain: reviewing treatment guidelines. Prim Care Companion CNS Disord. 2014 Oct 9;16(5).

Raison CL, Rutherford RE, Woolwine BJ, et al. A randomized controlled trial of the tumor necrosis factor antagonist infliximab for treatment-resistant depression: the role of baseline inflammatory biomarkers. JAMA Psychiatry. 2013 Jan;70(1):31–41.

Raskin S, Teitelbaum A, Zislin J, Durst R. Adjunctive lamotrigine as a possible mania inducer in bipolar patients. Am J Psychiatry. 2006 Jan;163(1):159–60.

Regeer EJ, Kupka RW, Have MT, et al. Low self-recognition and awareness of past hypomanic and manic episodes in the general population. Int J Bipolar Disord. 2015 Dec;3(1):22.

Reid JG, Gitlin MJ, Altshuler LL. Lamotrigine in psychiatric disorders. J Clin Psychiatry. 2013 Jul;74(7):675–84.

Rej S, Segal M, Low NC, et al. The McGill Geriatric Lithium-Induced Diabetes Insipidus Clinical Study (McGLIDICS). Can J Psychiatry. 2014 Jun;59(6):327–34.

Rihmer Z, Akiskal H. Do antidepressants t(h)reat(en) depressives? Toward a clinically judicious formulation of the antidepressant-suicidality FDA advisory in light of declining national suicide statistics from many countries. J Affect Disord. 2006;94:3–13.

Ricken R, Bermpohl F, Schlattmann P, et al. Long-term treatment with supraphysiological doses of thyroid hormone in affective disorders—effects on bone mineral density. J Affect Disord. 2012 Jan;136 (1–2):e89–94.

Robakis TK, Holtzman J, Stemmle PG, et al. Lamotrigine and GABAA receptor modulators interact with menstrual cycle phase and oral contraceptives to regulate mood in women with bipolar disorder. J Affect Disord. 2015 Apr 1;175:108–15.

Roberts SM, Sylvia LG, Reilly-Harrington N. *The Bipolar II Disorder Workbook: Managing Recurring Depression, Hypomania, and Anxiety.* New Harbinger, 2014.

Roser P, Vollenweider FX, Kawohl W. Potential antipsychotic properties of central cannabinoid (CB1) receptor antagonists. World J Biol Psychiatry. 2010 Mar;11(2 Pt 2):208–19.

Roose SP, Nurnberger JI, Dunner DL, Blood DK, Fieve RR. Cardiac sinus node dysfunction during lithium treatment. Am J Psychiatry. 1979 Jun;136(6):804–6.

Sachs GS. Strategies for improving treatment of bipolar disorder: integration of measurement and management. Acta Psychiatr Scand Suppl. 2004;(422):7–17.

Sachs G. The bipolarity index as a tool for assessment and creating rapport: an expert interview with Gary Sachs. Medscape Psychiatry 2005;10(1). http://www.medscape.org/viewarticle/503893; accessed 5/11/2015.

Sachs GS, Nierenberg AA, Calabrese JR, et al. Effectiveness of adjunctive antidepressant treatment for bipolar depression. N Engl J Med. 2007 Apr 26;356(17):1711–22.

Saito S, Shioda K, Nisijima K. Anger with murderous impulse induced by lamotrigine. Gen Hosp Psychiatry. 2014 Jul–Aug;36(4):451.e1–2.

Sala R, Gill MK, Birmaher B. Differentiating pediatric bipolar spectrum disorders from attention-deficit/hyperactivity disorder. Psychiatric Annals. 2014; 44:410–415.

Sansone RA and Sawyer RJ. Aripiprazole withdrawal: a case report. Innov Clin Neurosci. 2013 May;10(5-6):10-2.

Sani G, Napoletano F, Vöhringer PA, et al. Mixed depression: clinical features and predictors of its onset associated with antidepressant use. Psychother Psychosom. 2014a;83(4):213–21.

Sani G, Vöhringer PA, Napoletano F, et al. Koukopoulos' diagnostic criteria for mixed depression: a validation study. J Affect Disord. 2014b;164:14–8.

Schaffler L, Bourgeois BF, Luders HO. Rapid reversibility of autoinduction of carbamazepine metabolism after temporary discontinuation. Epilepsia; 1994;35:195–8.

Schier AR, Ribeiro NP, Silva AC et al. Cannabidiol, a *Cannabis sativa* constituent, as an anxiolytic drug. Rev Bras Psiquiatr. 2012 Jun;34 Suppl 1:S104–10.

Schneck CD, Miklowitz DJ, Miyahara S, et al. The prospective course of rapid-cycling bipolar disorder: findings from the STEP-BD. Am J Psychiatry. 2008 Mar;165(3):370–7.

Schrauzer GN and Shrestha KP. Lithium in drinking water. Brit J Psychiatry. 2010, 196 (2) 159-160.

Selle V, Schalkwijk S, Vázquez GH, Baldessarini RJ. Treatments for acute bipolar depression: meta-analyses of placebo-controlled, monotherapy trials of anticonvulsants, lithium and antipsychotics. Pharmacopsychiatry. 2014 Mar;47(2):43–52.

Shelton RC, Stahl SM. Risperidone and paroxetine given singly and in combination for bipolar depression. J Clin Psychiatry. 2004 Dec;65(12):1715–9.

Shin JH, Gadde KM, Østbye T, Bray GA. Weight changes in obese adults 6-months after discontinuation of double-blind zonisamide or placebo treatment. Diabetes Obes Metab. 2014 Aug;16(8):766–8.

Sidhu J, Job S, Singh S, Philipson R. The pharmacokinetic and pharmacodynamic consequences of the co-administration of lamotrigine and a combined oral contraceptive in healthy female subjects. Br J Clin Pharmacol. 2006 Feb;61(2):191–9.

Silk KR. Management and effectiveness of psychopharmacology in emotionally unstable and borderline personality disorder. J Clin Psychiatry. 2015 Apr;76(4):e524–5.

Silva GE, Vana KD, Goodwin JL, Sherrill DL, Quan SF. Identification of patients with sleep disordered breathing: comparing the four-variable screening tool, STOP, STOP-Bang, and Epworth Sleepiness Scales. J Clin Sleep Med. 2011 Oct 15;7(5):467–72.

Sinclair LI, Christmas DM, Hood SD, et al. Antidepressant-induced jitteriness/anxiety syndrome: systematic review. Br J Psychiatry. 2009 May;194(6):483–90.

Singh T. Aripiprazole-induced weight gain. Psychiatry (Edgmont). 2005 Jun;2(6):19.

Sit D, Wisner KL, Hanusa BH, Stull S, Terman M. Light therapy for bipolar disorder: a case series in women. Bipolar Disord. 2007 Dec;9(8):918–27.

Solé B, Bonnin CM, Mayoral M, et al. Functional remediation for patients with Bipolar II disorder: improvement of functioning and subsyndromal symptoms. Eur Neuropsychopharmacol. 2015 Feb; 25(2):257–64.

Sommer BR, Mitchell EL, Wroolie TE. Topiramate: effects on cognition in patients with epilepsy, migraine headache and obesity. Ther Adv Neurol Disord. 2013 Jul;6(4):211–27.

Spedding S. Vitamin D and depression: a systematic review and meta-analysis comparing studies with and without biological flaws. Nutrients. 2014 Apr 11;6(4):1501–18.

Spoov J, Lahdelma L. Should thyroid augmentation precede lithium augmentation—a pilot study. J Affect Disord. 1998 Jun;49(3):235–9.

Stamm TJ, Lewitzka U, Sauer C, et al. Supraphysiologic doses of levothyroxine as adjunctive therapy in bipolar depression: a randomized, double-blind, placebo-controlled study. J Clin Psychiatry. 2014 Feb;75(2):162–8.

Stancer HC, Persad E. Treatment of intractable rapid-cycling manic-depressive disorder with levothyroxine. Arch Gen Psychiatry. 1982; 39(3):311–2.

Stoffers J, Völlm BA, Rücker G, et al. Pharmacological interventions for borderline personality disorder. Cochrane Database Syst Rev. 2010 Jun 16;(6):CD005653.

Stoll AL, Severus WE, Freeman MP, et al. Omega 3 fatty acids in bipolar disorder: a preliminary double-blind, placebo-controlled trial. Arch Gen Psychiatry. 1999 May;56(5):407–12.

Sublette ME, Ellis SP, Geant AL, Mann JJ. Meta-analysis of the effects of eicosapentaenoic acid (EPA) in clinical trials in depression. J Clin Psychiatry. 2011 Dec;72(12):1577–84.

Suppes T, McElroy SL, Sheehan DV, et al. A randomized, double-blind, placebo-controlled study of ziprasidone monotherapy in bipolar disorder with co-occurring lifetime panic or generalized anxiety disorder. J Clin Psychiatry. 2014 Jan;75(1):77–84.

Swann AC, Lafer B, Perugi G, et al. Bipolar mixed states: an international society for bipolar disorders task force report of symptom structure, course of illness, and diagnosis. Am J Psychiatry. 2013 Jan;170(1):31–42.

Swartz HA, Frank E, Cheng Y. A randomized pilot study of psychotherapy and quetiapine for the acute treatment of Bipolar II depression.
Bipolar Disord. 2012 Mar;14(2):211–6.

Takeshima M, Oka T. Association between the so-called "activation syndrome" and Bipolar II disorder, a related disorder, and bipolar suggestive features in outpatients with depression. J Affect Disord. 2013
Oct;151(1):196–202.

Tampi RR, Balderas M, Carter KV, et al. Citalopram, QTc prolongation,
and torsades de pointes. Psychosomatics. 2015 Jan–Feb;56(1):36–43.

Taylor DM, Cornelius V, Smith L, Young AH. Comparative efficacy and
acceptability of drug treatments for bipolar depression: a multiple-treat-
ments meta-analysis. Acta Psychiatr Scand. 2014 Dec;130(6):452–69.

Teff KL, Rickels K, Alshehabi E, Rickels MR. Metabolic impairments
precede changes in hunger and food intake following short-term
administration of second-generation antipsychotics. J Clin Psychopharmacol. 2015 Oct;35(5):579–82.

Teicher MH, Glod C, Cole JO. Emergence of intense suicidal pre-
occupation during fluoxetine treatment. Am J Psychiatry. 1990
Feb;147(2):207–10.

Tek C, Ratliff J, Reutenauer E, Ganguli R, O'Malley SS. A randomized,
double-blind, placebo-controlled pilot study of naltrexone to coun-
teract antipsychotic-associated weight gain: proof of concept. J Clin
Psychopharmacol. 2014 Oct;34(5):608–12.

Terman M, Terman JS. Controlled trial of naturalistic dawn simulation
and negative air ionization for seasonal affective disorder. Am J Psychiatry. 2006 Dec;163(12):2126–33.

Thase ME. Antidepressants and rapid-cycling Bipolar II disorder: dogma,
definitions and deconstructing discrepant data. Br J Psychiatry. 2013
Apr;202(4):251–2.

Thase ME, Jonas A, Khan A, et al. Aripiprazole monotherapy in non-
psychotic Bipolar I depression: results of 2 randomized, placebo-
controlled studies. J Clin Psychopharmacol. 2008 Feb;28(1):13–20.

Tiihonen M, Liewendahl K, Waltimo O, Ojala M, Välimäki M. Thyroid
status of patients receiving long-term anticonvulsant therapy assessed
by peripheral parameters: a placebo-controlled thyroxine therapy
trial. Epilepsia. 1995 Nov;36(11):1118–25.

Tohen M, Vieta E, Calabrese J, et al. Efficacy of olanzapine and olanzapine-fluoxetine combination in the treatment of Bipolar I depression. Arch Gen Psychiatry 2003;60:1079–88.

Torrent C, Bonnin Cdel M, Martínez-Arán A, et al. Efficacy of functional remediation in bipolar disorder: a multicenter randomized controlled study. Am J Psychiatry. 2013 Aug;170(8):852–9.

Turner EH, Matthews AM, Linardatos E, et al. Selective publication of antidepressant trials and its influence on apparent efficacy. N Engl J Med. 2008 Jan 17;358(3):252–60.

Tyler E, Jones S, Black N, Carter LA, Barrowclough C. The relationship between bipolar disorder and cannabis use in daily life: an experience sampling study. PLoS One. 2015 Mar 4;10(3):e0118916.

University of Washington Department of Family Medicine. Non-drug ways to manage PMS. 2012. http://www.fammed.wisc.edu/sites/default/files/webfm-uploads/documents/outreach/im/handout_pms.pdf; accessed 7/31/15.

Valentí M, Pacchiarotti I, Rosa AR, et al. Bipolar mixed episodes and antidepressants: a cohort study of Bipolar I disorder patients. Bipolar Disord. 2011 Mar;13(2):145–54.

Valentí M, Pacchiarotti I, Undurraga J, et al. Risk factors for rapid cycling in bipolar disorder. Bipolar Disord. 2015 Aug;17(5):549–59.

Van Dijk S, Segal Z. *The Dialectical Behavior Therapy Skills Workbook for Bipolar Disorder: Using DBT to Regain Control of Your Emotions and Your Life*. New Harbinger, 2009.

Vázquez GH, Romero E, Fabregues F, Pies R, Ghaemi N, Mota-Castillo M. Screening for bipolar disorders in Spanish-speaking populations: sensitivity and specificity of the Bipolar Spectrum Diagnostic Scale-Spanish version. Compr Psychiatry. 2010 Sep–Oct;51(5):552–6.

Vita A, De Peri L, Sacchetti E. Lithium in drinking water and suicide prevention: a review of the evidence. Int Clin Psychopharmacol. 2015 Jan;30(1):1–5.

Vieta E, Suppes T. Bipolar II disorder: arguments for and against a distinct diagnostic entity. Bipolar Disord. 2008 Feb;10(1 Pt 2):163–78.

Vieta E, Valentí M. Pharmacological management of bipolar depression: acute treatment, maintenance, and prophylaxis. CNS Drugs. 2013 Jul;27(7):515–29.

Wang PW, Yang YS, Chandler RA, Nowakowska C, Alarcon AM, Culver J, Ketter TA. Adjunctive zonisamide for weight loss in euthymic bipolar disorder patients: a pilot study. J Psychiatr Res. 2008 May;42(6):451–7.

Wang XQ, Xiong J, Xu WH, et al. Risk of a lamotrigine-related skin rash: current meta-analysis and postmarketing cohort analysis. Seizure. 2015 Feb;25:52–61.

Wegner I, Edelbroek PM, Bulk S, Lindhout D. Lamotrigine kinetics within the menstrual cycle, after menopause, and with oral contraceptives. Neurology. 2009 Oct 27;73(17):1388–93.

Wehr TA, Goodwin FK. Rapid cycling in manic-depressives induced by tricyclic antidepressants. Arch Gen Psychiatry. 1979 May;36(5):555–9.

Wehr TA, Sack DA, Rosenthal NE, Cowdry RW. Rapid cycling affective disorder: contributing factors and treatment responses in 51 patients. Am J Psychiatry. 1988a;145:179–84.

Wehr TA, Turner EH, Shimada JM, et al. Treatment of rapidly cycling bipolar patient by using extended bed rest and darkness to stabilize the timing and duration of sleep. Biol Psychiatry. 1998b Jun 1;43(11):822–8.

Weinberger JF, Raison CL, Rye DB, et al. Inhibition of tumor necrosis factor improves sleep continuity in patients with treatment resistant depression and high inflammation. Brain Behav Immun. 2015 Jul;47:193–200.

Weisler RH, Nolen WA, Neijber A, Hellqvist A, Paulsson B, Trial 144 Study Investigators. Continuation of quetiapine versus switching to placebo or lithium for maintenance treatment of Bipolar I disorder (Trial 144: a randomized controlled study). J Clin Psychiatry. 2011 Nov;72(11):1452–64.

West AE, Weinstein SM, Peters AT, et al. Child- and family-focused cognitive-behavioral therapy for pediatric bipolar disorder: a randomized clinical trial. J Am Acad Child Adolesc Psychiatry. 2014 Nov;53(11):1168–78.

Wetmore CM, Mokdad AH. In denial: misperceptions of weight change among adults in the United States. Prev Med. 2012 Aug;55(2):93–100.

Wiffen PJ, Derry S, Moore RA, Kalso EA. Carbamazepine for chronic neuropathic pain and fibromyalgia in adults. Cochrane Database Syst Rev. 2014 Apr 10;4:CD005451.

Wilding J, Van Gaal L, Rissanen A, et al. A randomized double-blind placebo-controlled study of the long-term efficacy and safety of topiramate in the treatment of obese subjects. Int J Obes Relat Metab Disord. 2004 Nov;28(11):1399–410.

Wirz-Justice A, Quinto C, Cajochen C, Werth E, Hock C. A rapid-cycling bipolar patient treated with long nights, bedrest, and light. Biol Psychiatry. 1999 Apr 15;45(8):1075–7.

Wolf R, Ruocco V. Triggered psoriasis. Adv Exp Med Biol. 1999;455:221–5.

Wolpert EA, Goldberg JF, Harrow M. Rapid cycling in unipolar and bipolar affective disorders. Am J Psychiatry. 1990;147:725–8.

Xenitidis K, Campbell C, Eppel AB. Antidepressants in rapid-cycling bipolar disorder. Br J Psychiatry. 2013 Jul;203(1):75

Xia G, Gajwani P, Muzina DJ, et al. Treatment-emergent mania in unipolar and bipolar depression: focus on repetitive transcranial magnetic stimulation. Int J Neuropsychopharmacol. 2008 Feb;11(1):119–30.

Young AH. Invited commentary on... Lithium levels in drinking water and risk of suicide. Br J Psychiatry 2009 ; 194: 466.

Zavodnick AD, Ali R. Lamotrigine in the treatment of unipolar depression with and without comorbidities: a literature review. Psychiatr Q. 2012 Sep;83(3):371–83.

Zilkens RR, Bruce DG, Duke J, Spilsbury K, Semmens JB. Severe psychiatric disorders in mid-life and risk of dementia in late- life (age 65–84 years): a population based case-control study. Curr Alzheimer Res. 2014;11(7):681–93.

Zimmerman M. Improving the recognition of borderline personality disorder in a bipolar world. J Pers Disord. 2015 Apr 20;1–16.

Zimmerman M, Galione JN. Screening for bipolar disorder with the Mood Disorders Questionnaire: a review. Harv Rev Psychiatry. 2011 Sep-Oct;19(5):219-28.

Zimmerman M, Galione JN, Ruggero CJ, et al. Screening for bipolar disorder and finding borderline personality disorder. J Clin Psychiatry. 2010a;71(9):1212–7.

Zimmerman M, Ruggero CJ, Chelminski I, Young D. Is bipolar disorder overdiagnosed? J Clin Psychiatry. 2008 Jun;69(6):935-40.

Zimmerman M, Ruggero CJ, Chelminski I, Young D. Psychiatric diagnoses in patients previously overdiagnosed with bipolar disorder. J Clin Psychiatry. 2010b;71(1):26–31.

Zorrilla I, Aguado J, Haro JM et al. Cannabis and bipolar disorder: does quitting cannabis use during manic/mixed episode improve clinical/functional outcomes? Acta Psychiatr Scand. 2015 Feb;131(2):100–10.

Zuckoff M. Science, money drive a makeover. Boston Globe. 2000 May 7. http://ahrp.org/prozac-revisited-concerns-about-suicides-surface-boston-globe; accessed 9/6/2015.

Index

In this index, *f* denotes figure and *t* denotes table.

antidepressants (*continued*)
lithium versus, 167, 168
mixed states and, 29–30, 31
mood stabilizers versus, 44
PMDD and PMS and, 65, 66
psychotherapy versus, 31–32,
33, 35
PTSD and, 46
spectrum model of mood disorders and, 20–21, 21*f*
tapering of, 126, 178–183
See also specific drug
antipsychotics
lithium versus, 120–21, 122
overview of, 150–165, 161*t*
pregnancy and, 68, 69
side effects of, 26, 124
See also specific drug
anxiety, 23, 30–32, 183, 201
aripiprazole, 154–55, 156, 159
arrhythmias, 144
See also cardiac issues
AS. *See* activation syndrome (AS)
Asian-descent population, 129
attachment disturbance, 40–41
attention deficit disorders (ADD),
46–48
AutoMEQ. *See* Morningness-
Eveningness Questionnaire
(AutoMEQ)

Barcelona Bipolar Disorder Pro-
gram, 173
Bateman, A., 44
Bauer, M., 75, 143
BDNF levels, 139

behavioral changes. *See* lifestyle
modification
benzodiazepines, 29, 32–33, 50,
98
Berk, M., 200
biological clock resetting, 83–85
See also Social Rhythm Therapy
(SRT)
bipolar depression
medications for, 52, 52*t*, 53, 96,
103, 156
supraphysiologic thyroid
approach and, 142–43
T3 and T4 and, 140, 141, 147
TSH levels and, 139
Bipolar I
antipsychotics and, 51, 52
genetic influence and, 43
lithium levels and, 120
psychosis and, 12
renal issues and, 115
Bipolar I and II
antidepressants and, 167, 168,
169
lack of familiarity about,
54–55
mid-spectrum presentations
and, 49
suicide rates, 60
Bipolar II
borderlinity versus, 40
cyclic depression and, 52–53
lamotrigine and, 91
non-medication approaches,
50
Zeta-Jones and, 54–55